Origami
for kids

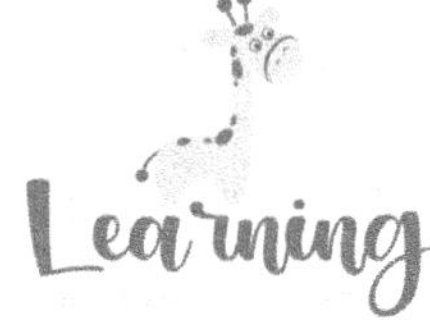

SPECIAL BONUS!

Want These 2 Books For <u>FREE</u>?

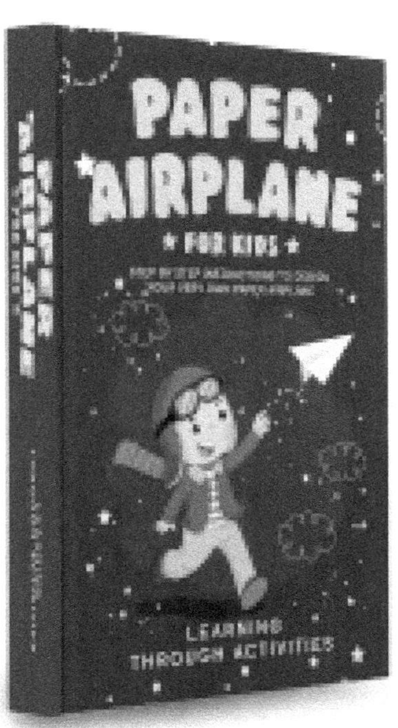

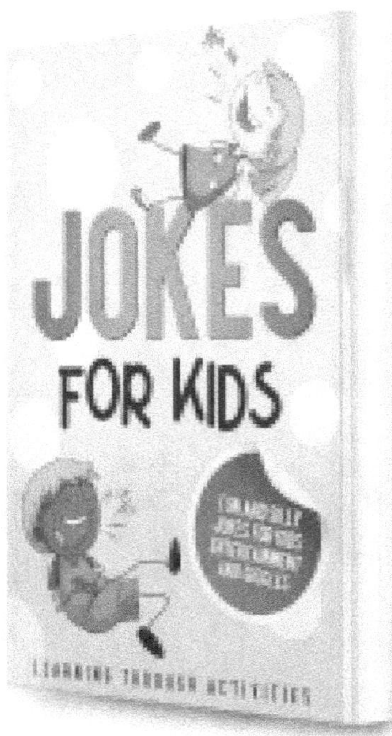

Get <u>FREE</u>, unlimited access to these and all of our new kids books by joining our community!

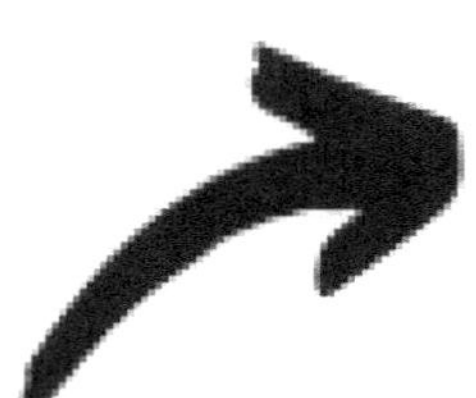

Scan W/ Your Camera To Join!

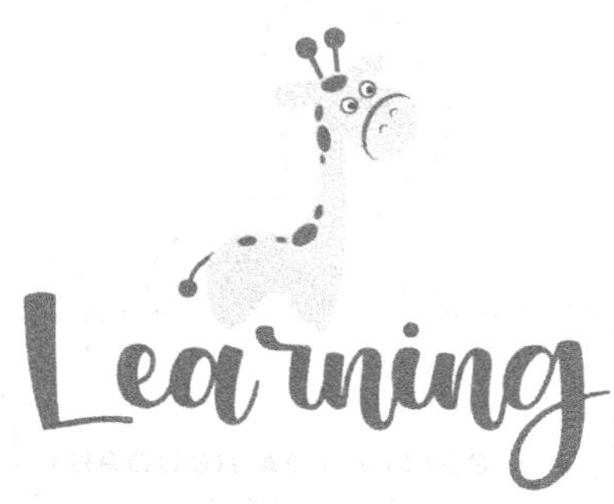

Table of Contents

Welcome to more Origami!

Origami is the art of transforming a sheet of paper into a sculpture without using scissors or glue.

A lot of benefits will come from mastering the art of origami such as improved concentration, abstract thinking, and hand-eye coordination.

In this book, you will find 40 impressive designs to create from easy to more difficult as you go through. Create your own Origami world with the designs in this book!

Symbols

- - - - - - - -   Valley fold, fold forward.

· · · · · · · ·   Mountain fold, fold backward.

——————   Crease line

Fold in this direction.

Turn over.

Shows the result after each step.

Square Sheet

All sheets have two shades to better show each step.

Tall Hat

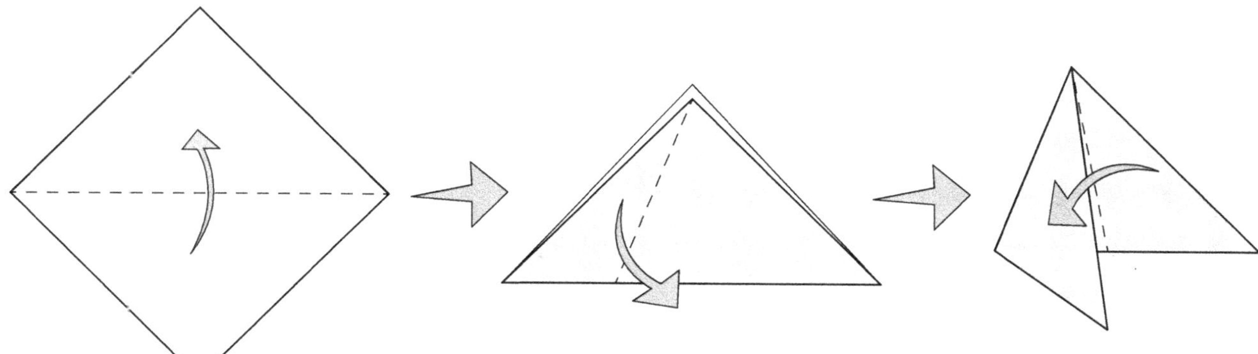

Step 1

Fold the sheet diagonally up in half.

Step 2

Fold the left corner in as shown.

Step 3

Fold the right corner over the left one.

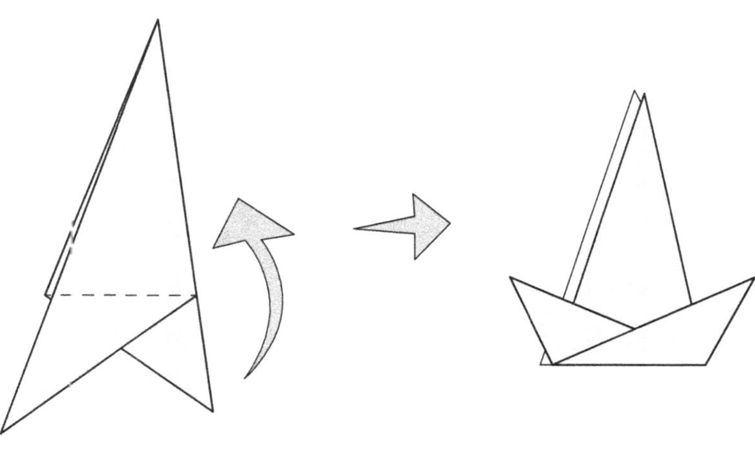

Step 4

Fold both bottom tips up as shown, then flatten the figure. Slightly separate both sides of the figure to finish the hat.

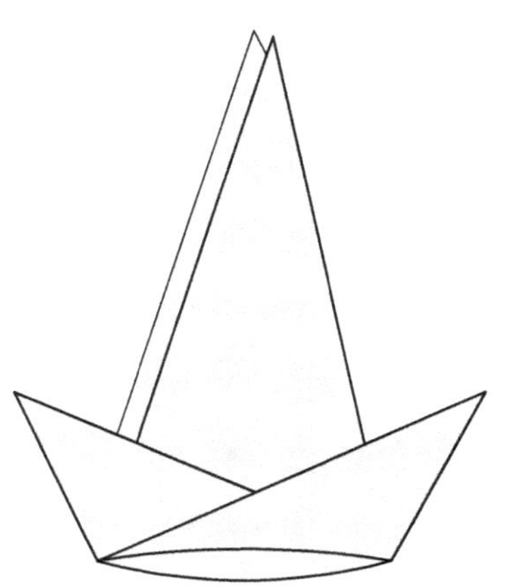

Cup

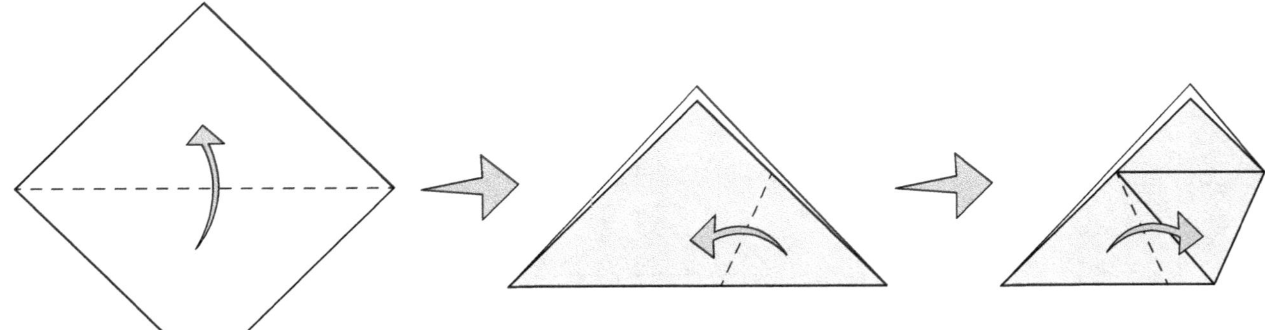

Step 1

Fold the sheet diagonally up in half.

Step 2

Fold the right corner in as shown.

Step 3

Fold the right corner over the left one.

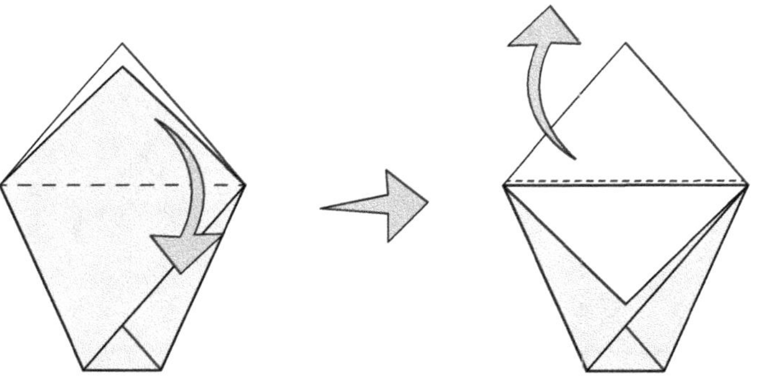

Step 4

Fold the top corner of the top layer forward down, then fold the top corner of the bottom layer back down and flatten.

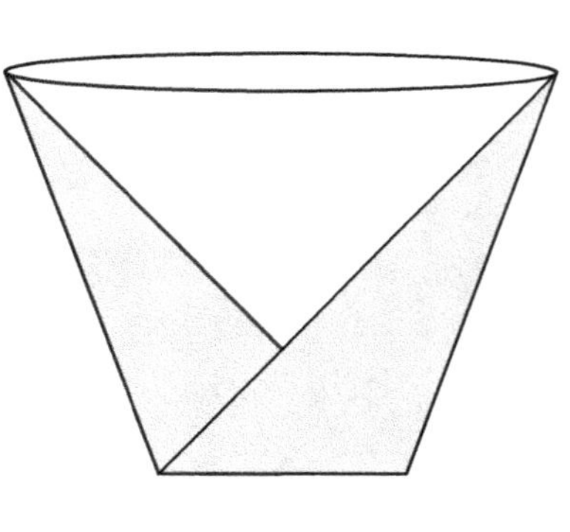

Envelope

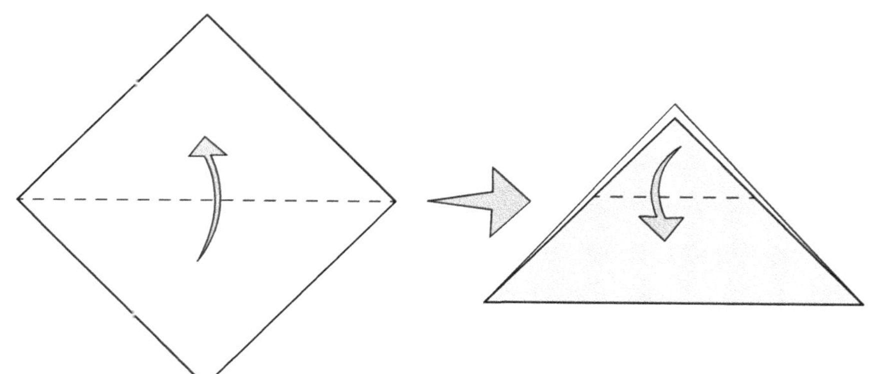

Step 1

Fold the sheet diagonally up in half, then fold the top corner of the top layer forward down as shown.

Step 2

Fold the top corner of the bottom layer forward down over the flap you just made, making sure to leave a small gap between the two folds.

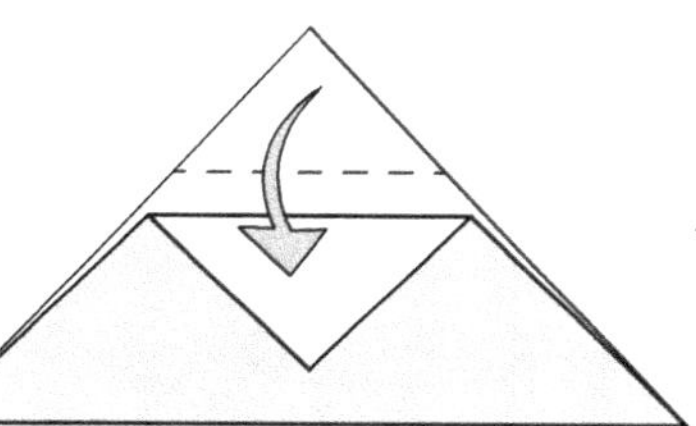

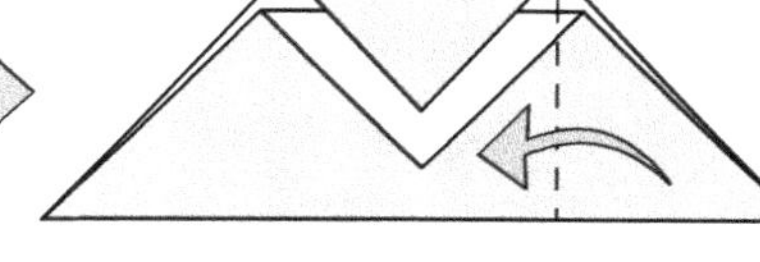

Step 3

Fold the right corner in as shown

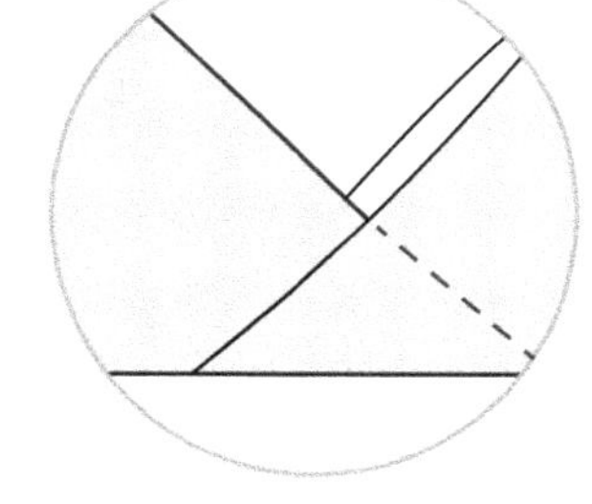

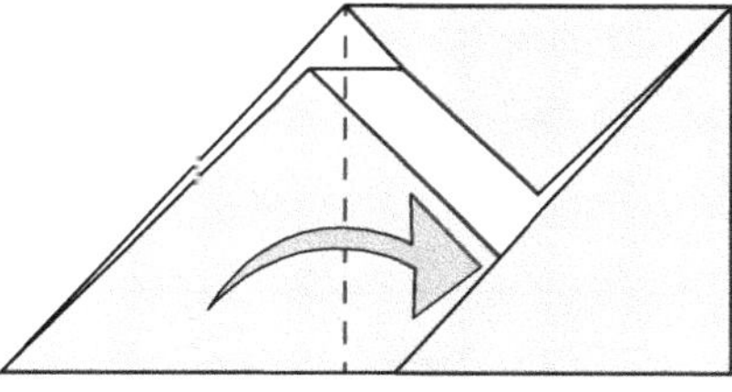

Step 4

Fold the left corner in and tuck it between both layers of the right corner you just folded.

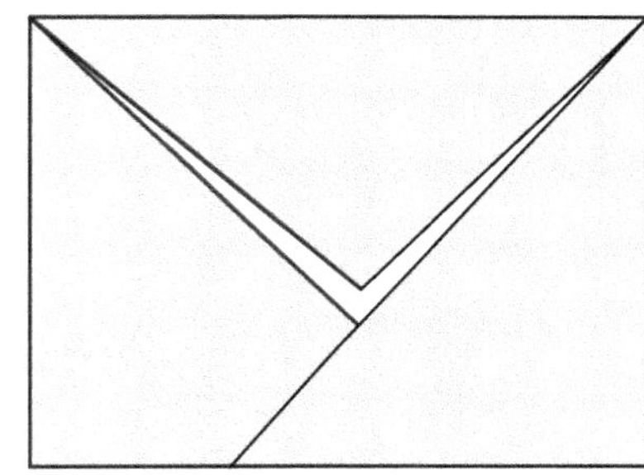

Envelope

Ship

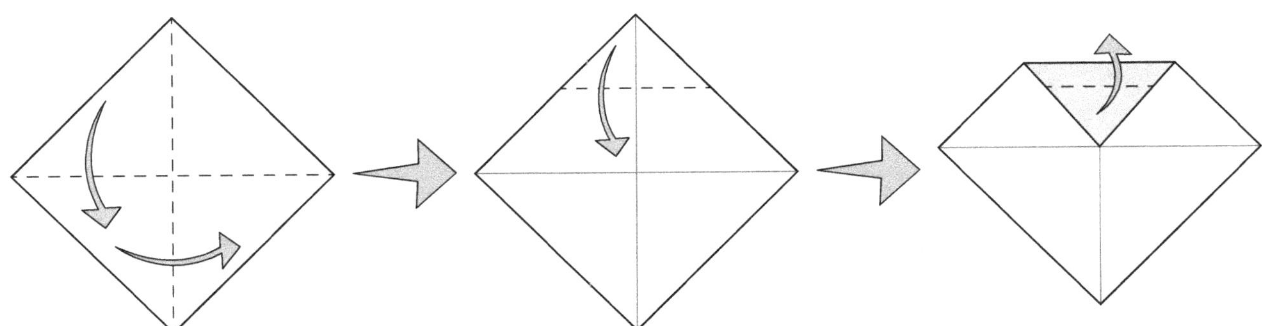

Step 1
Fold the sheet along both diagonals and unfold it.

Step 2
Fold the top corner down to the center of the sheet.

Step 3
Fold the corner back up, leaving a small gap between the two folds.

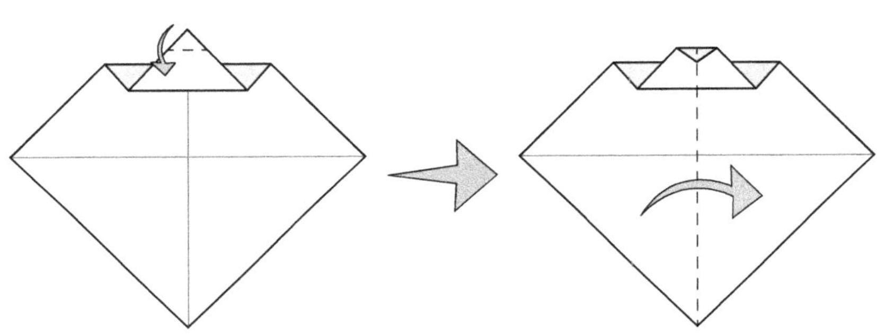

Step 4
Fold the tip down again as shown, then fold the entire figure in half.

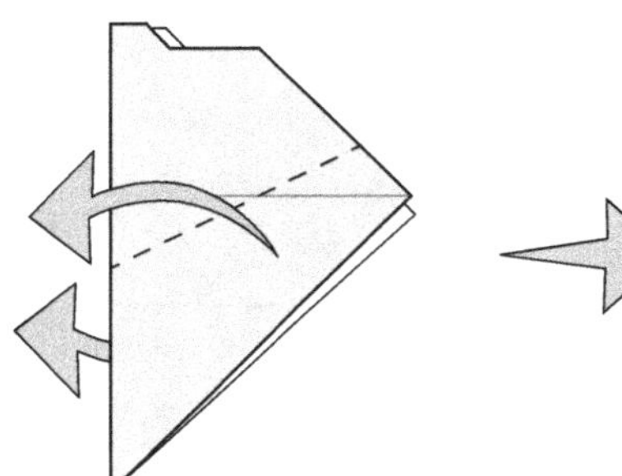

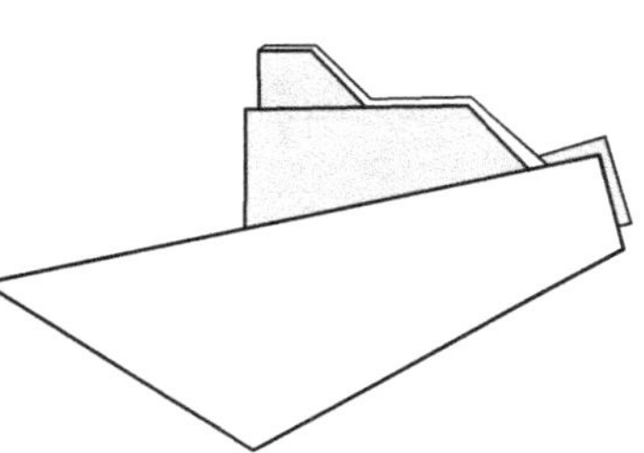

Step 5
Make a crease by folding the figure to both sides along the line shown, then use it to make an outside reverse fold and flatten.

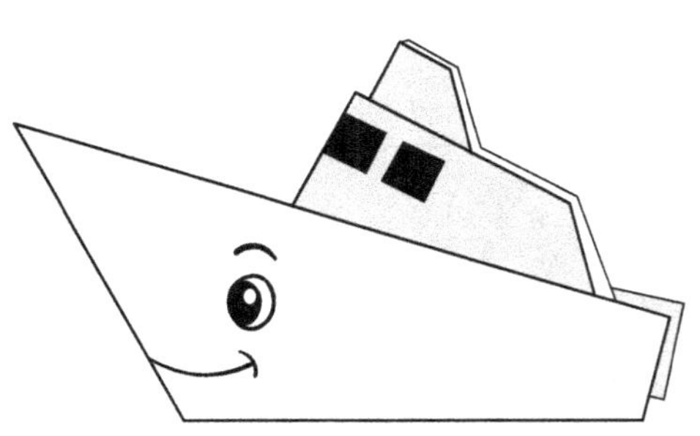

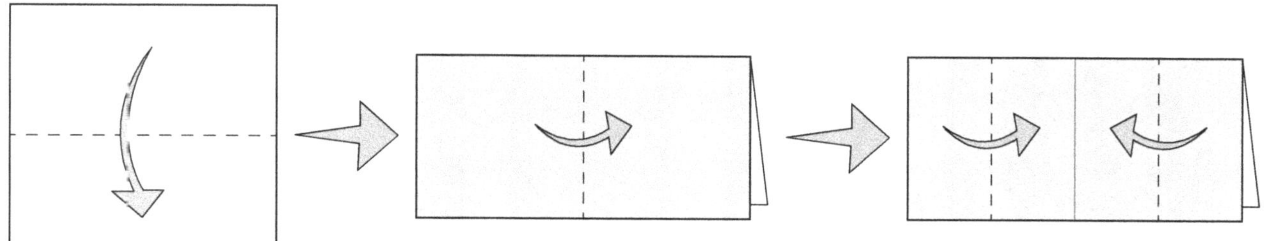

Step 1

Fold the sheet crosswise down in half.

Step 2

Fold in half again as shown and unfold.

Step 3

Bring both side edges to the vertical midline you just made.

Step 4

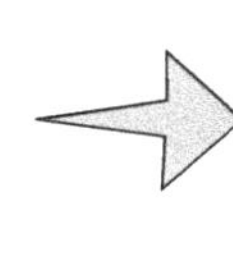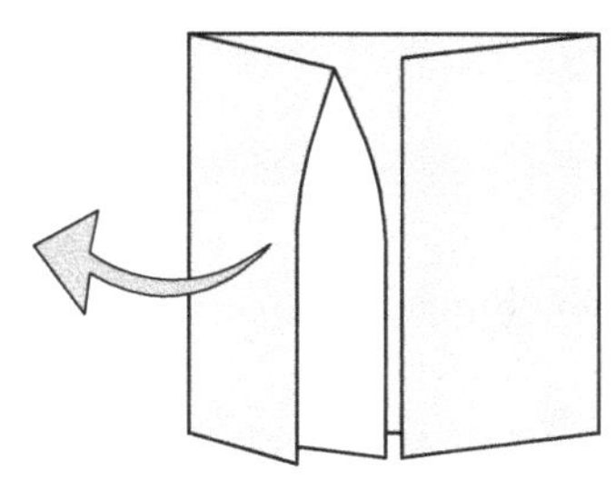

On the left side, separate both layers of paper until they are completely flat as shown, to do this keep the bottom layer right where it is while you slowly open and flatten the top layer.

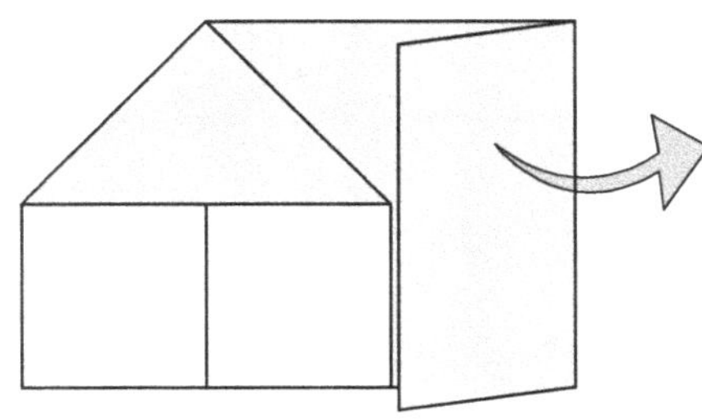

Step 5

Repeat the previous step for the right side.

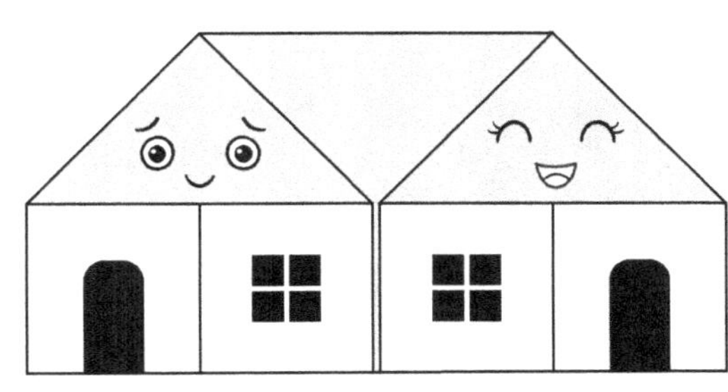

House

Dress

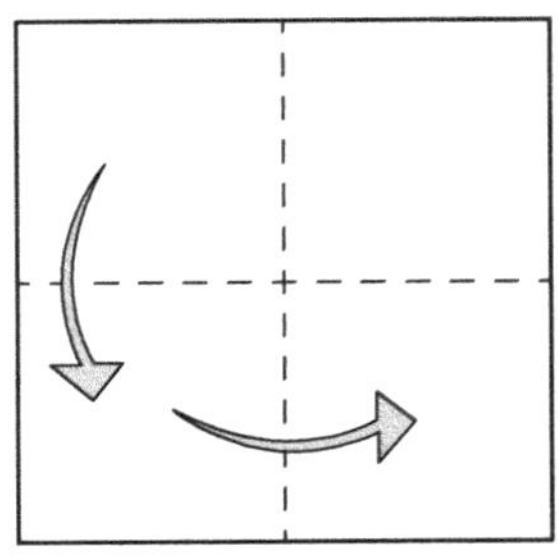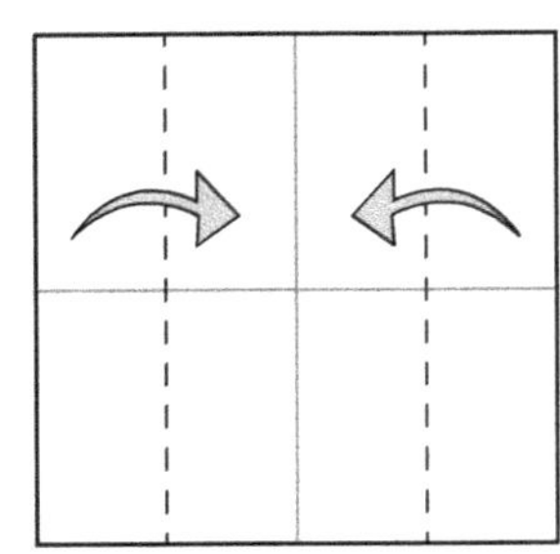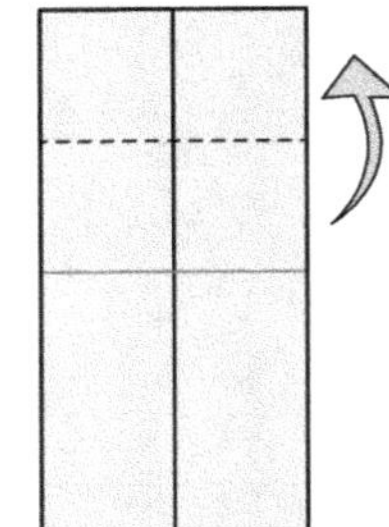

Step 1	Step 2	Step 3
Fold the paper sheet in half lengthwise and crosswise. Then unfold it.	Bring both side edges to the vertical midline you just made.	Fold the top half back in half again as shown.

Step 4

Fold the right side at an angle so that its corner ends past the vertical midline as shown. Then bring the top layer of that corner back again and flatten the figure until you get the drawing below.

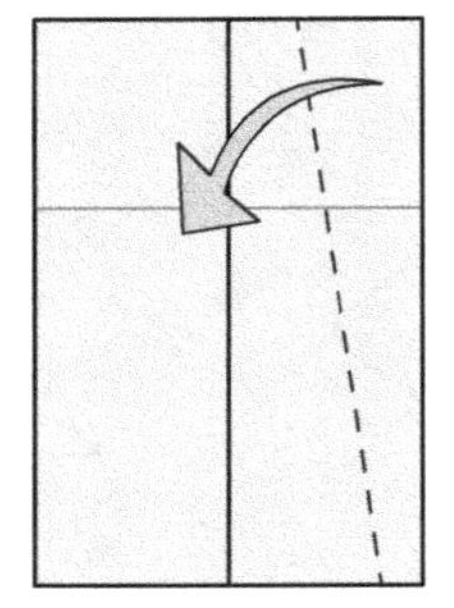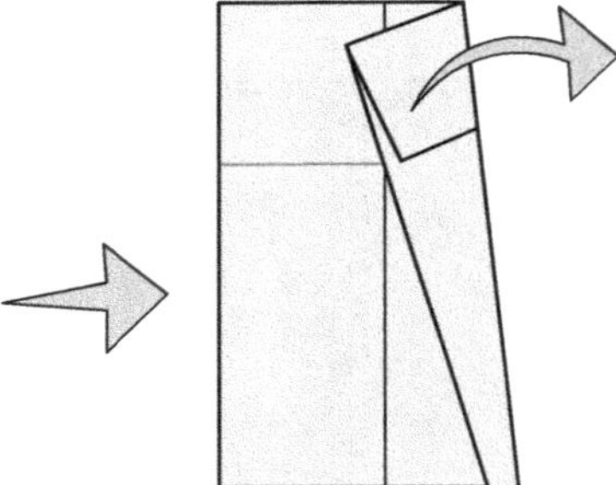

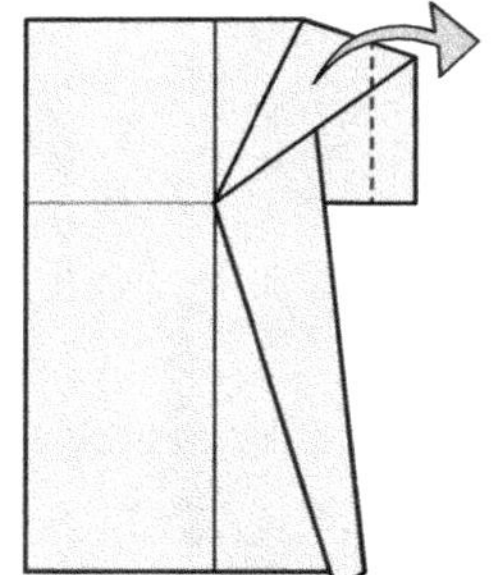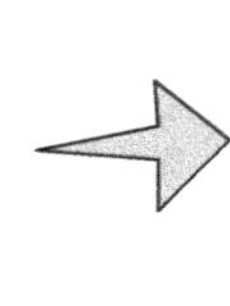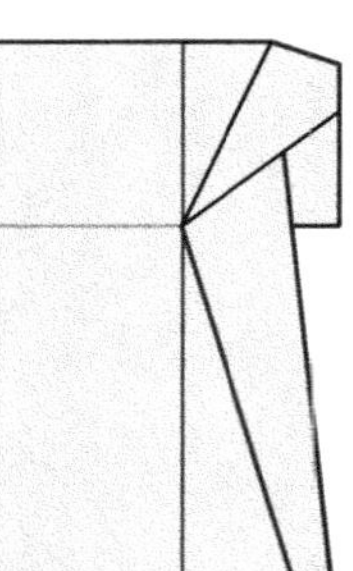

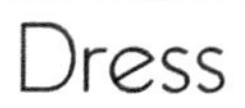

Step 5

Fold the flap you just made vertically back. Then repeat these last two steps for the left side of the figure.

Dress

Chick

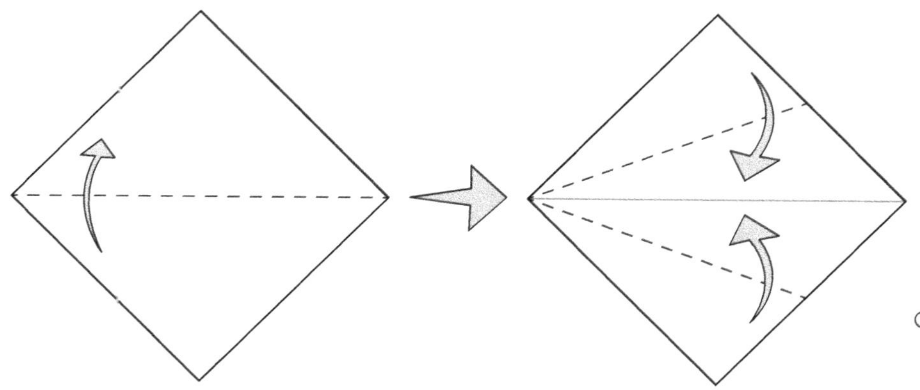

Fold the sheet diagonally up in half and unfold. Then bring the top and bottom corners to that horizontal midline as shown.

Step 2

Bring the left corner in to the edge of the folds from the previous step. Then do the same with the right corner.

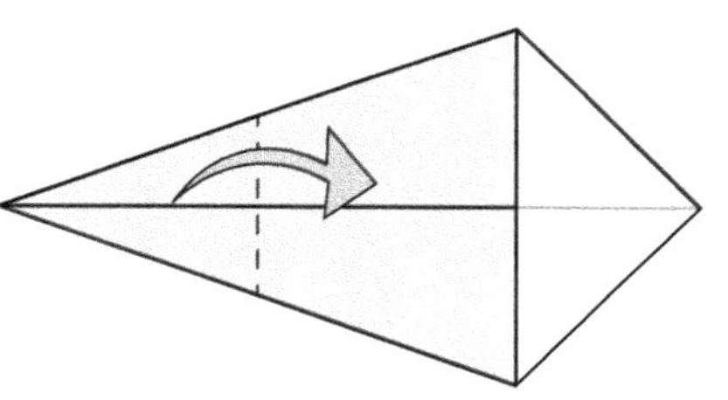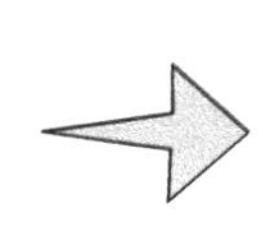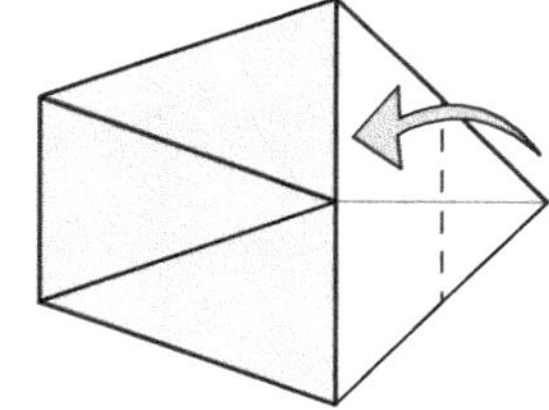

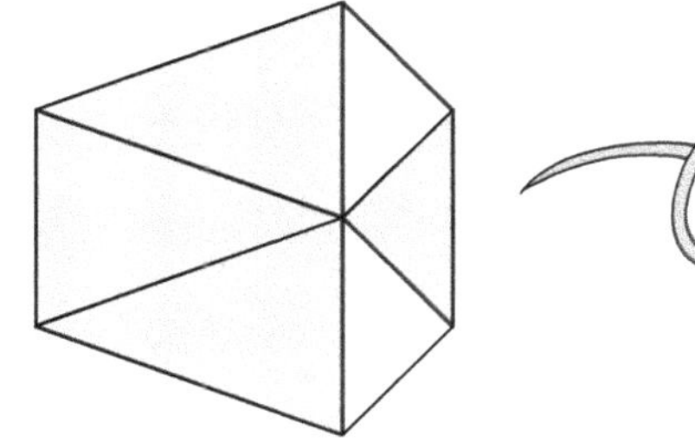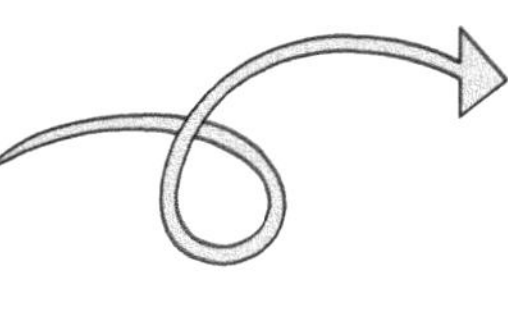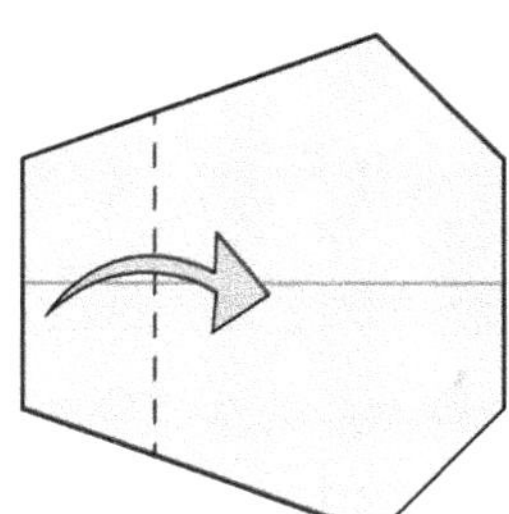

Step 3

Flip the figure over and fold the left edge in as shown.

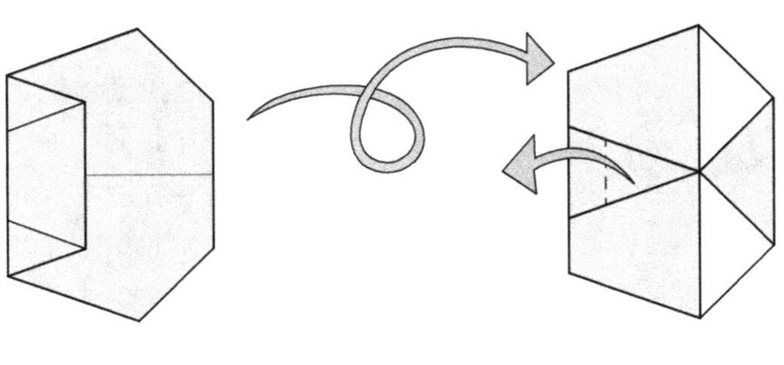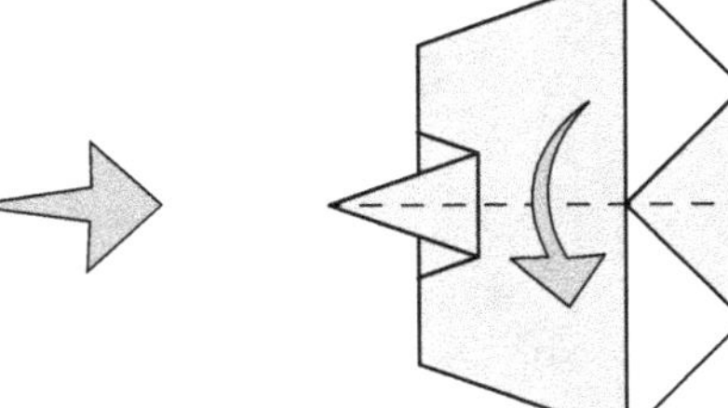

Flip the figure over again and fold the tip of the top layer out.

Fold the figure down in half.

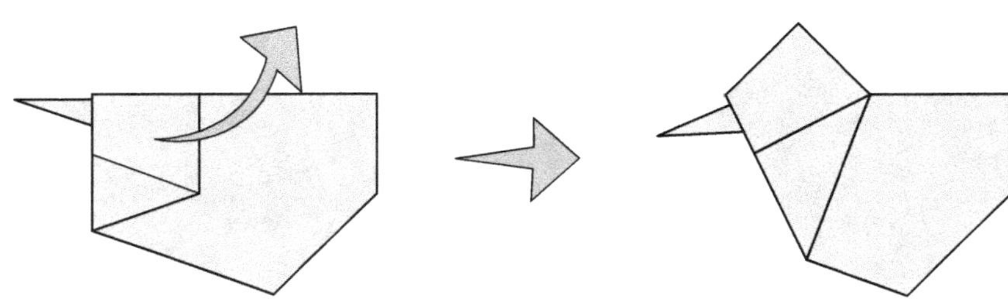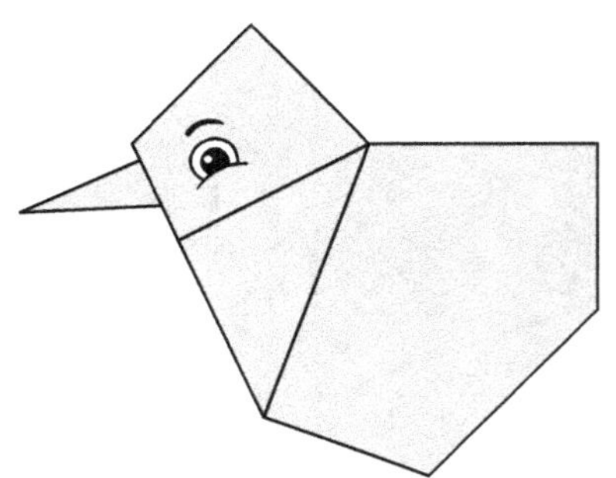

Carefully grab the flaps on either side of the figure's left side and gently pull them up until their bottom corners meet the top edge of the figure as shown, then flatten.

Cupcake

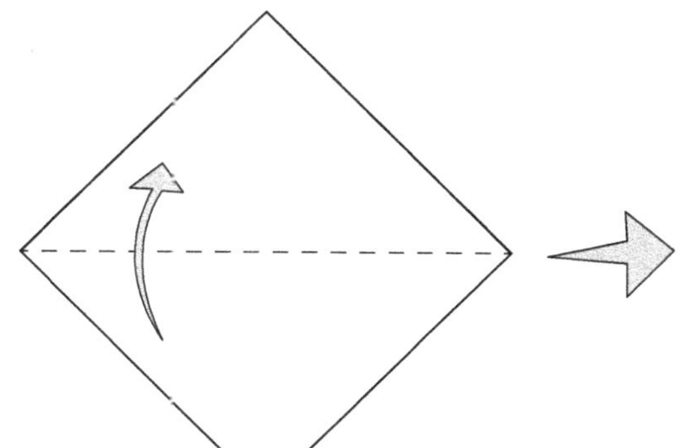 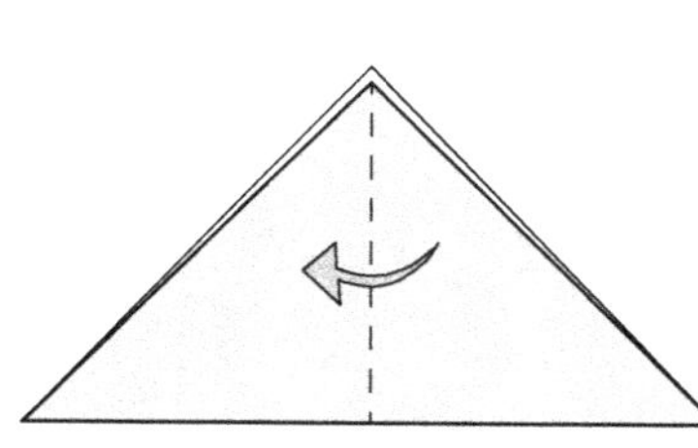

Fold the sheet diagonally up in half, then fold it in half again as shown.

Fold the tip of the top layer down and then back up, leaving a small gap between the two folds.

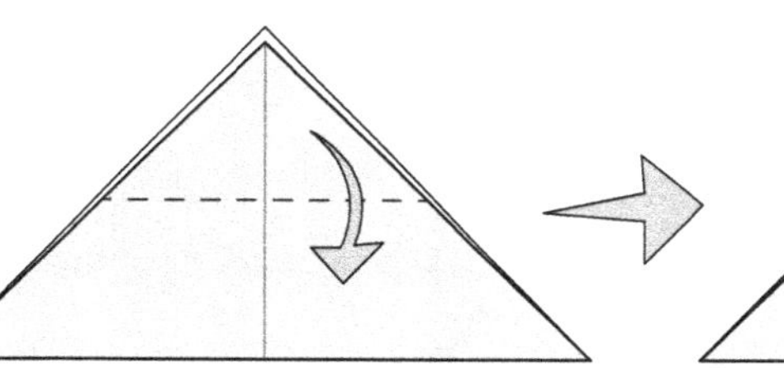 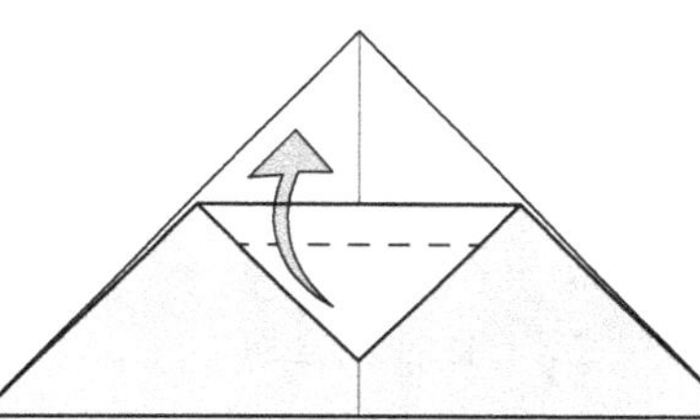

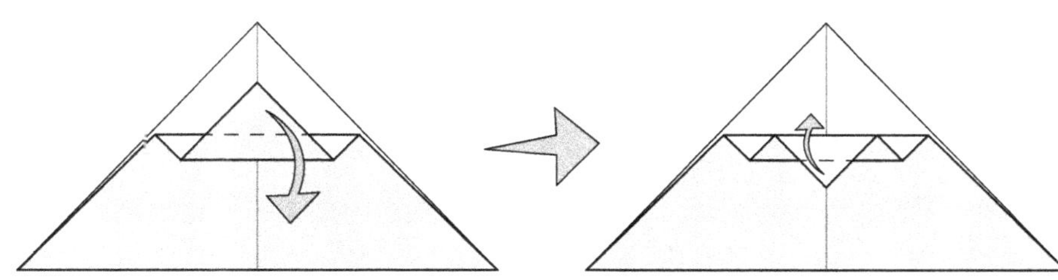

Fold the same tip down and then back up again.

Cupcake

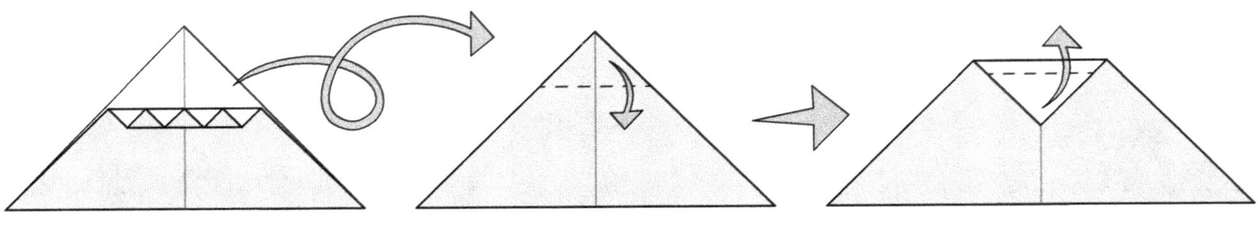

Step 4

Flip the figure over.

Step 5

Fold the tip of this layer down and then back up, leaving a small gap between the two folds.

Step 6

Flip the figure over again, then fold the tip of the bottom layer down over the top layer as shown.

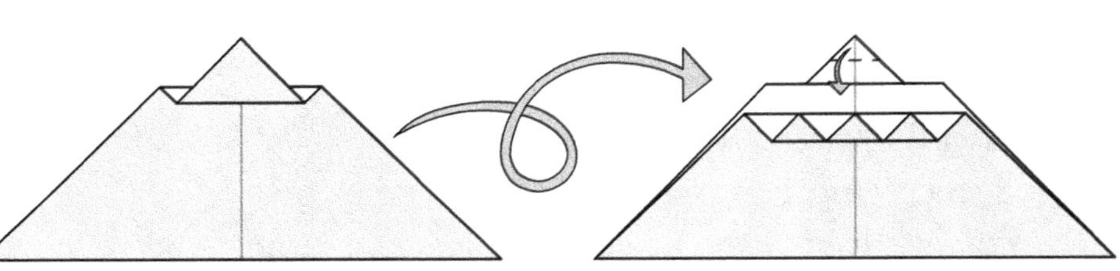

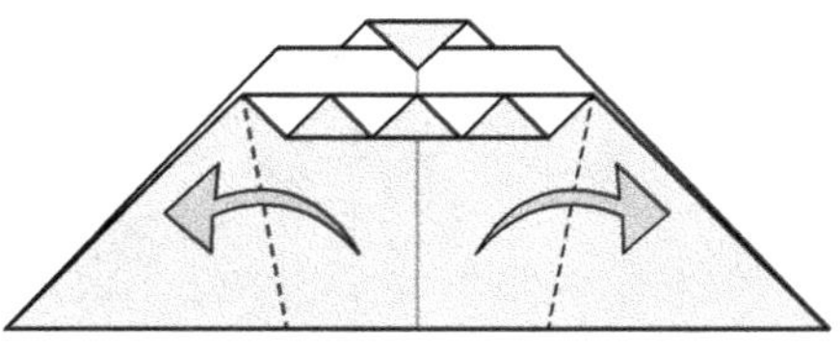

Step 7

Fold both side corners back as shown and flatten the figure.

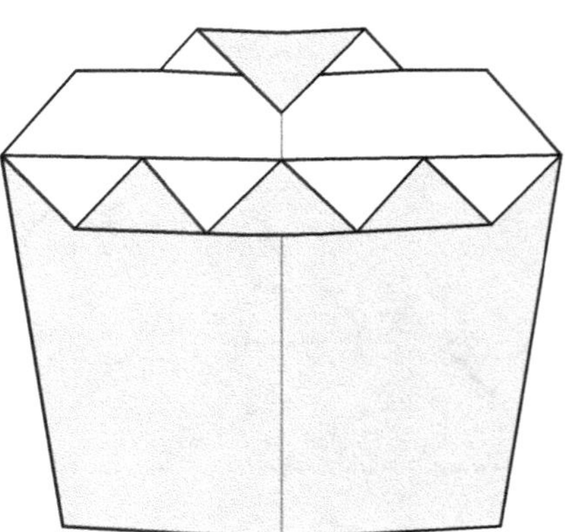

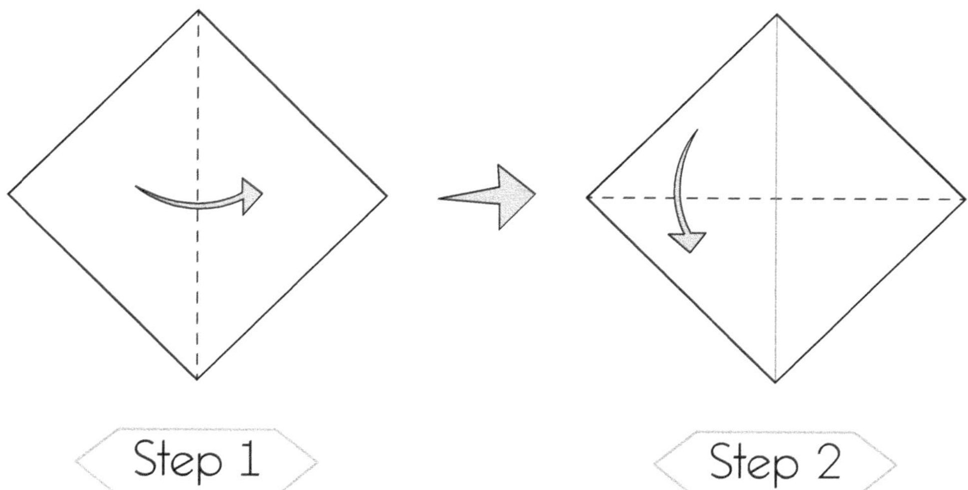

Step 1

Fold the sheet along one of its diagonals and unfold.

Step 2

Now fold the sheet down in half along the other diagonal.

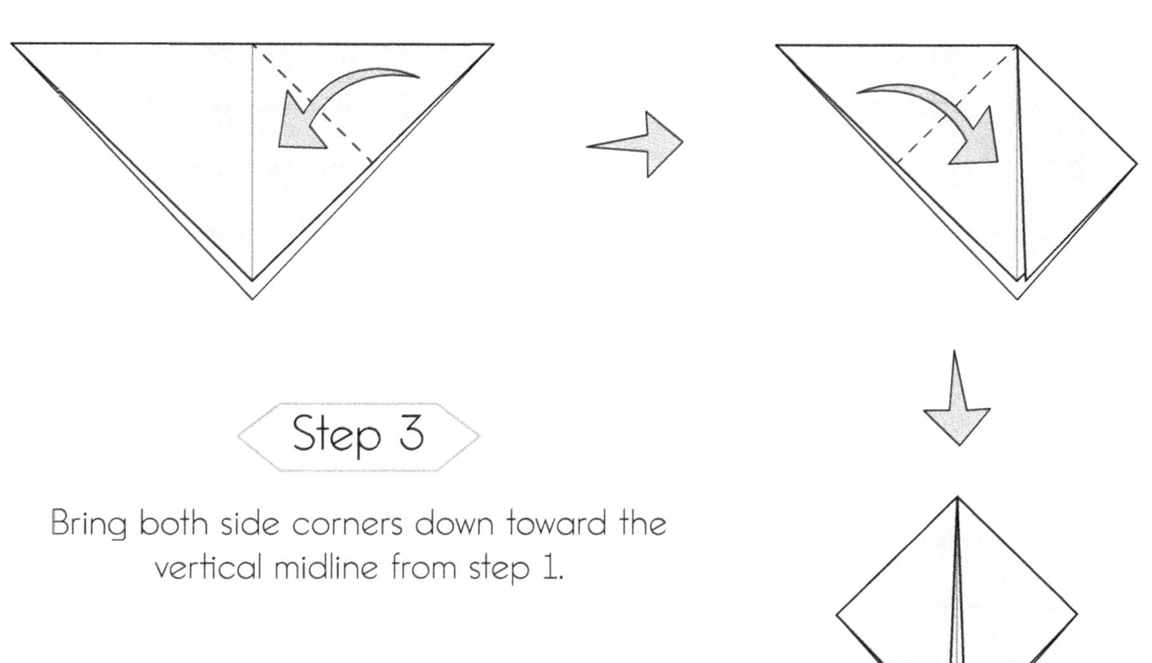

Step 3

Bring both side corners down toward the vertical midline from step 1.

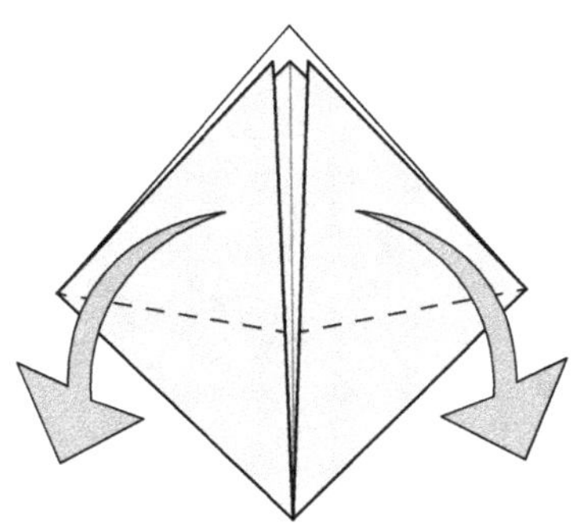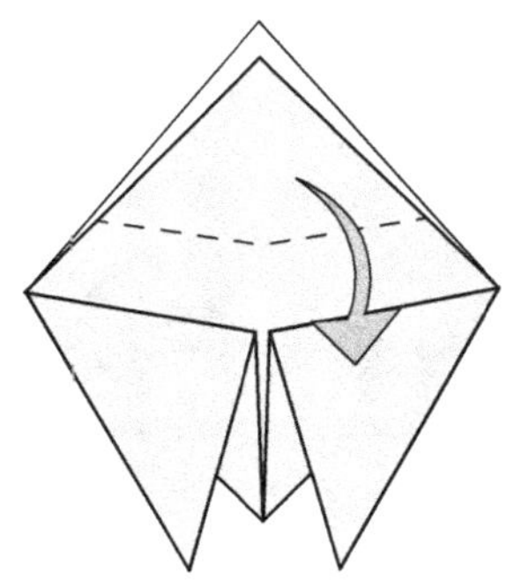

Step 4

Turn the figure upside down and fold the flaps from the previous step down, then fold the tip of the next layer of paper down as shown.

Step 5

Fold the last layer of paper down as well.

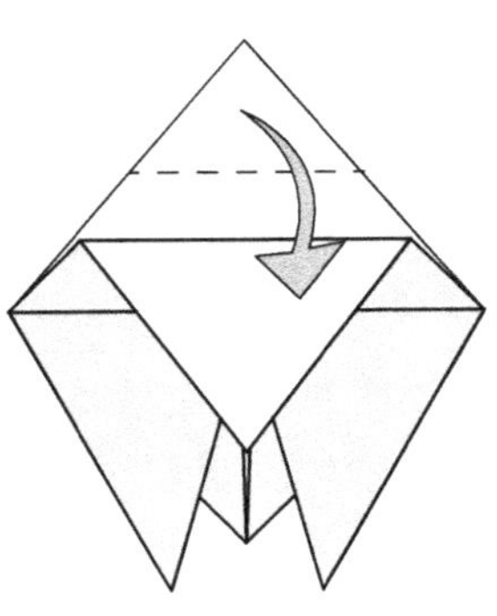

Step 6

Fold both side corners back at an angle as shown.

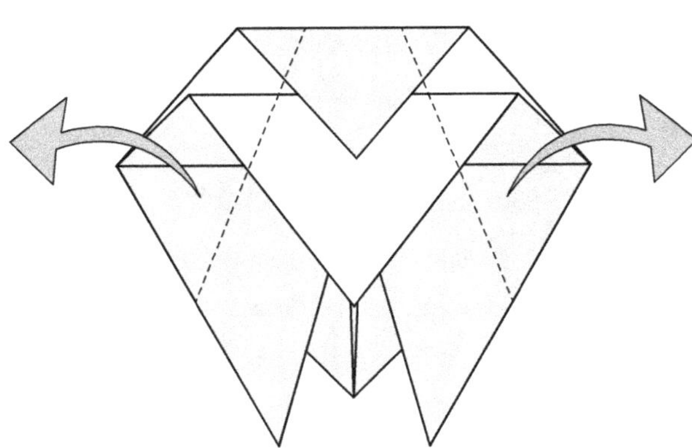

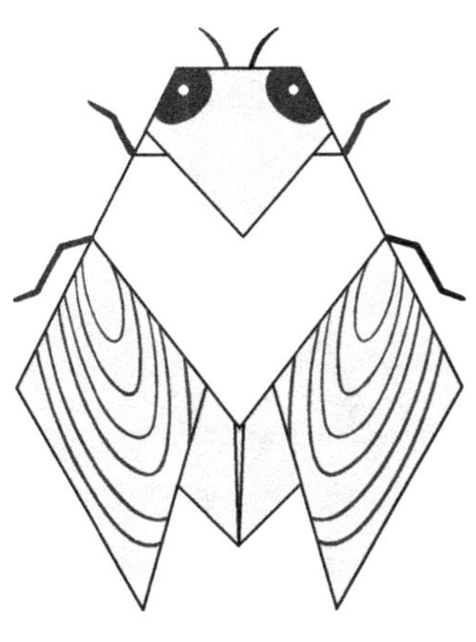

Cicada

Bee

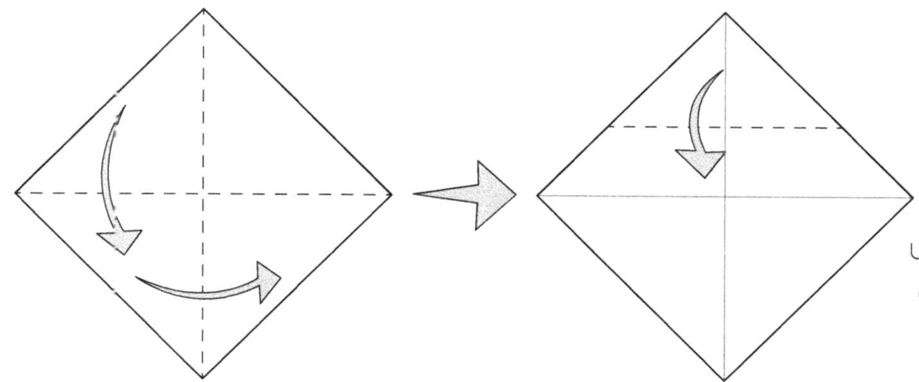

Step 1

Fold the sheet along both diagonals and unfold, then bring the top corner down a little past the horizontal midline.

Step 2

Flip the figure over and bring both side corners down toward the vertical midline.

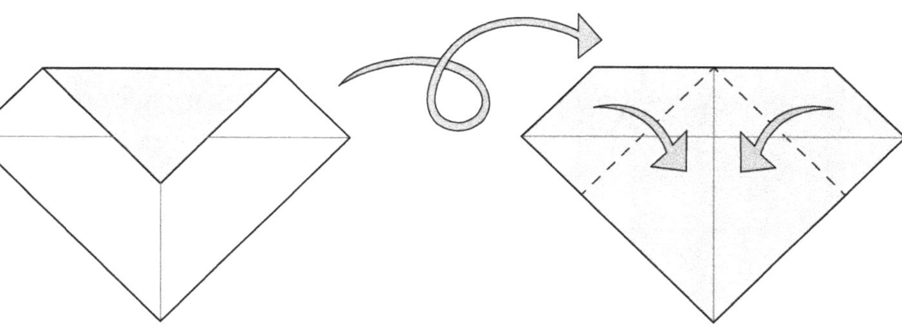

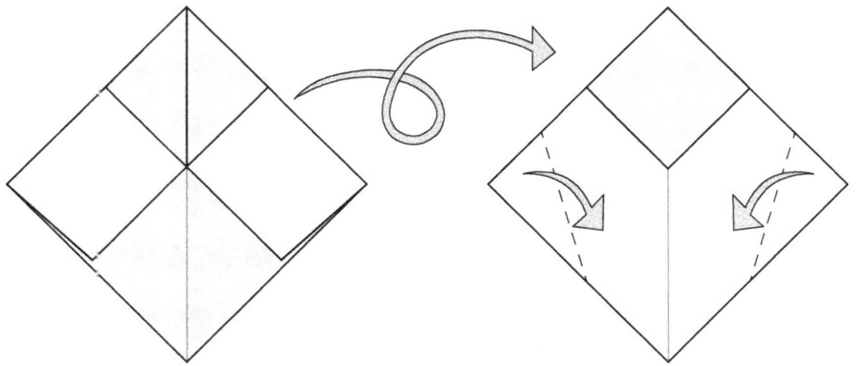

Step 3

Flip the figure over again. Fold and then unfold the side corners as shown to make creases.

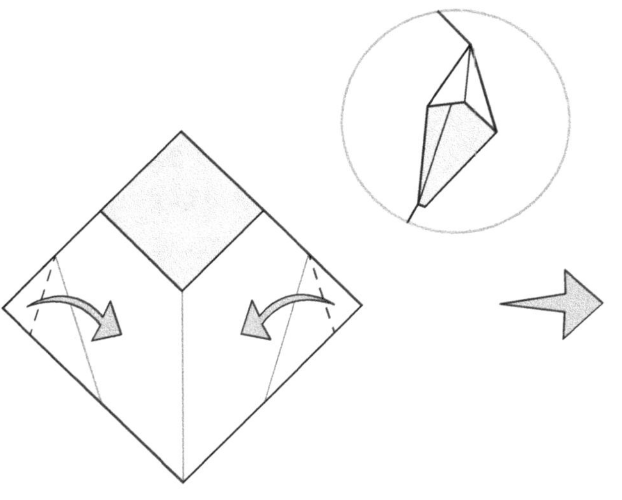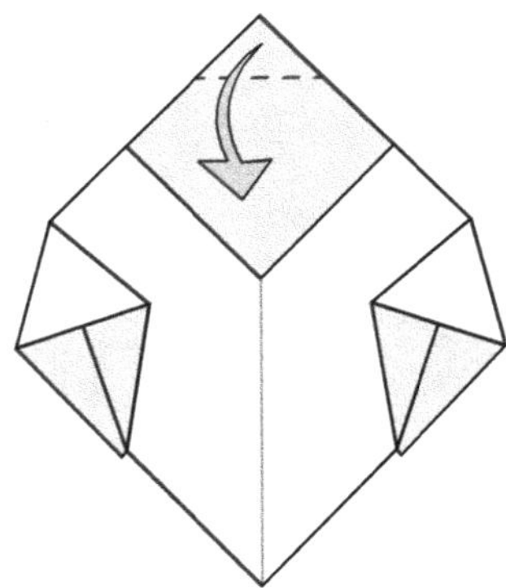

Use the creases you just made to separate both layers of paper and fold the top layer forward in. Then flatten the figure and fold the tip down as shown.

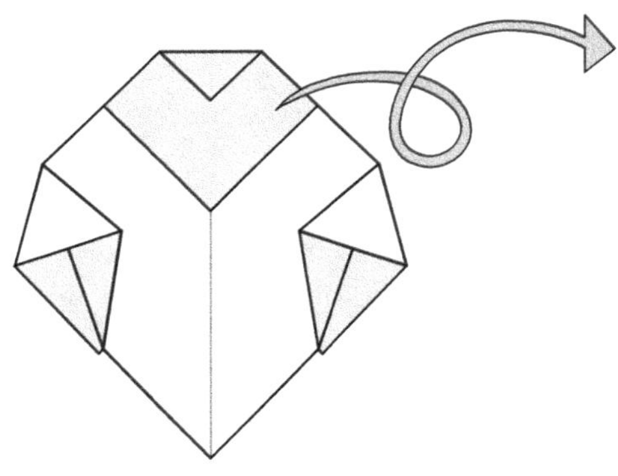

Flip the figure over.

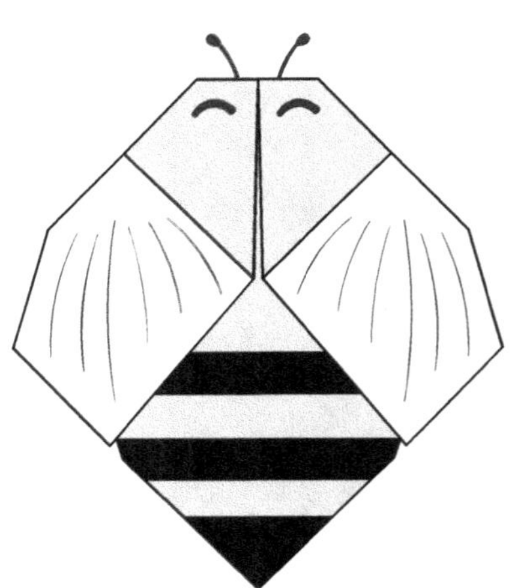

Samurai Helmet

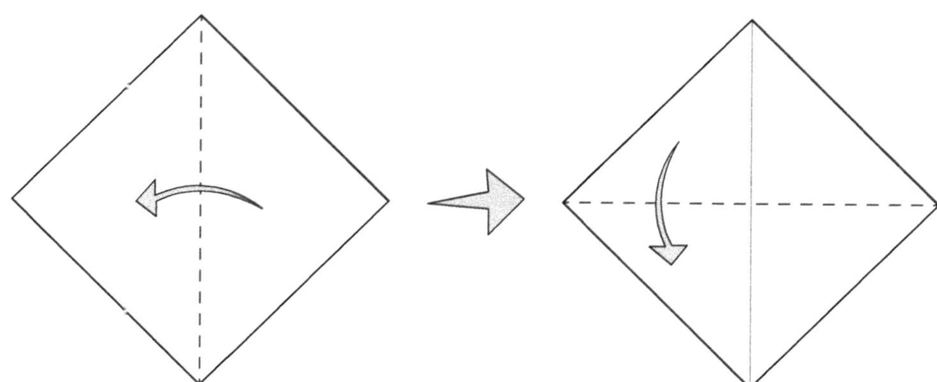

Step 1

Fold the sheet along its vertical diagonal and unfold, then fold it down in half along the other diagonal.

Step 2

Bring both side corners down toward the vertical midline you just made, then fold them halfway back up as shown.

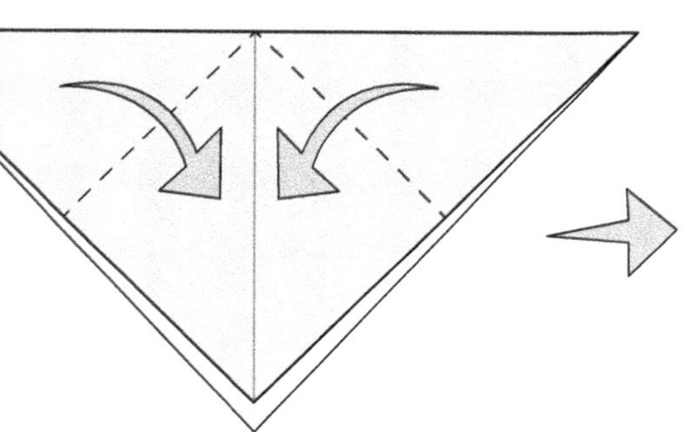

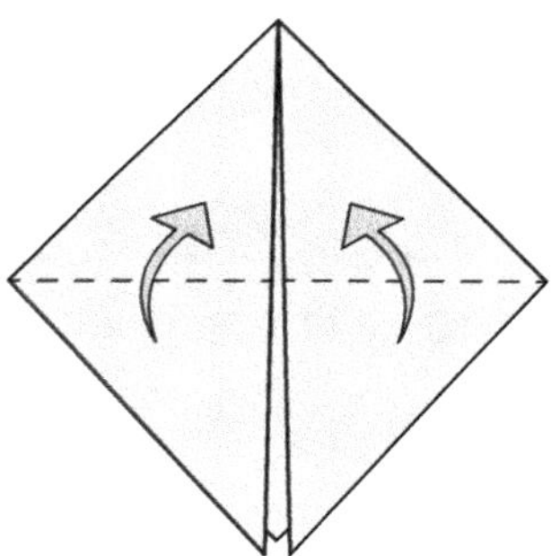

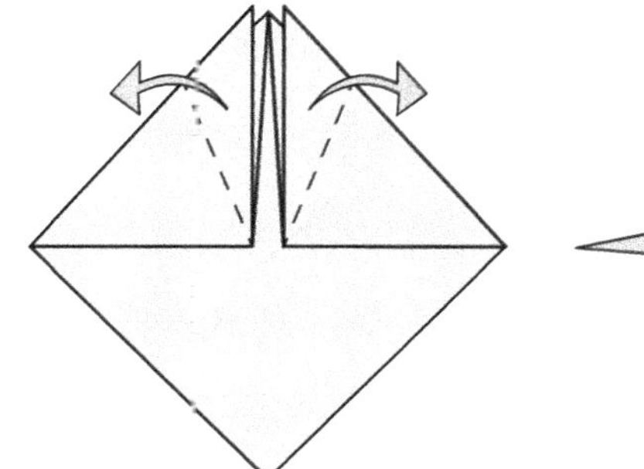

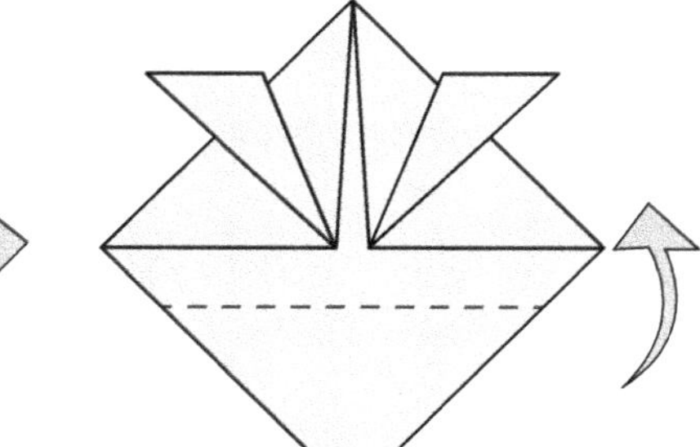

Step 3

Fold the tips of the flaps you just made outward, then fold the bottom corner up as shown.

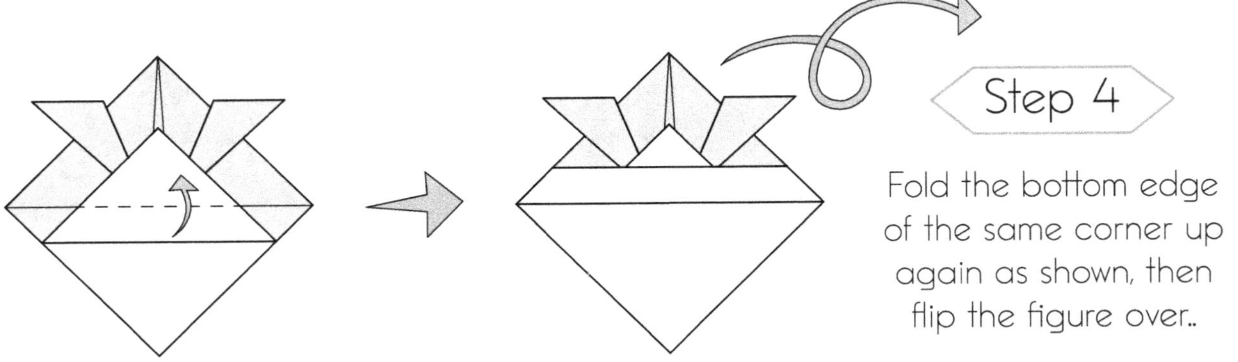

Fold the bottom edge of the same corner up again as shown, then flip the figure over..

Fold the bottom corner up twice in a row, just like you did on the other side.

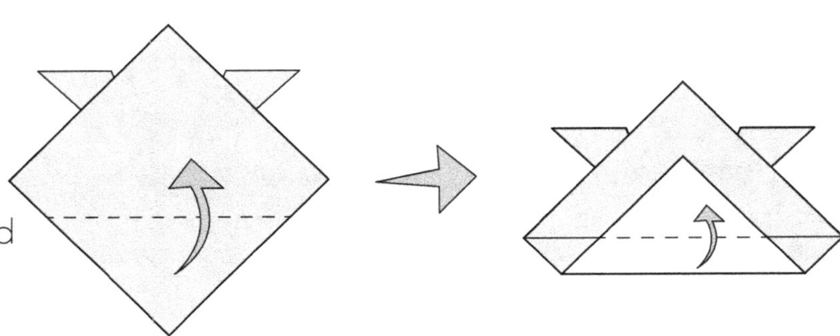

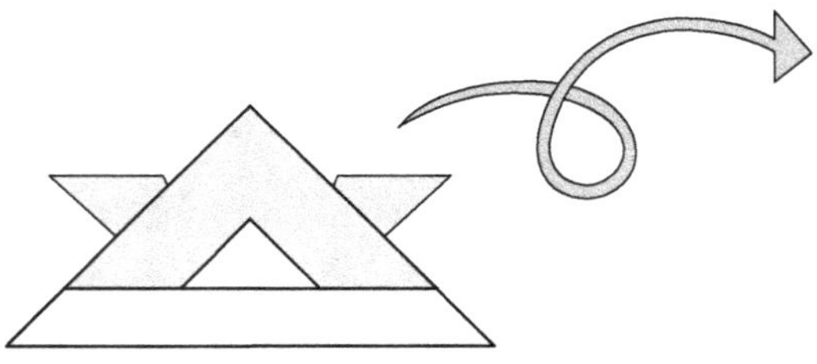

Flip the figure over.

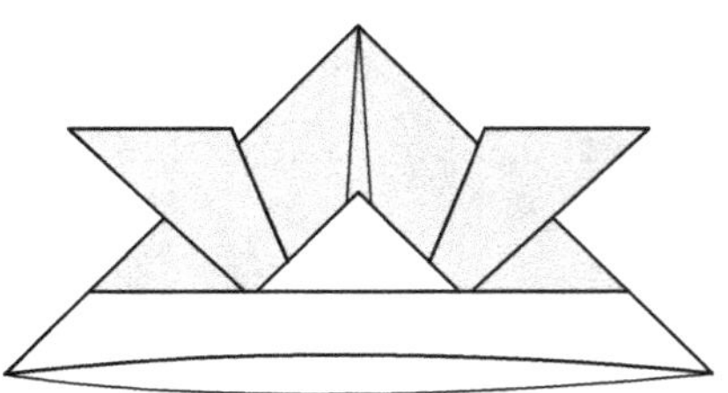

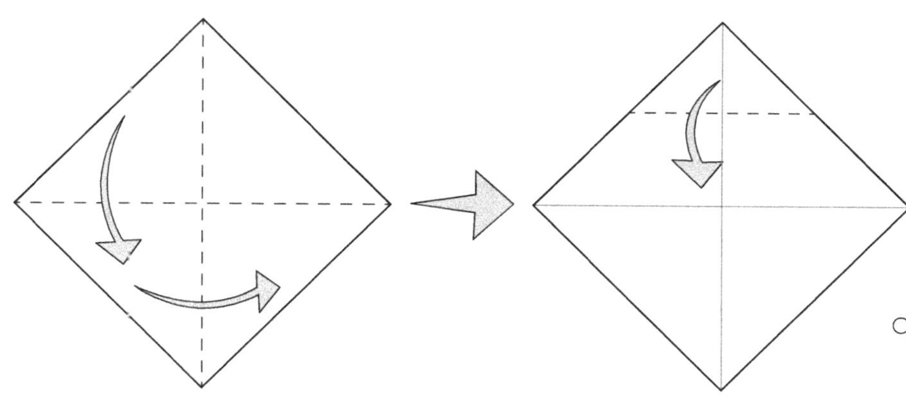

Fold the sheet along both diagonals and unfold, then bring the top corner down to the center of the sheet, where the two creases meet.

Fold both side corners in at an angle as shown, then flip the figure over.

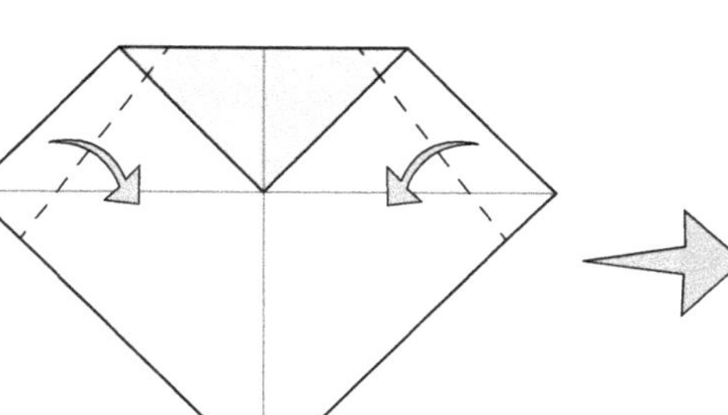
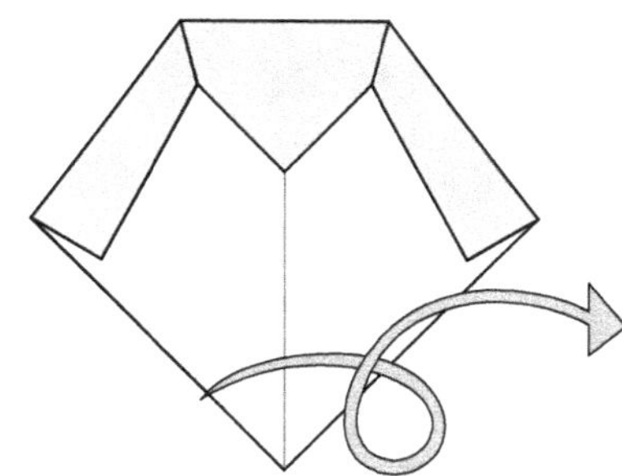

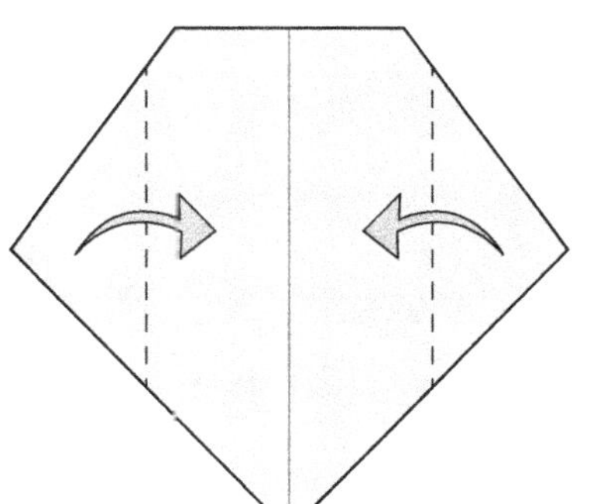
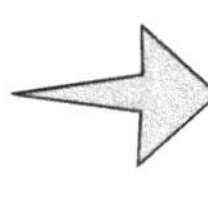
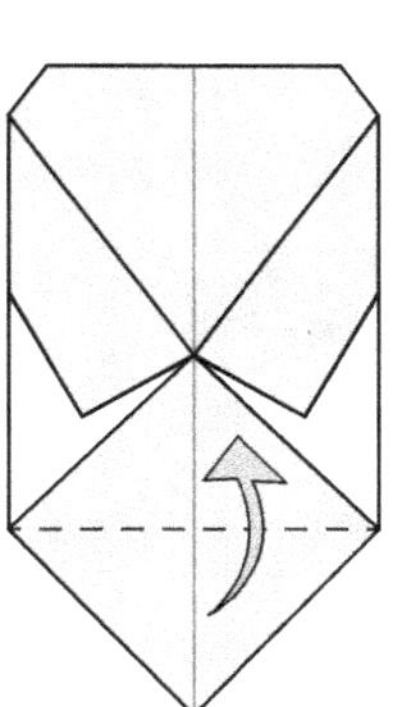

Bring both side corners in toward the vertical midline, then bring the bottom corner up to meet them.

Dracula

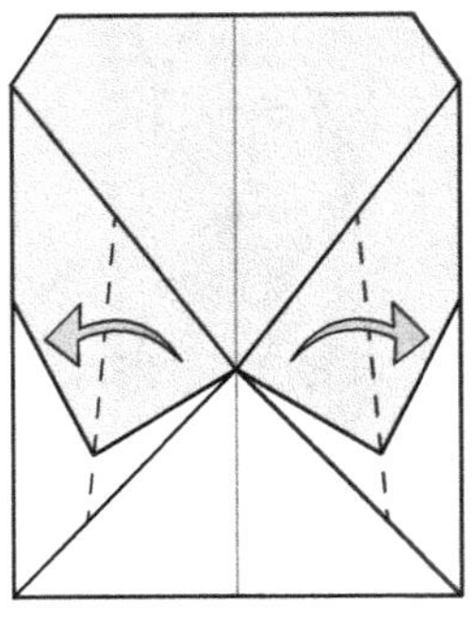 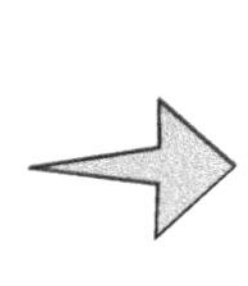 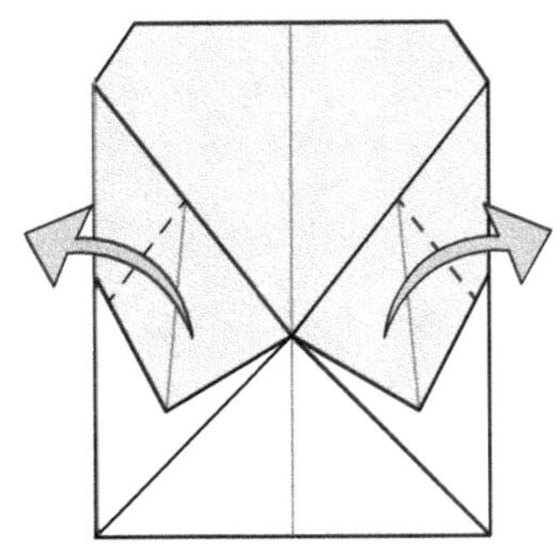 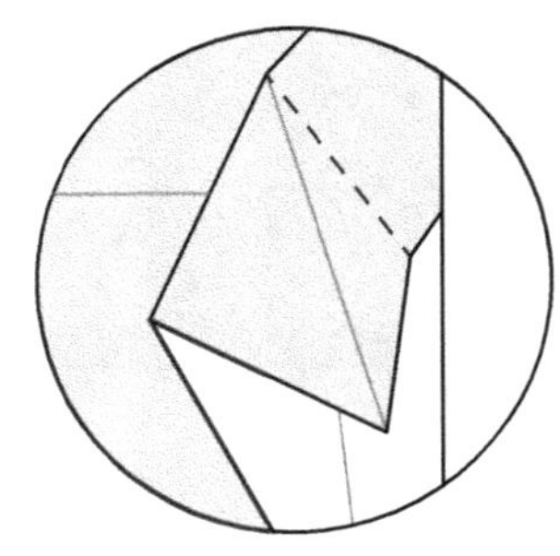

Step 4

Fold both corners back out as shown, then unfold them to make two creases.

Step 5

Use those creases you just made to open the top layer and fold it out as shown to make Dracula's ears.

Step 6

Fold both bottom corners up along the bottom edge of the ears as shown.

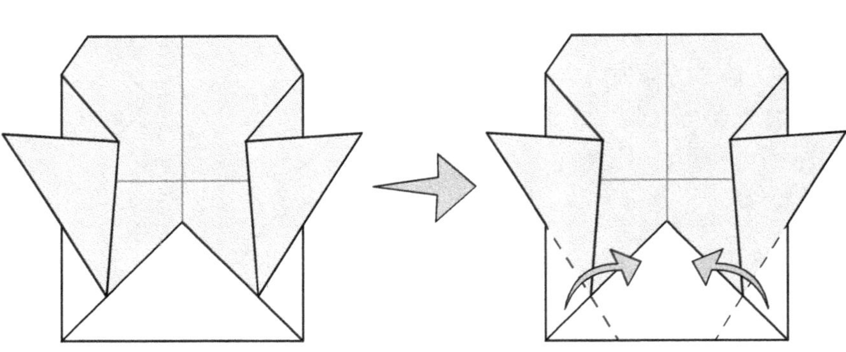

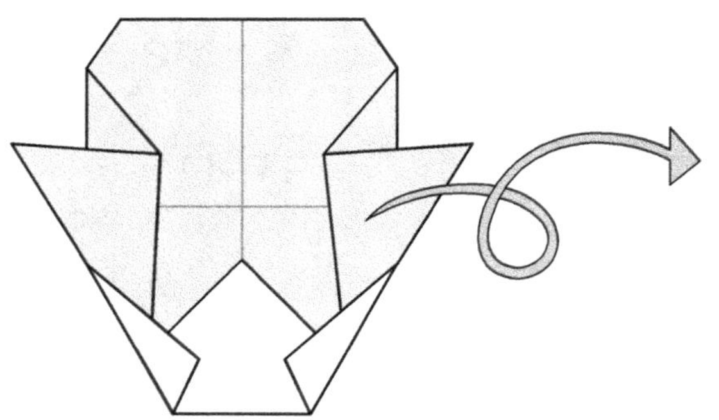

Step 7

Flip the figure over.

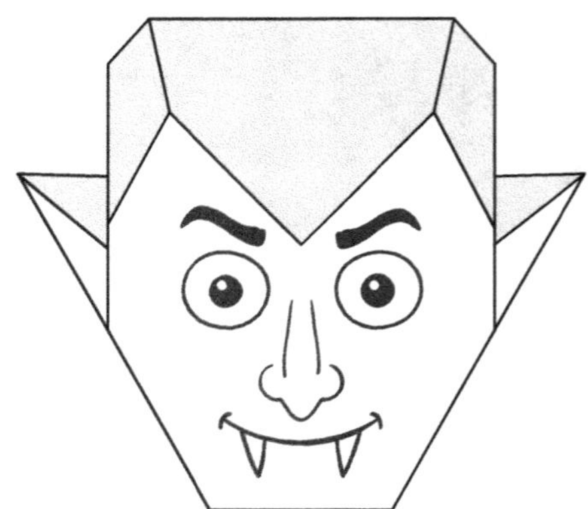

Dracula

Mushroom

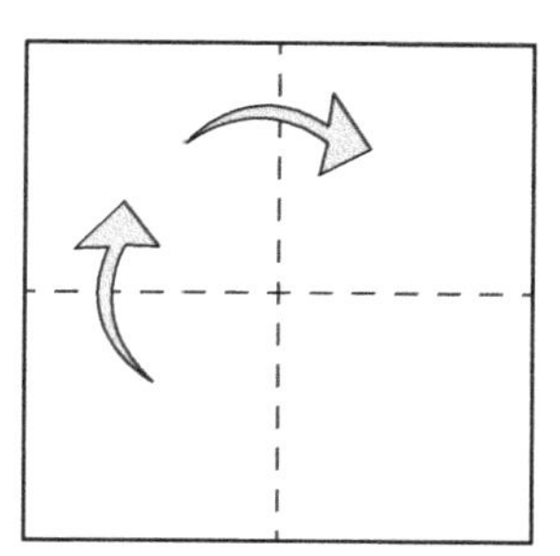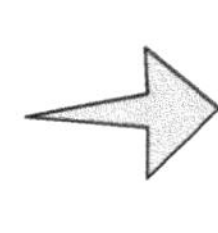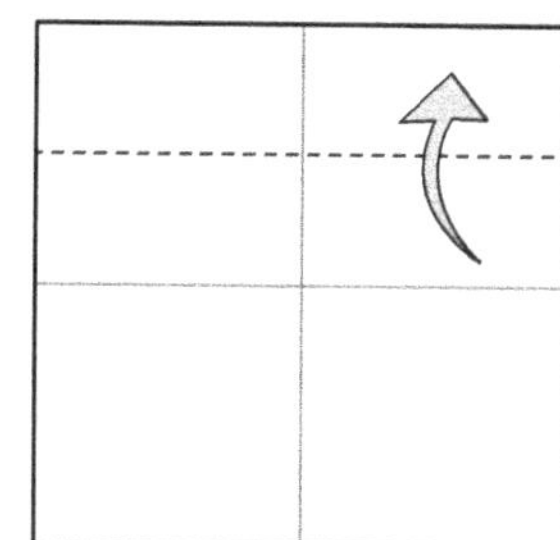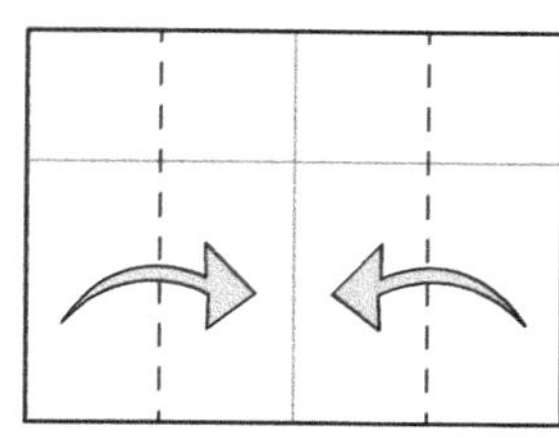

Step 1

Fold the paper sheet in half lengthwise and crosswise. Then unfold it.

Step 2

Fold the top edge backward to the horizontal midline.

Step 3

Fold both side edges in toward the vertical midline.

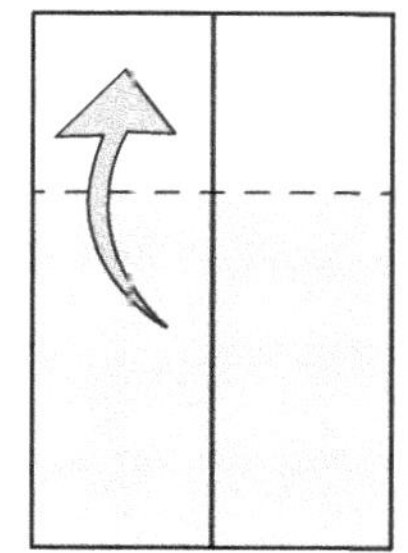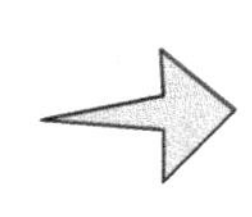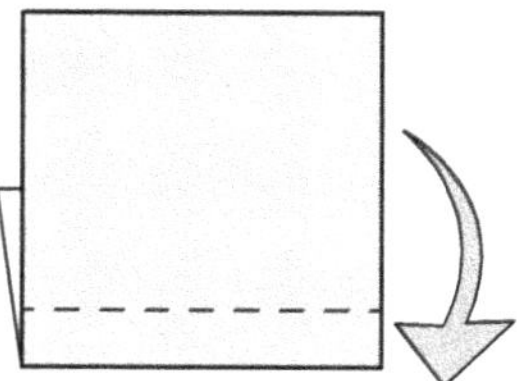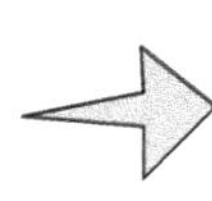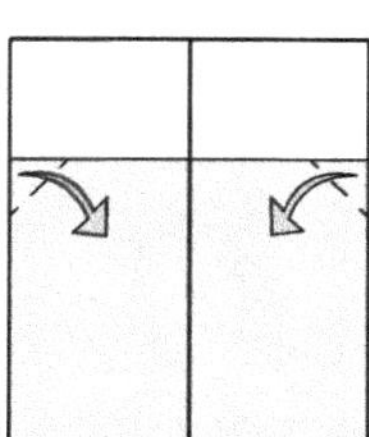

Step 4

Fold the bottom of the figure up along he horizontal midline from Step 1.

Step 5

Now fold the same section back down, leaving a small gap between the two folds.

Step 6

Fold the corners of the top layer down as shown, then unfold them.

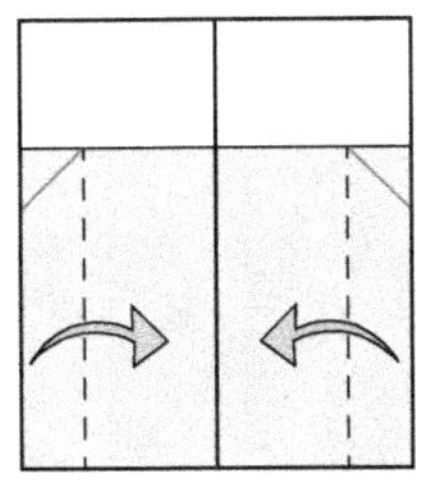 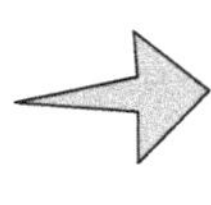 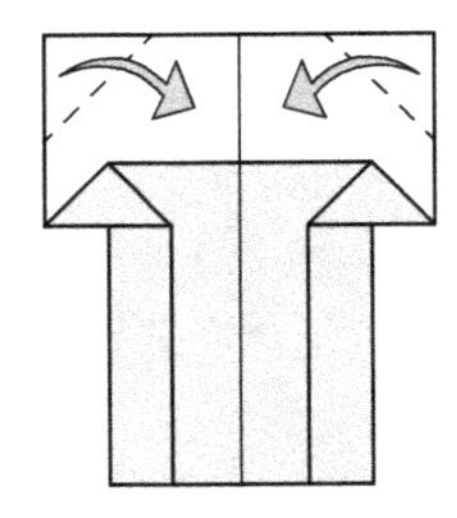

Use the creases you just made to fold the sides of the top layer in as shown. As you fold in the sides, flatten the top until you get a triangle on each side. Then fold the top corners down.

Fold the bottom corners up.

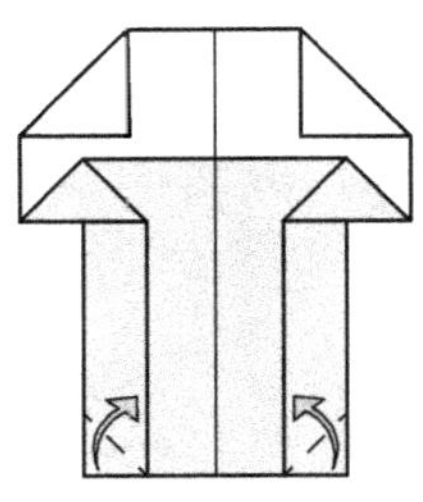 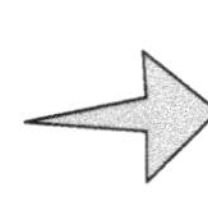 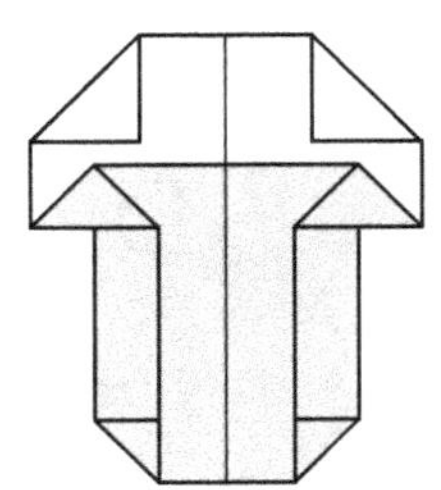

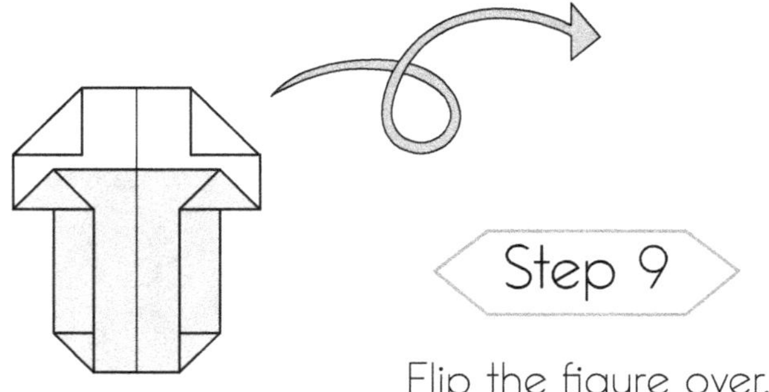

Flip the figure over.

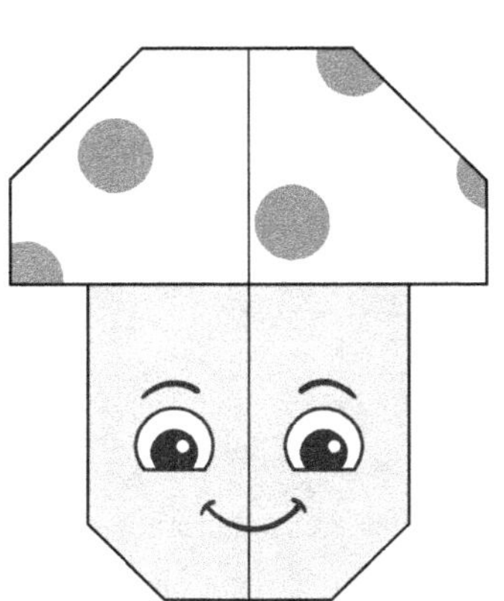

Mushroom

Lantern

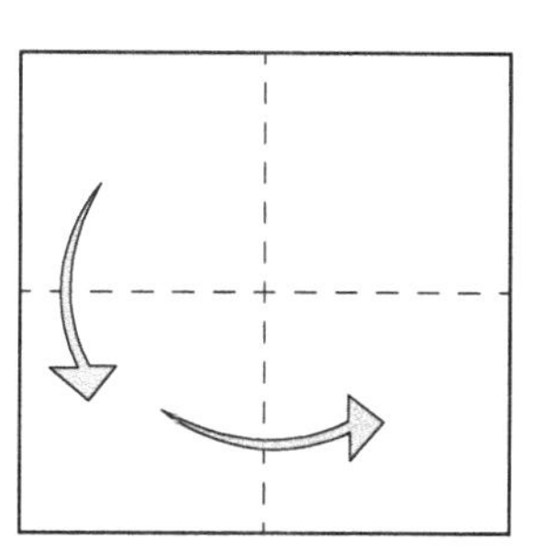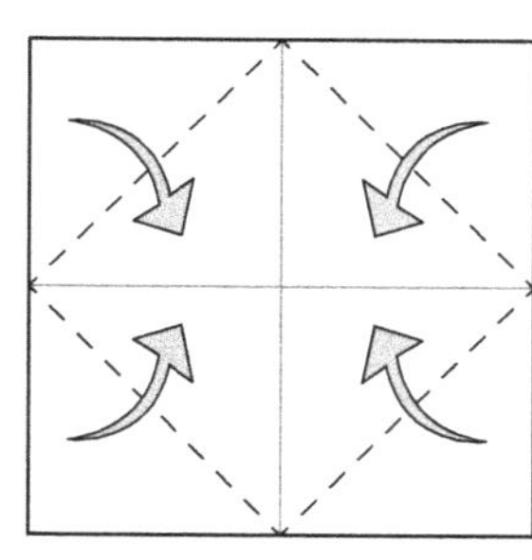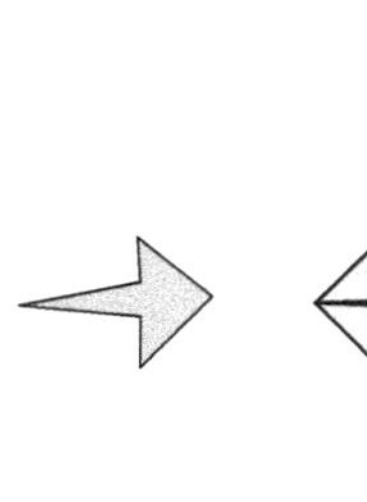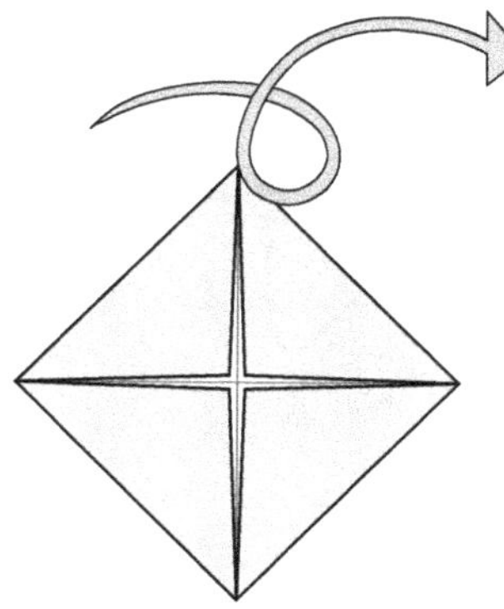

Step 1

Fold the paper sheet in half lengthwise and crosswise. Then unfold it.

Step 2

Bring all corners to the center of the sheet where the two creases from previous step meet.

Step 3

Flip the figure over.

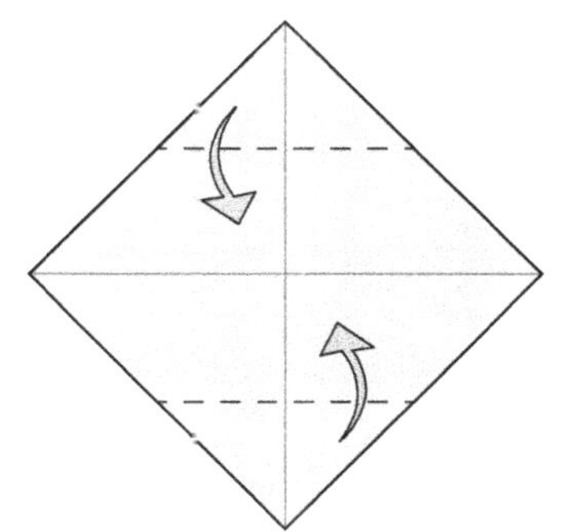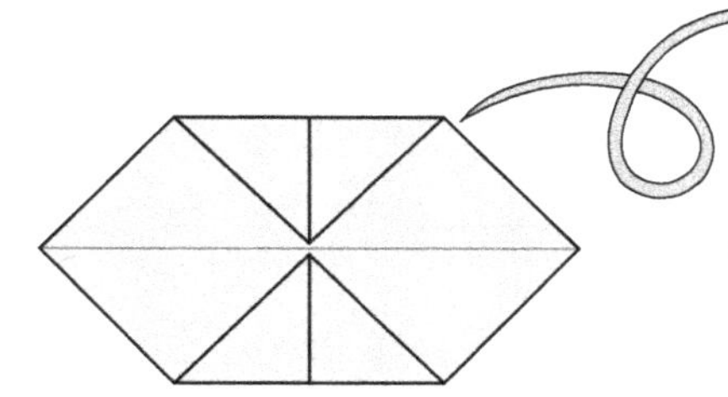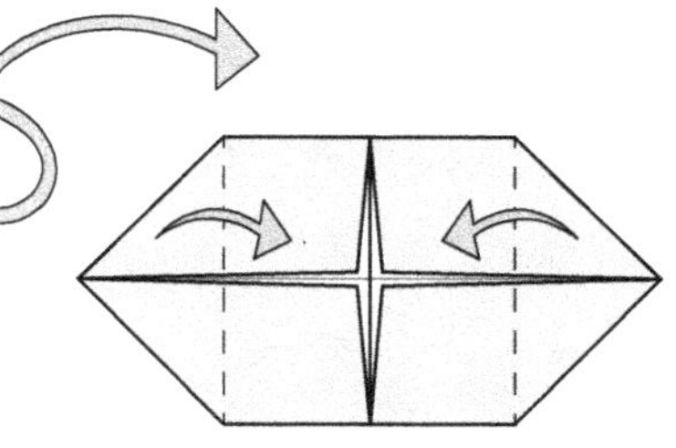

Step 4

Bring the top and bottom edges to the center of the figure as well, then flip the figure over again.

Step 5

Now fold the side corners in to the center of the figure.

Lantern

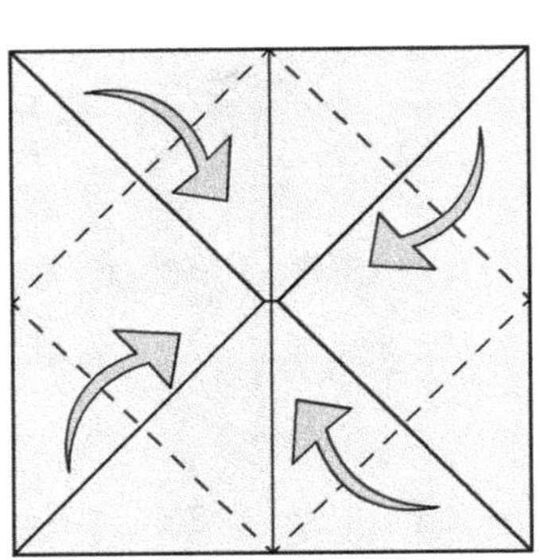 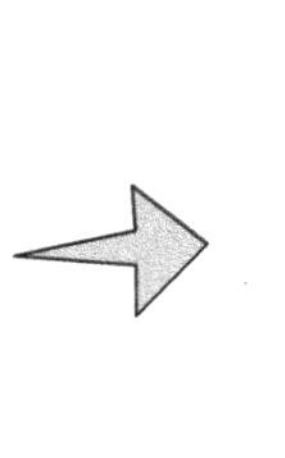 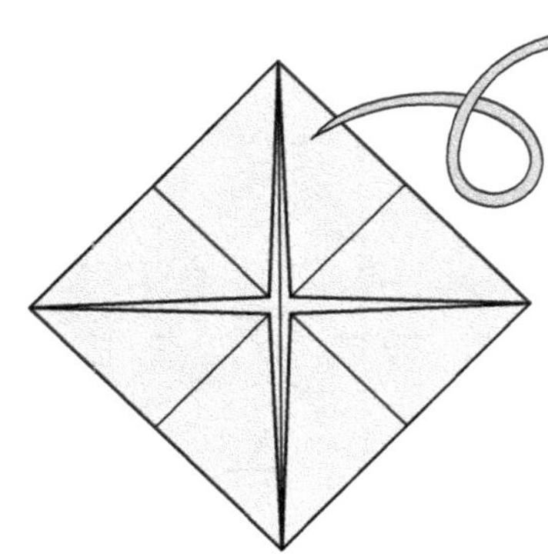

Repeat Step 2, that is, bring all corners to the center of the figure, then flip the figure over.

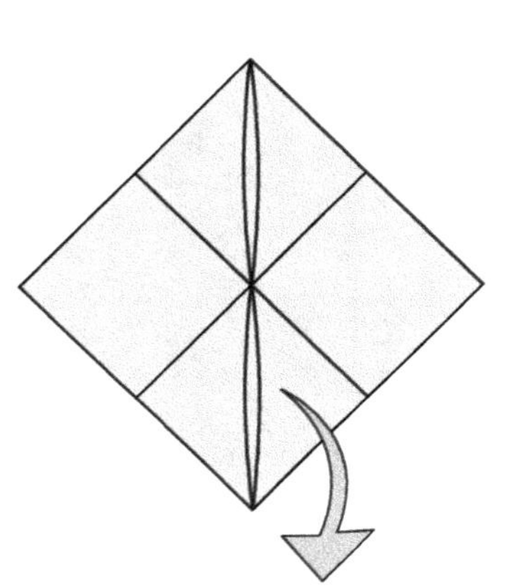 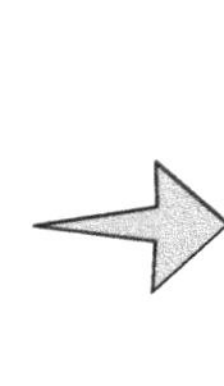 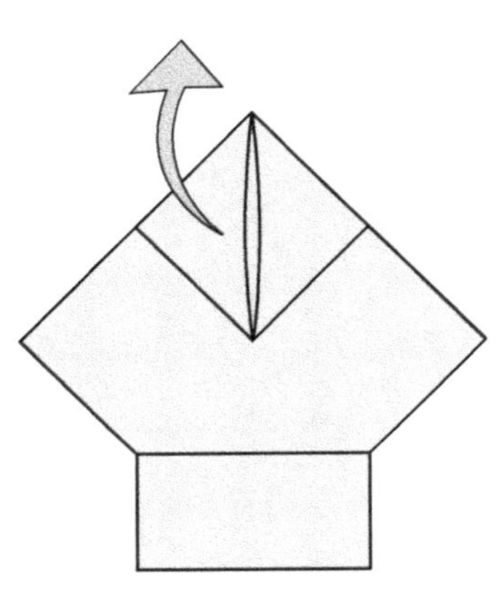

You will see that the bottom corner is made up of two flaps, open them carefully while pulling them down and flatten to get a rectangle. Repeat the process for the top corner.

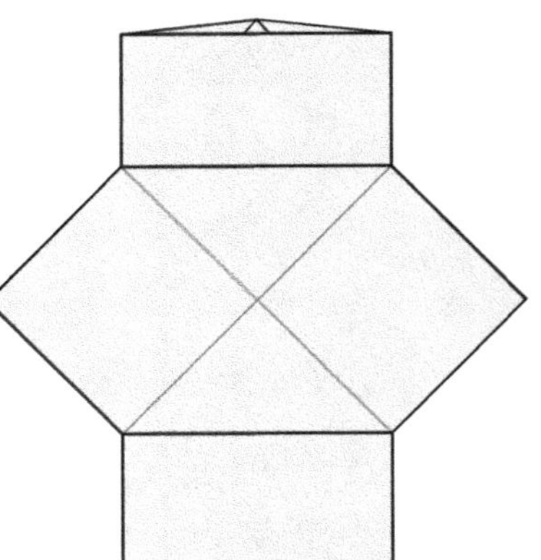

Strawberry

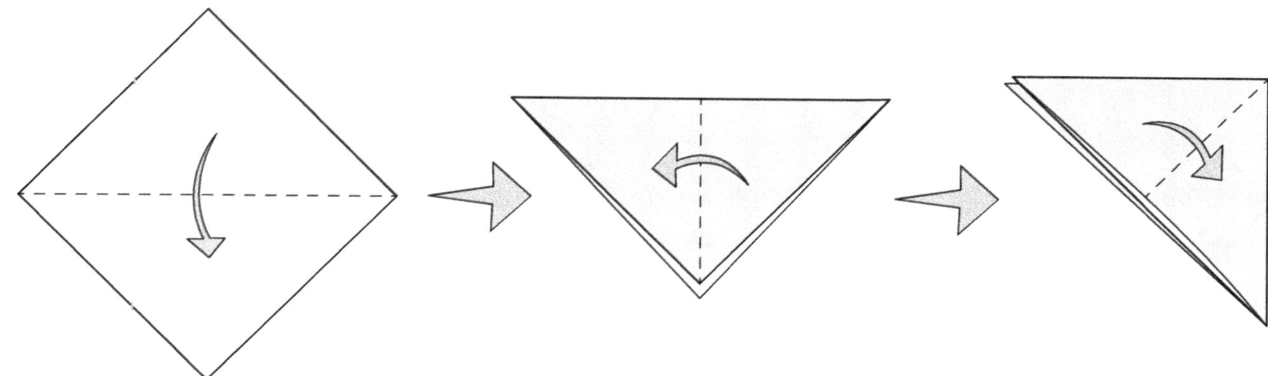

Step 1

Fold the sheet diagonally down in half.

Step 2

Fold the figure in half.

Step 3

Fold the top layer diagonally down and unfold it to make a crease.

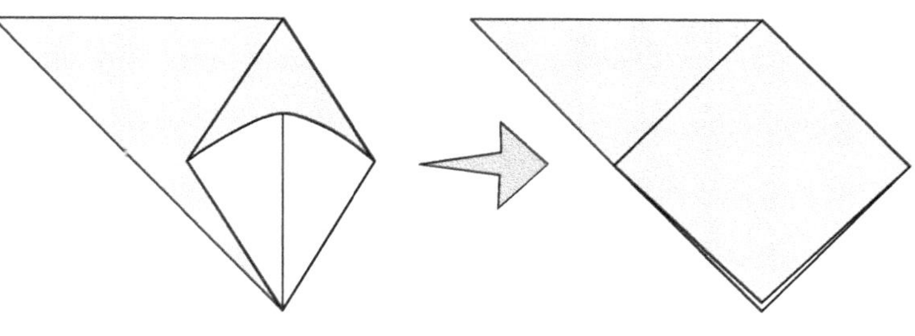

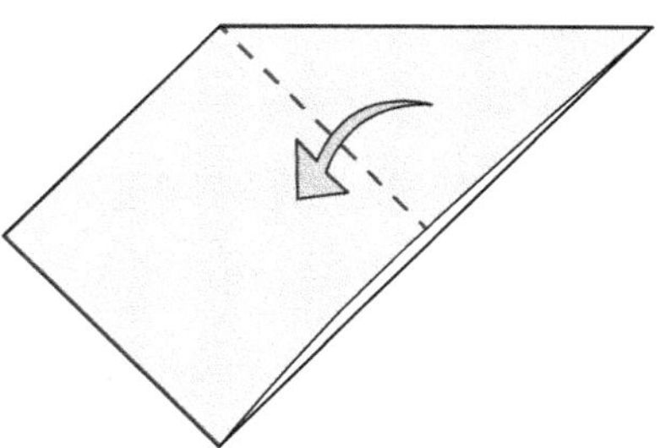

Step 4

Pull this top layer to the right along the crease you just made and flatten as shown.

Step 5

Flip the figure over and repeat steps 3 and 4.

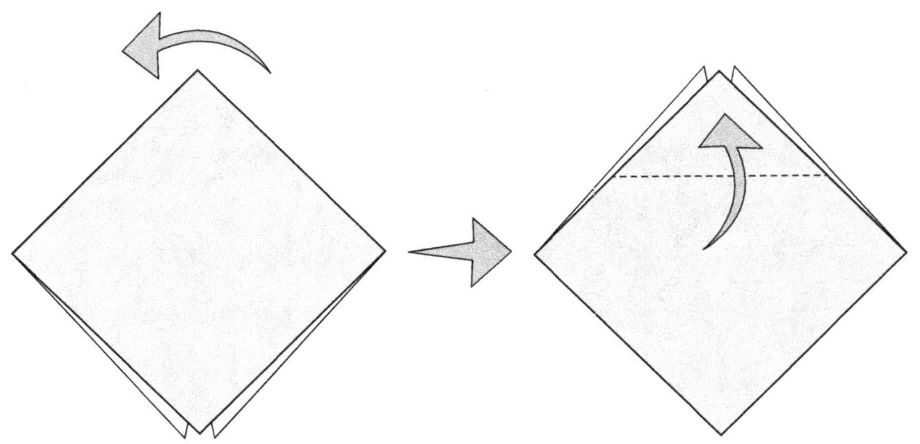

Turn the figure upside down and fold the tip of the top layer backward as shown.

Now fold the tips of the layer just below forward over the top layer, then fold the side corners backward as shown.

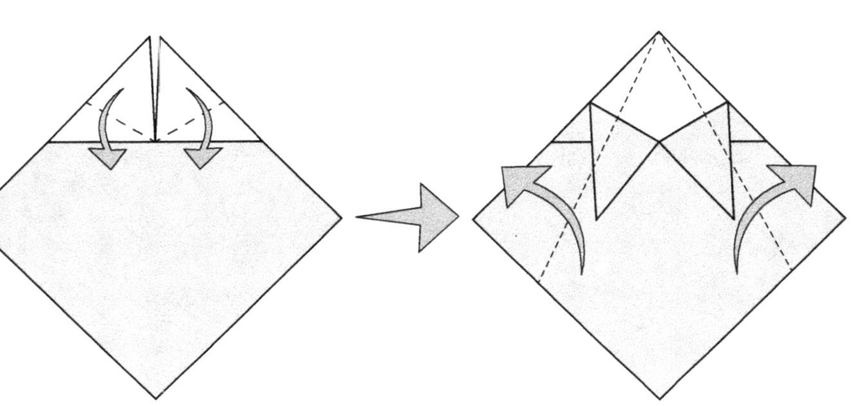

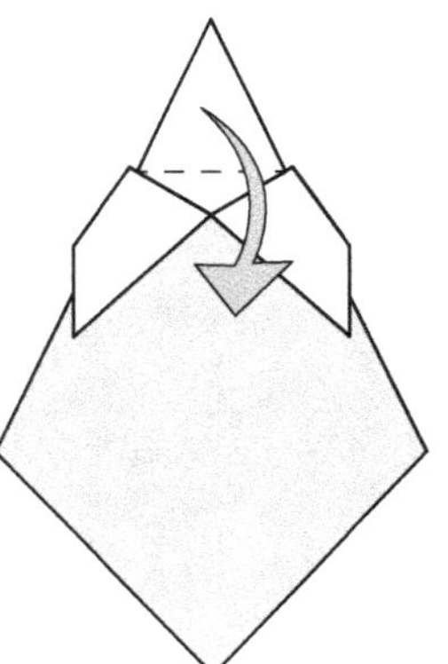

Fold the top corner down over the top layer.

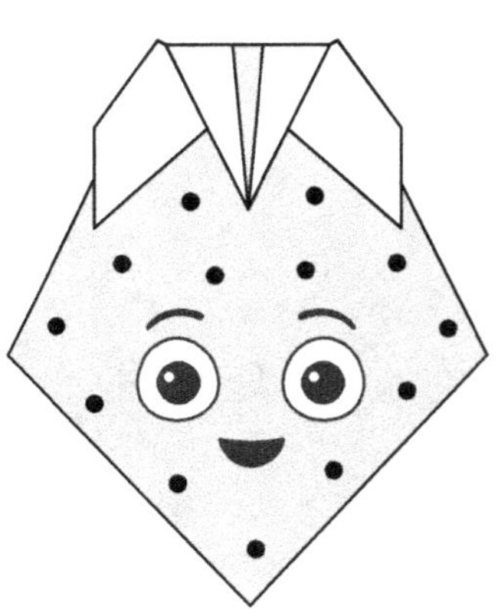

Jack-O'-Lantern

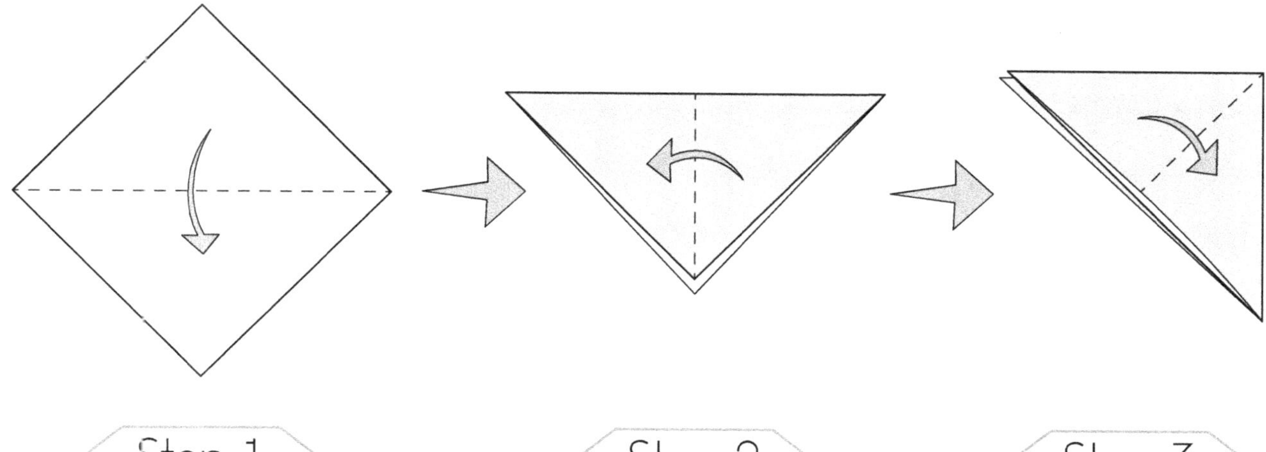

Step 1

Fold the sheet diagonally down in half.

Step 2

Fold the figure in half.

Step 3

Fold the top layer diagonally down and unfold to make a crease.

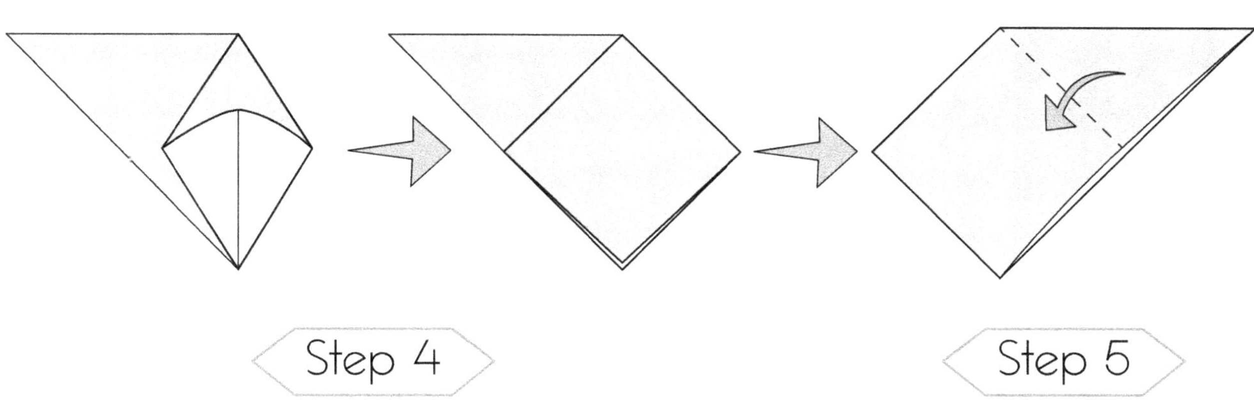

Step 4

Pull this top layer to the right along the crease you just made and flatten as shown.

Step 5

Flip the figure over and repeat steps 3 and 4.

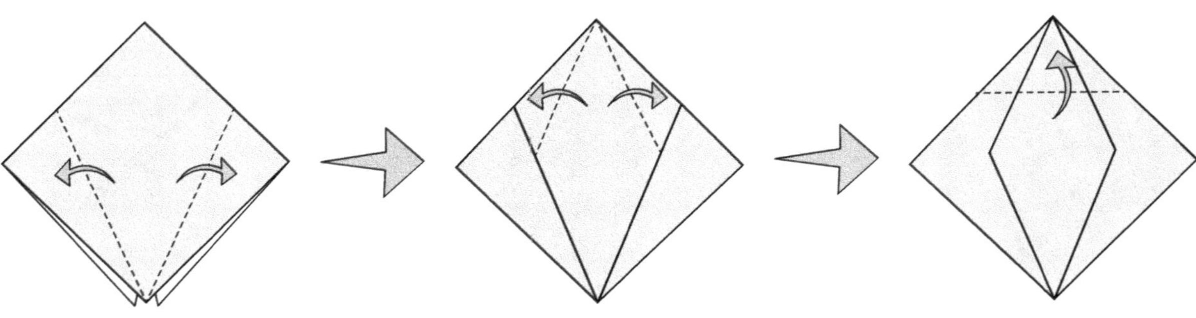

Step 6

Fold the bottom of the side corners of the top layer backward.

Step 7

Now fold the top of the side corners of the same layer backward as well.

Step 8

Fold the upper corner of the figure back.

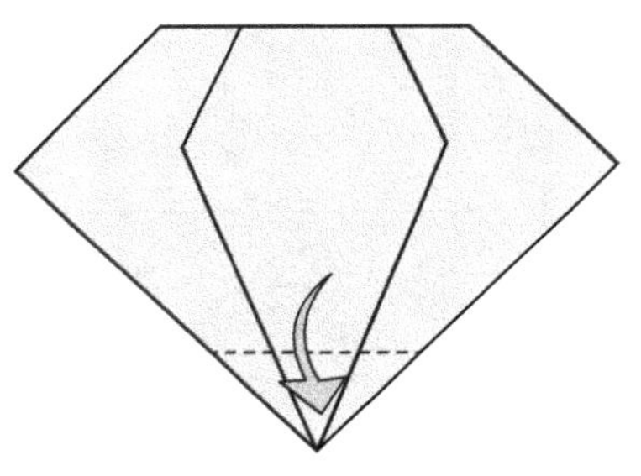

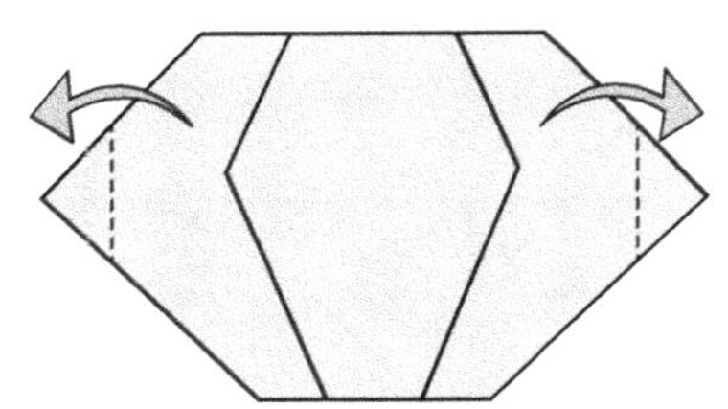

Step 9

Repeat the previous step for the bottom corner.

Step 10

Do the same for the side corners.

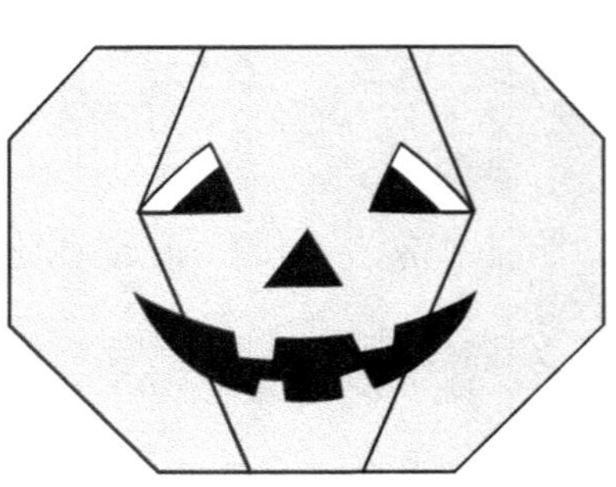

Jack-O'-Lantern

Sunglasses

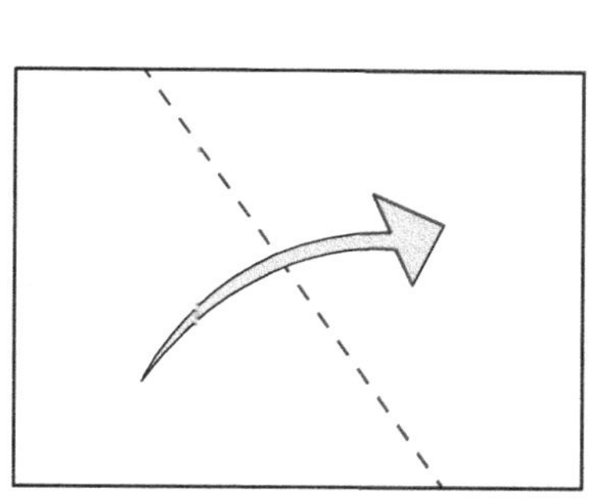

Step 1

Take an A4 sheet and bring the bottom left corner up until it meets the top right corner and flatten it.

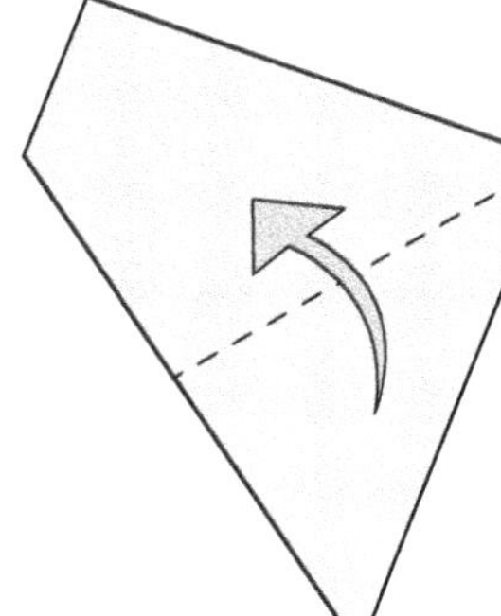

Step 2

Fold the figure up in half as shown.

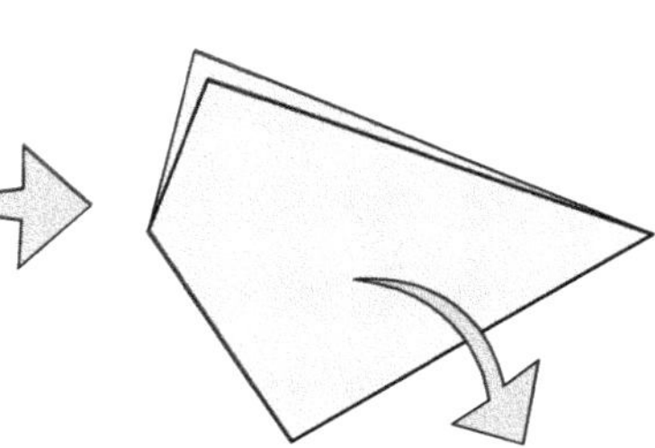

Step 3

Unfold everything you've done so far.

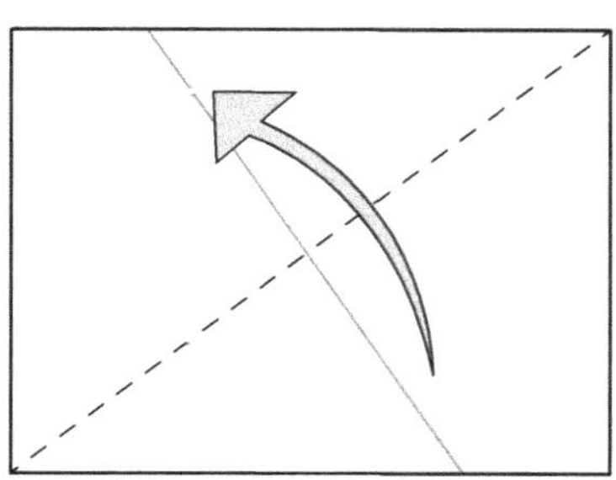

Step 4

Now fold the bottom right corner up until the bottom edge of the sheet meets the crease from Step 1. Then fold the new bottom edge up to the point where the two layers of paper form a V shape as shown.

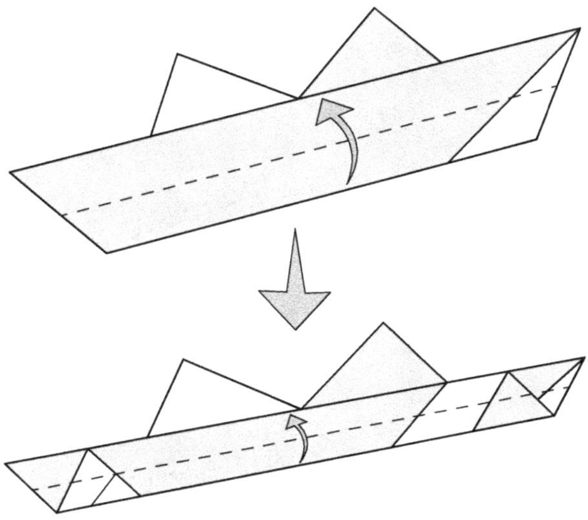

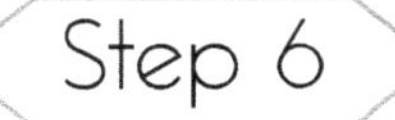

Fold the bottom edge back
up twice in a row.

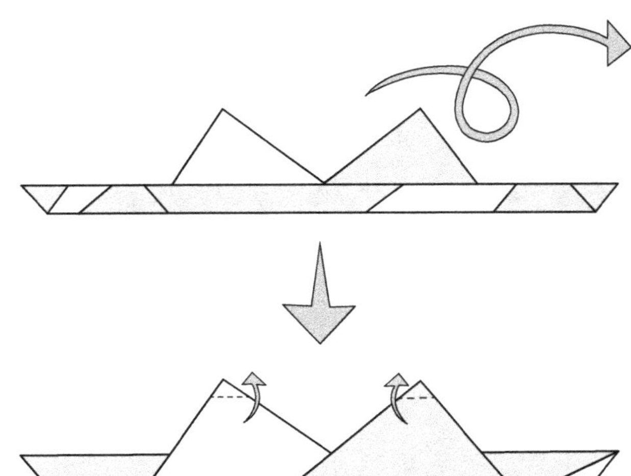

Flip the figure over and fold the
tips of the V-shape back.

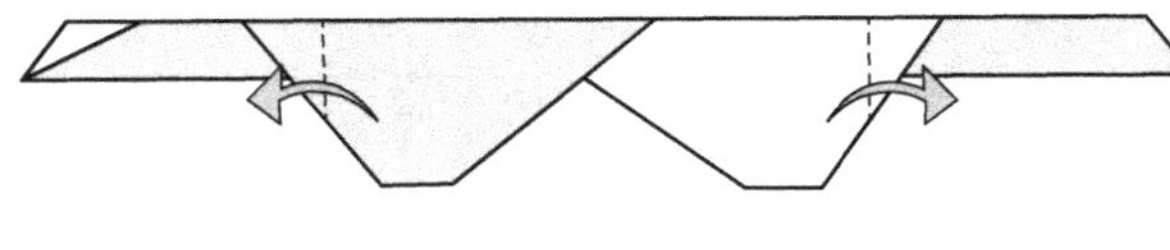

Rotate the figure as shown
and fold both sides halfway back.

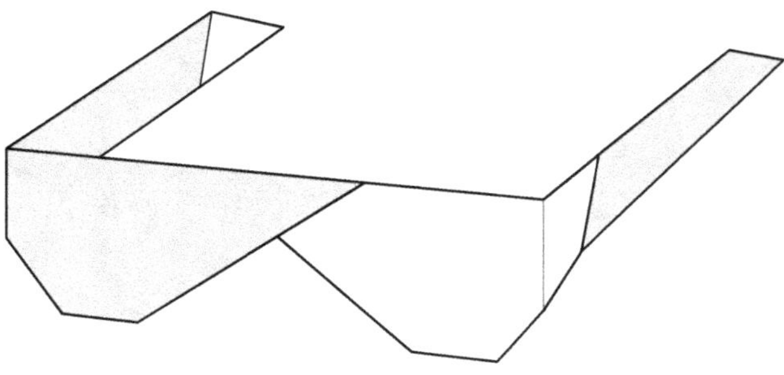

Sunglasses

Step 1

Take a square sheet and cut in half, then fold one of the pieces in half and unfold it.

Step 2

Bring the top and bottom edges to the crease you just made.

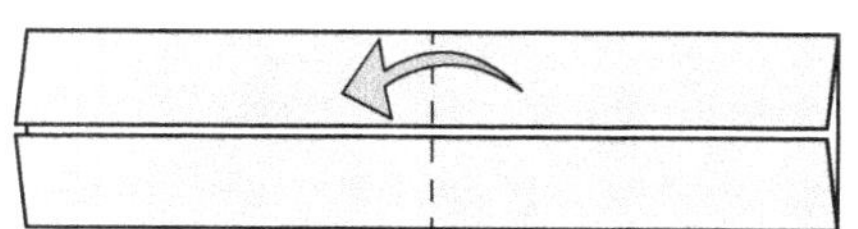

Step 3

Fold the figure in half to the left.

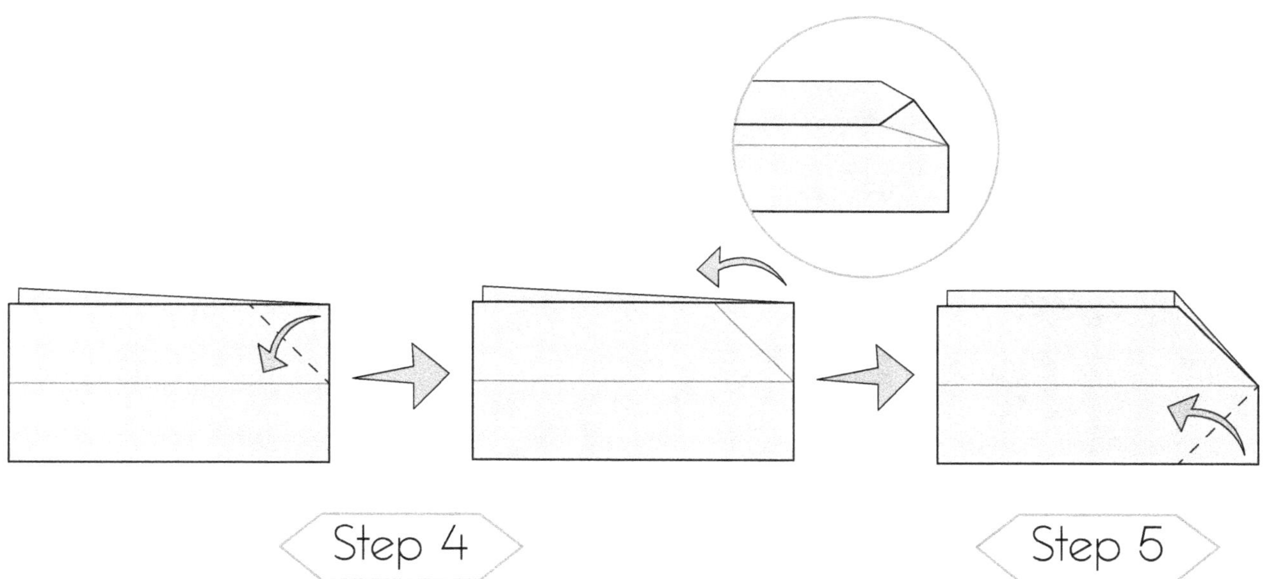

Step 4

Fold the top right corner diagonally down and unfold it to make a crease. Then use that crease to make an inside reverse fold as shown.

Step 5

Repeat the previous step for the bottom right corner.

Ring

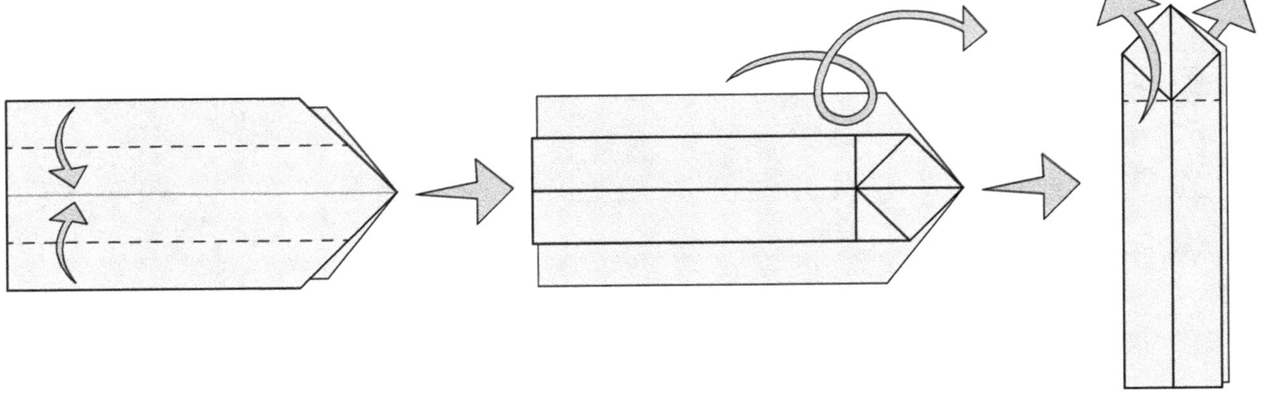

Step 6

Bring the top and bottom edges of the top layer to the midline, flip the figure over, and repeat on the other side. Now rotate the figure and fold both 'arms' halfway up as shown.

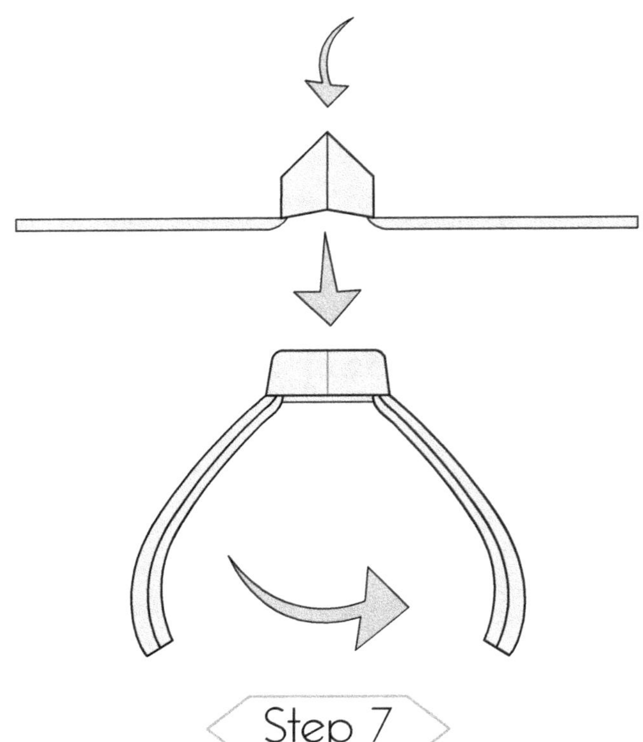

Step 7

Push the center of the figure to flatten it, then curve the 'arms' until you can fit the end of one inside the other to lock them in place.

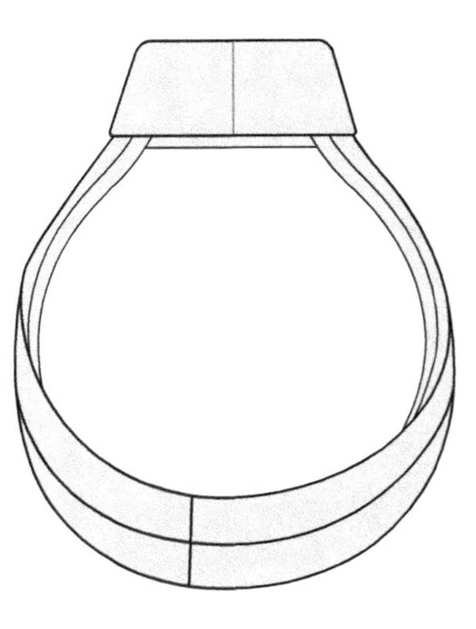

Ring

Big House

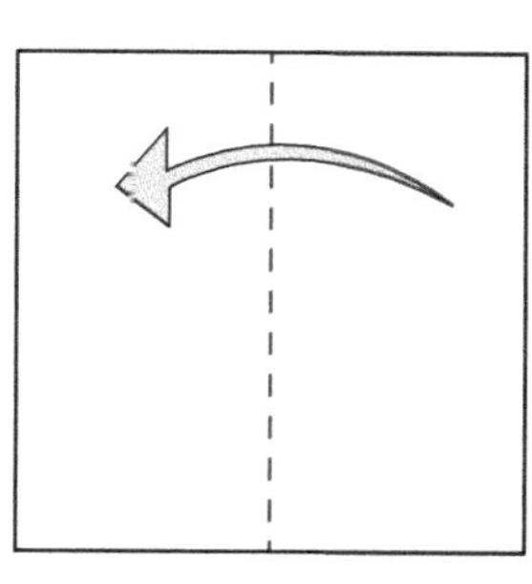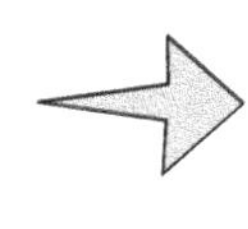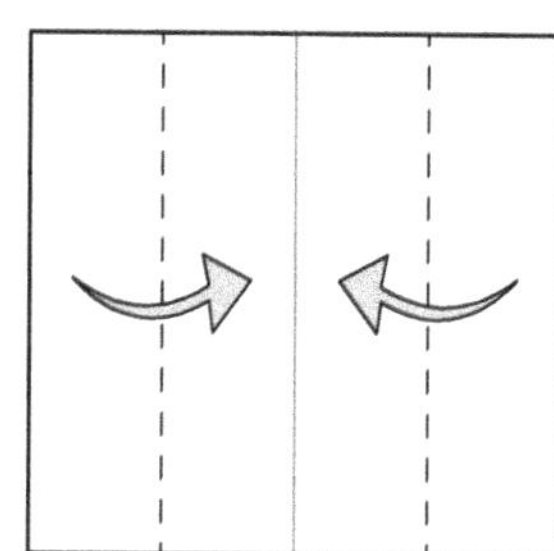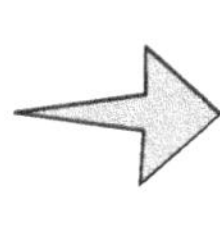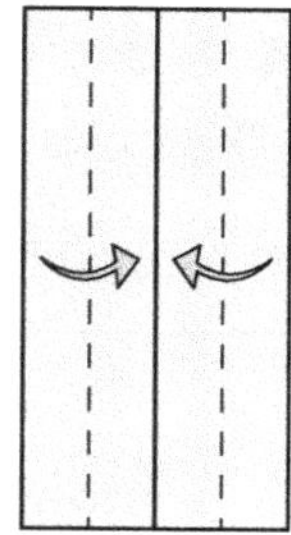

Step 1

Fold the paper sheet
lengthwise and unfold it.

Step 2

Bring both side edges in toward the
vertical midline you just made, then
fold them again.

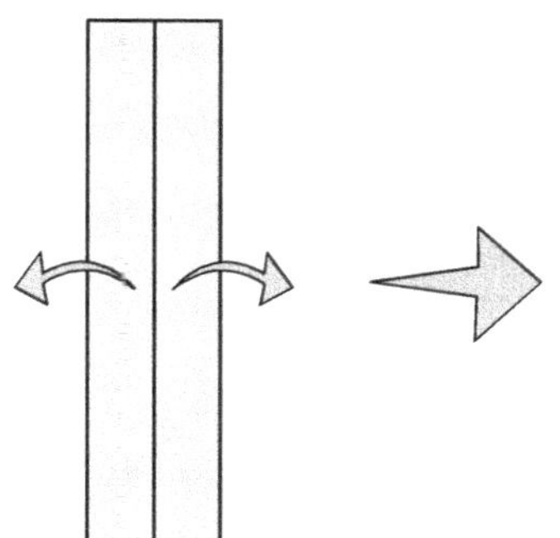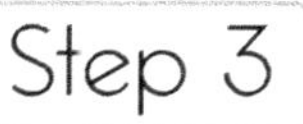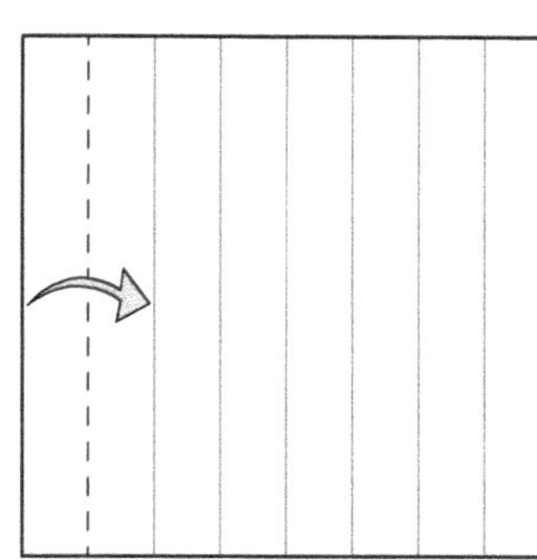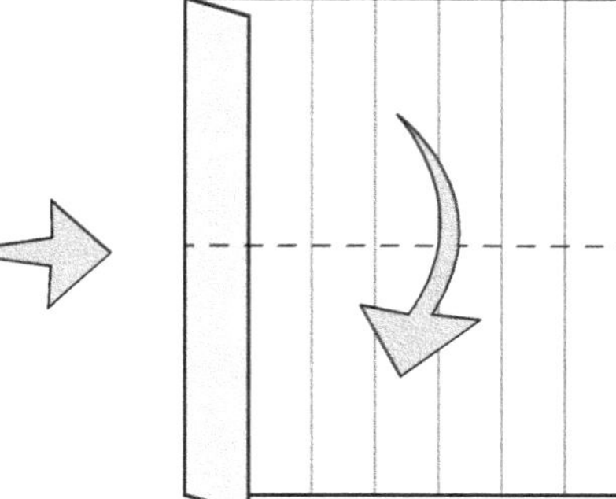

Step 3

Unfold everything.

Step 4

Bring the left edge to
the second vertical
crease as shown.

Step 5

Fold the figure in
half crosswise.

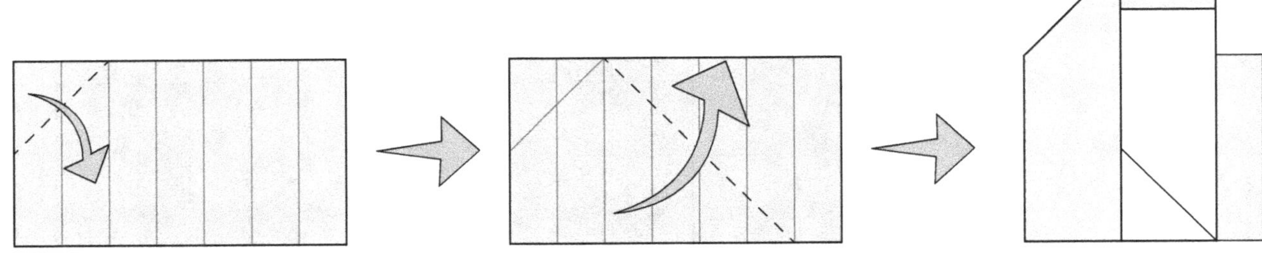

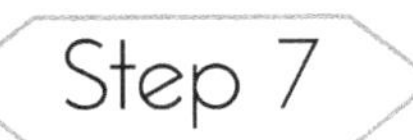

Step 6

Fold the upper left corner diagonally down to make a crease and unfold it.

Step 7

Bring the top layer of the figure along the diagonal line shown, using the crease from the previous step to flatten the figure.

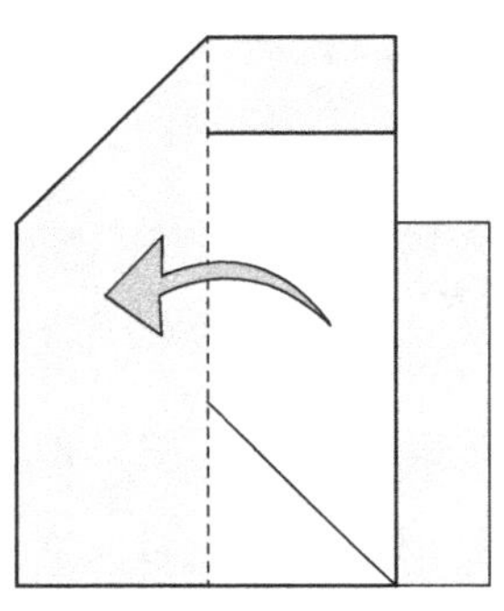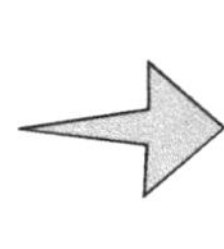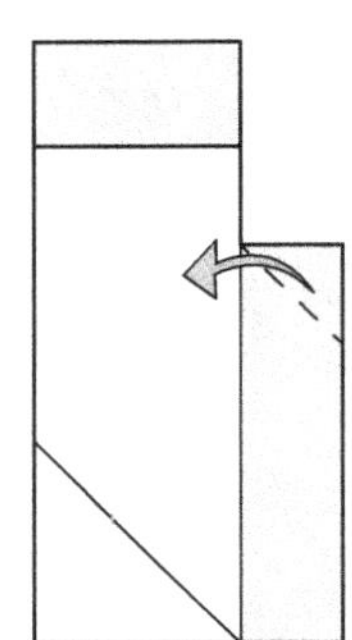

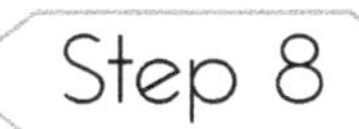

Step 9

Fold the top layer on the right side in. While separating both layers of paper on that side, flatten its top until it forms a triangle.

Step 8

Fold the left side of the figure backward as shown.

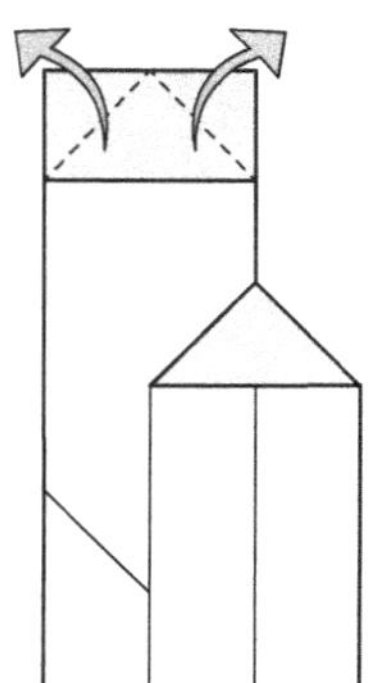

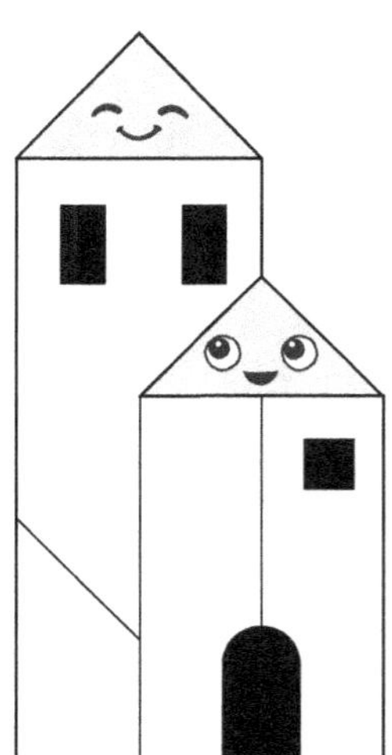

Step 10

Fold the corners on top backwards to form a triangle.

Big House

Little Bird

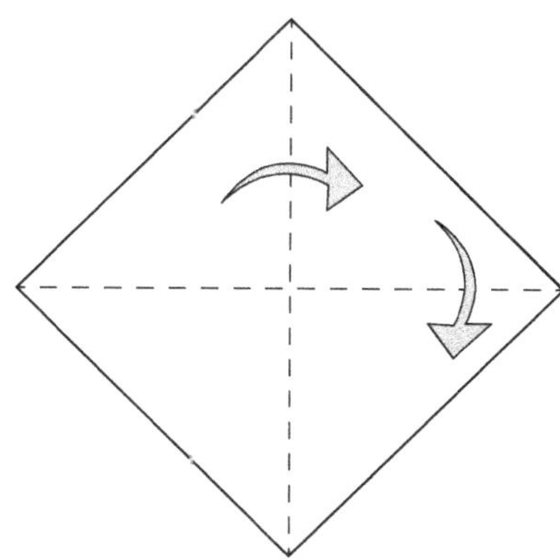

Fold the sheet along both diagonals and unfold.

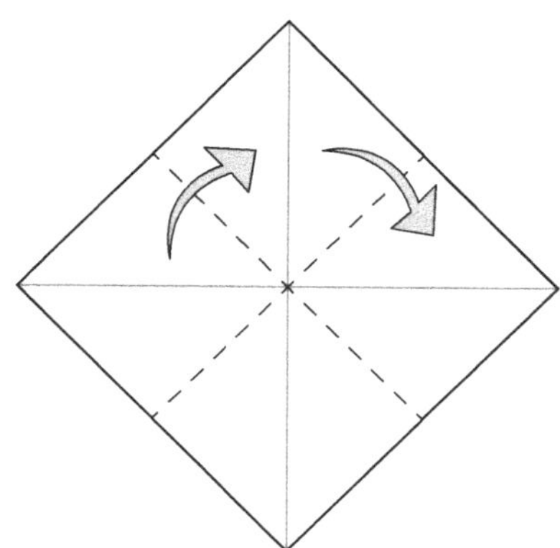

Now fold it lengthwise and crosswise, then unfold.

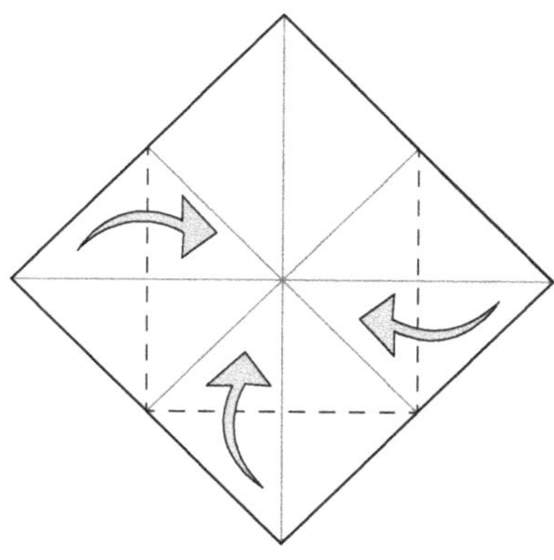

Bring the bottom and side corners to the center of the sheet where all the creases meet, leaving the top corner unfolded.

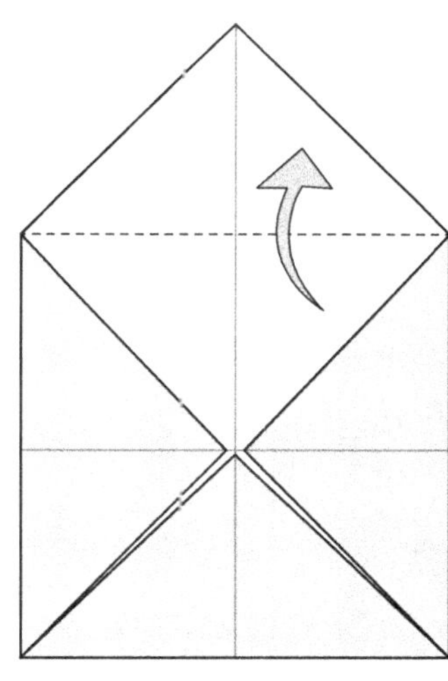

Fold the top corner, but backward this time.

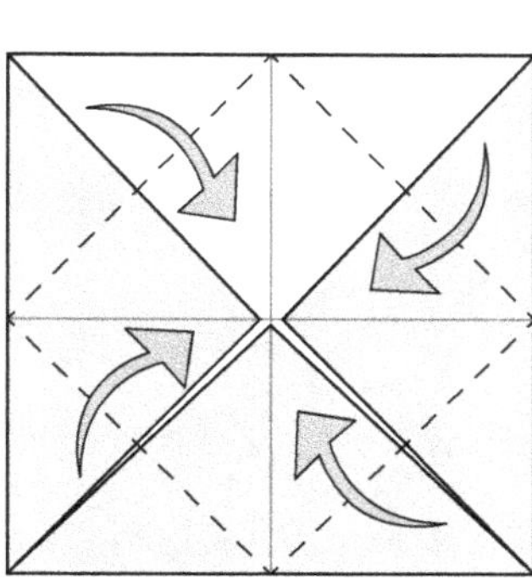

Now bring all corners to the center of the sheet.

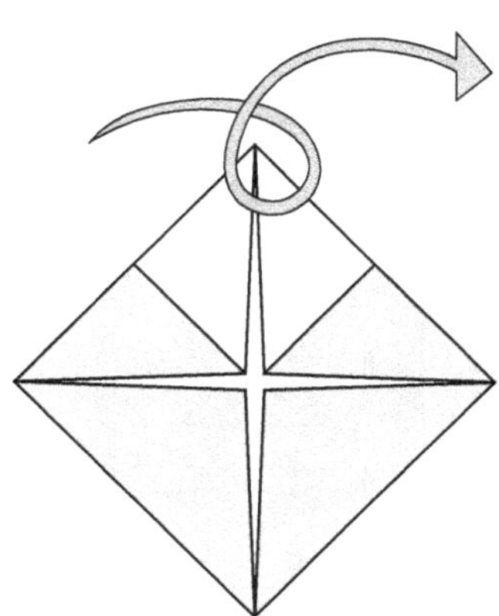

Flip over the figure.

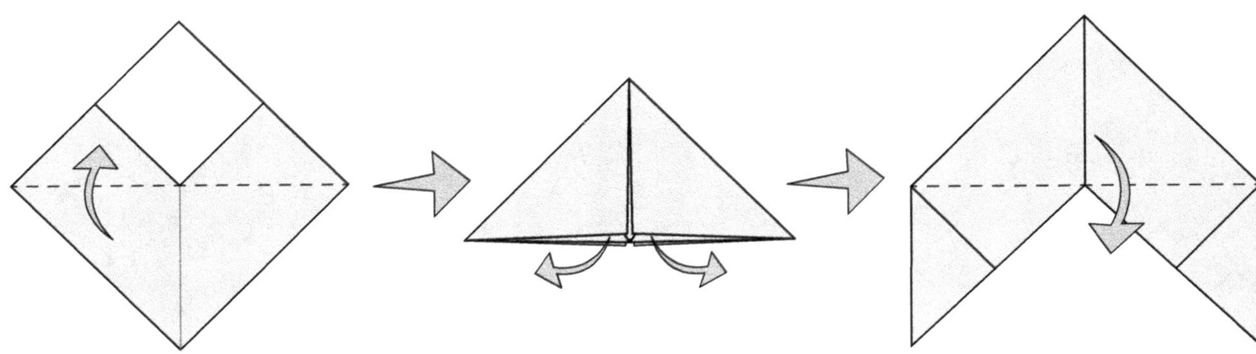

Step 7

Fold the figure up in half.

Step 8

Pull the corners you will see in the middle of the figure right under the top layer.

Step 9

Bring the top corner back down.

Step 10

Fold the figure forward in half, while pulling the flap at the top out so that it ends up sticking out from the folded figure.

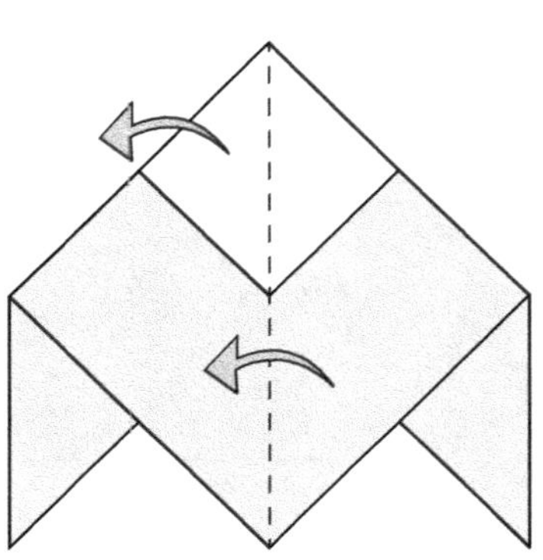

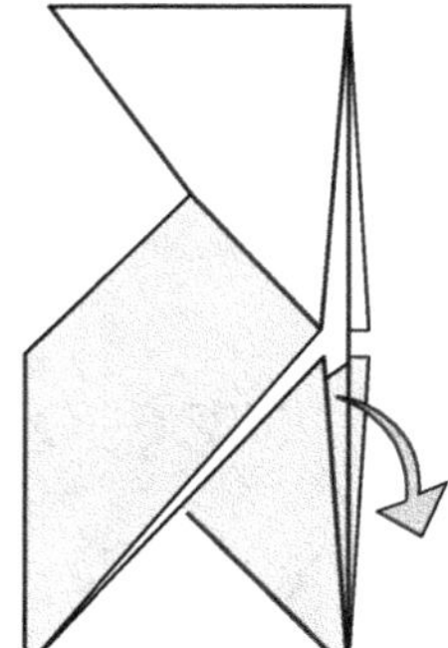

Step 11

In the bottom right corner you will see a flap on its middle layer. Pull it out to make the bird's tail.

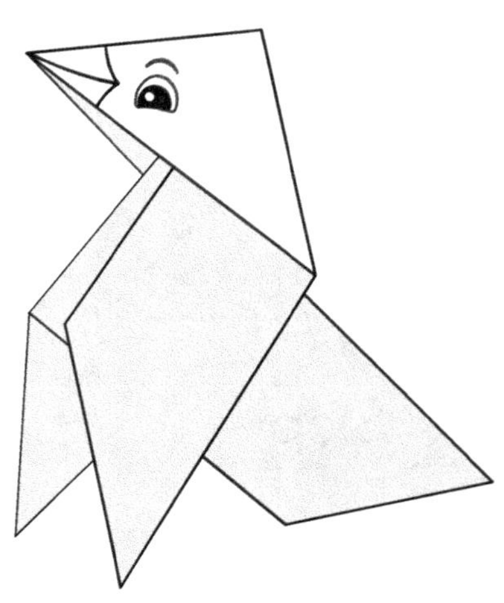

Little Bird

Pinwheel

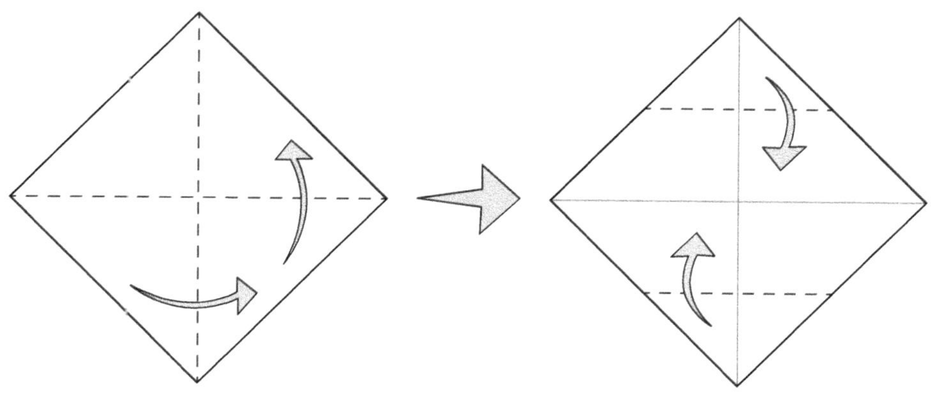

Fold the sheet along both diagonals and unfold. Then bring the top and bottom corners to the center of the sheet where the two creases meet.

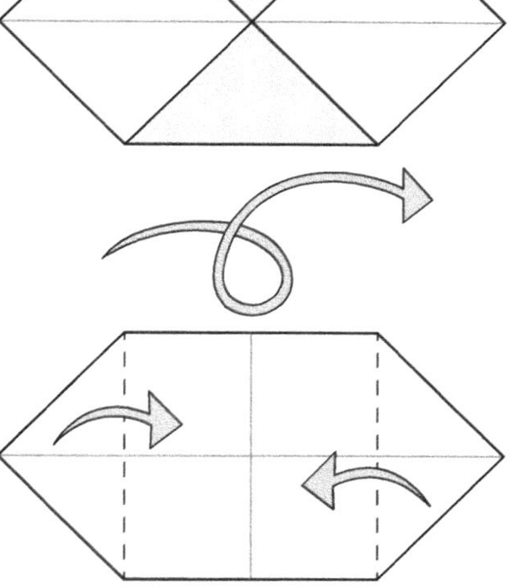

Flip the figure over and bring both side corners to the center of the sheet as well.

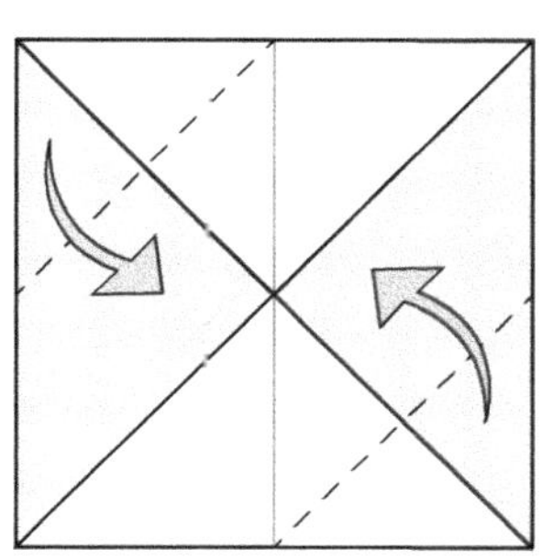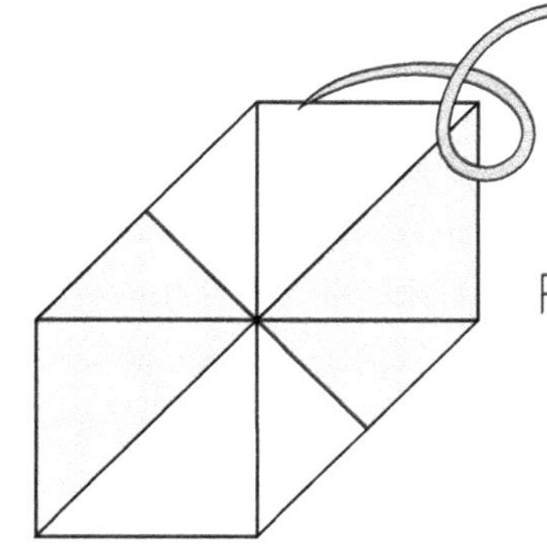

Fold the top left and bottom right corners to the center of the sheet, then flip the figure over.

Pinwheel

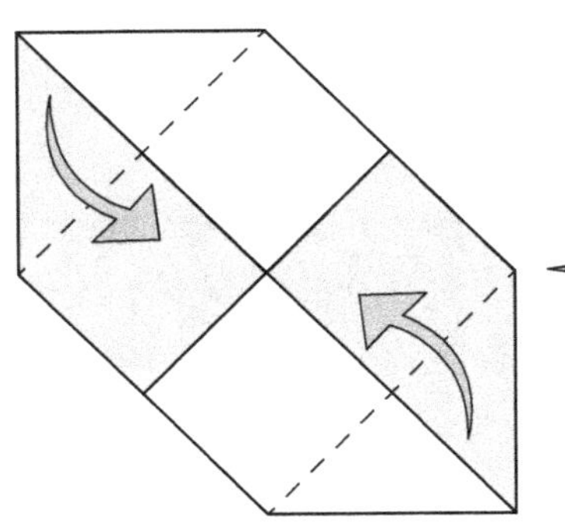

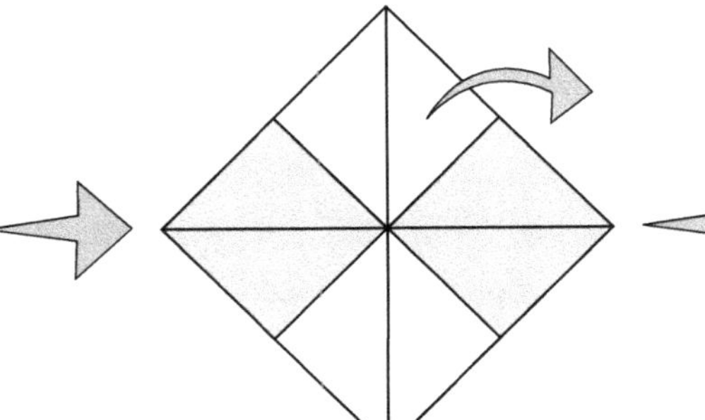

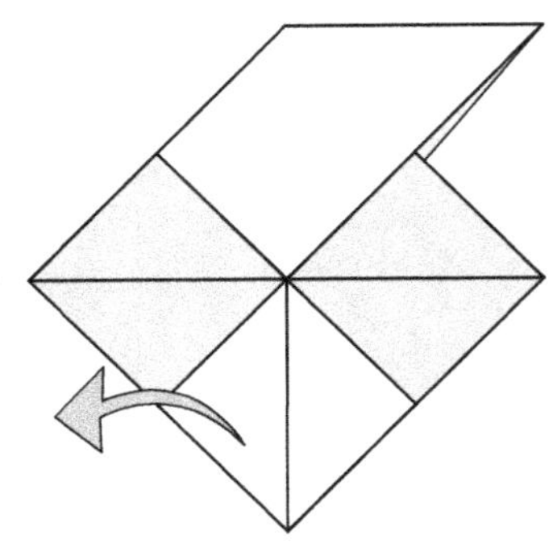

Step 4

Fold the top left and bottom right corners to the center of the sheet again.

Step 5

If you open up the top layer on the right side of the top corner a little bit, you'll see that there's a flap just below it. Pull it out and flatten it to make one of the pinwheel blades.

Step 6

Repeat the previous step on the left side of the bottom corner.

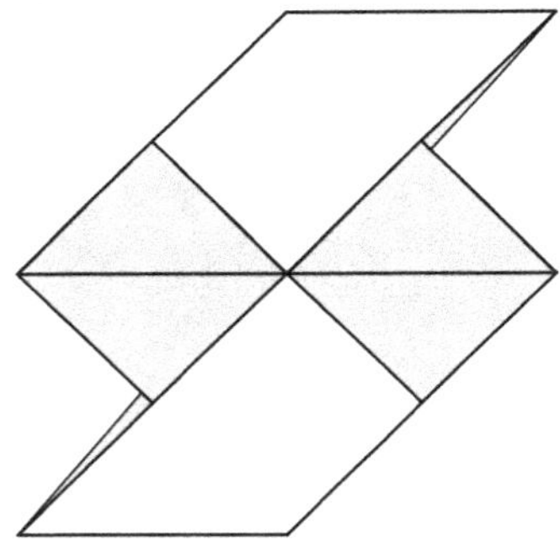

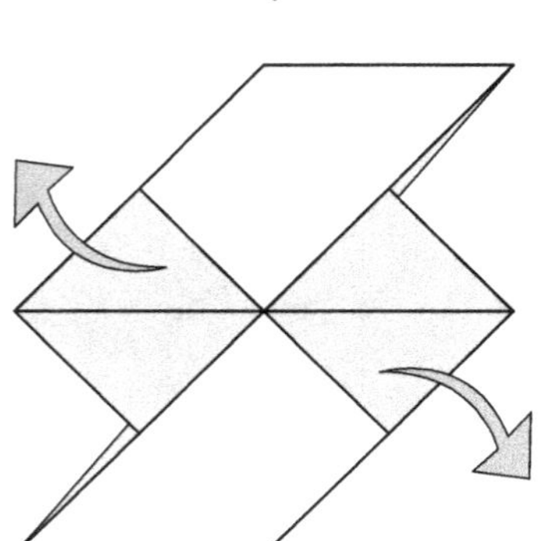

Step 7

Flip the figure over and repeat the previous two steps on that side to make the remaining two blades.

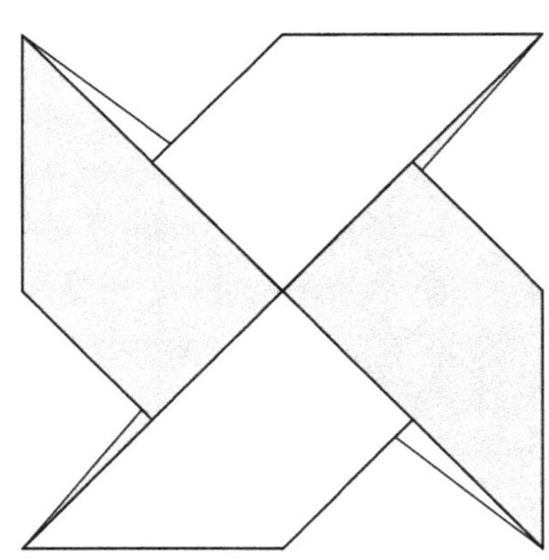

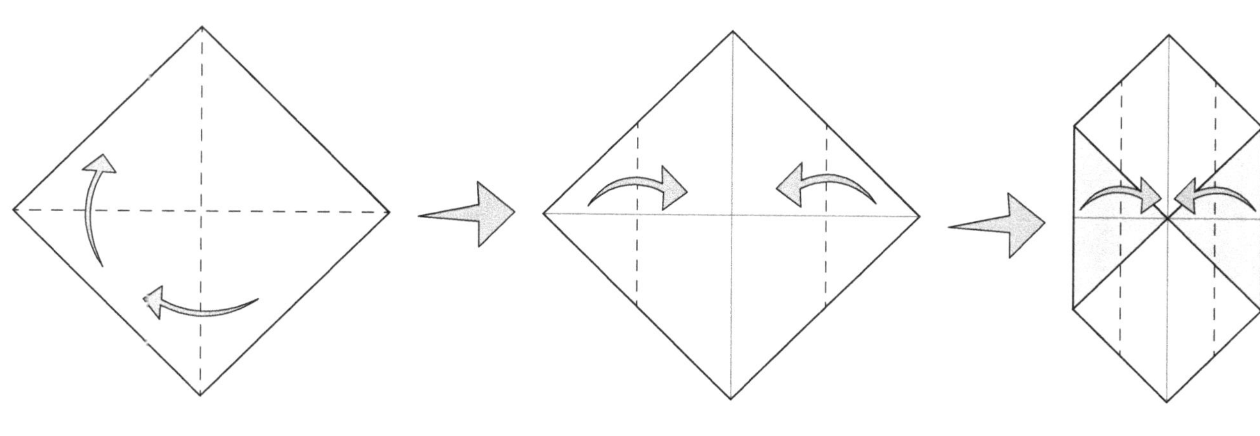

Step 1

Fold the sheet along both diagonals and unfold.

Step 2

Bring both side corners to the center of the sheet, where the two creases meet.

Step 3

Now fold the side edges to the center of the sheet.

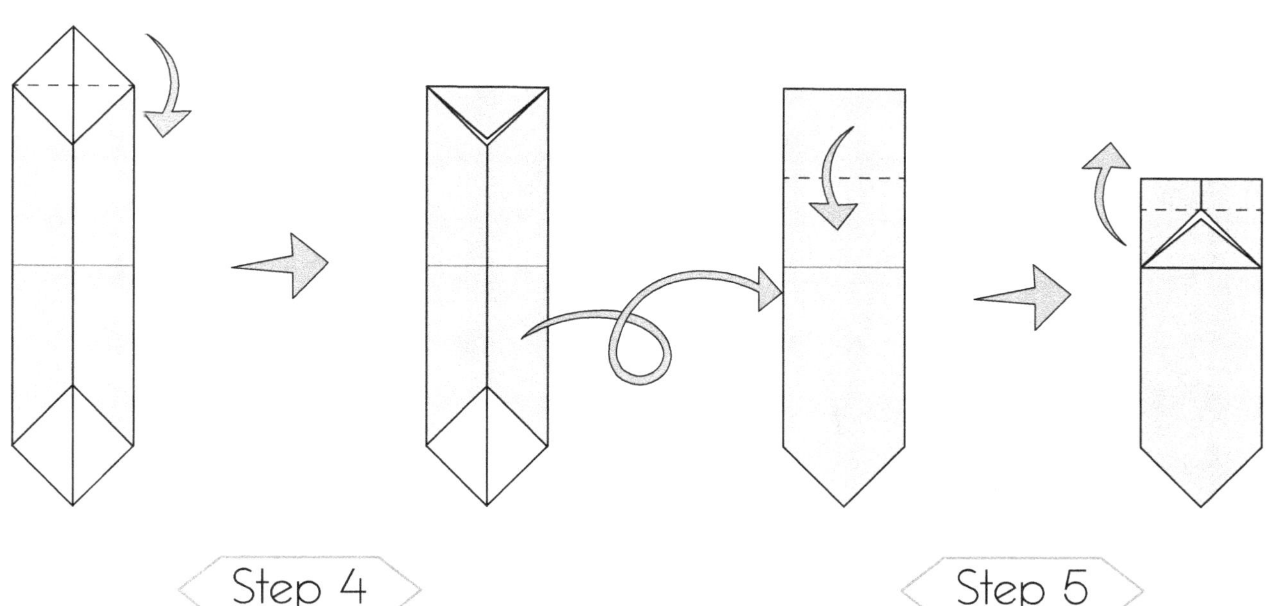

Step 4

Fold the top corner down as shown, then flip the figure over.

Step 5

Fold the top edge down to the midline and then up again, leaving a small gap between the two folds.

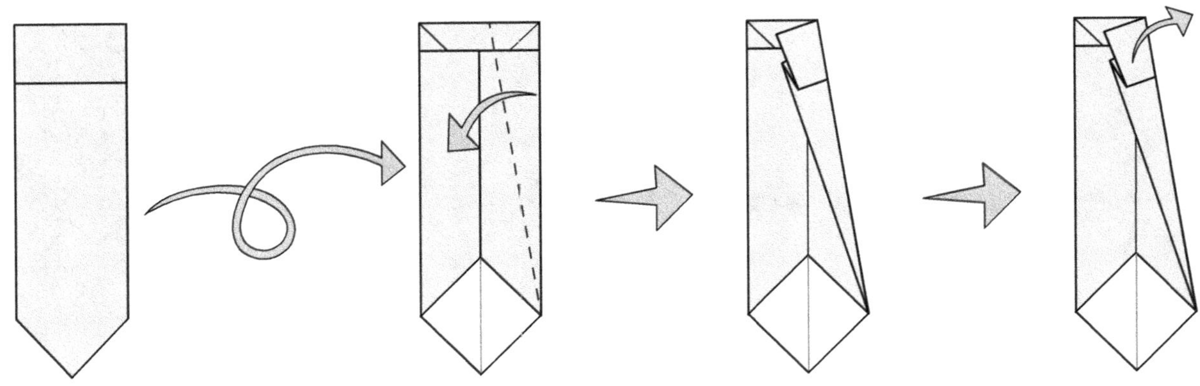

Flip the figure over.

Fold the right side diagonally inward as shown. Then fold its top corner back out and flatten.

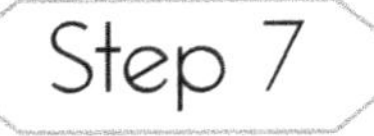

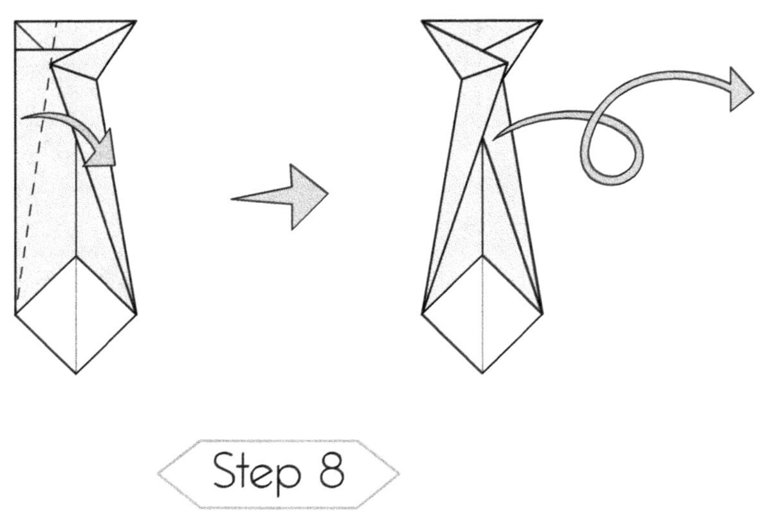

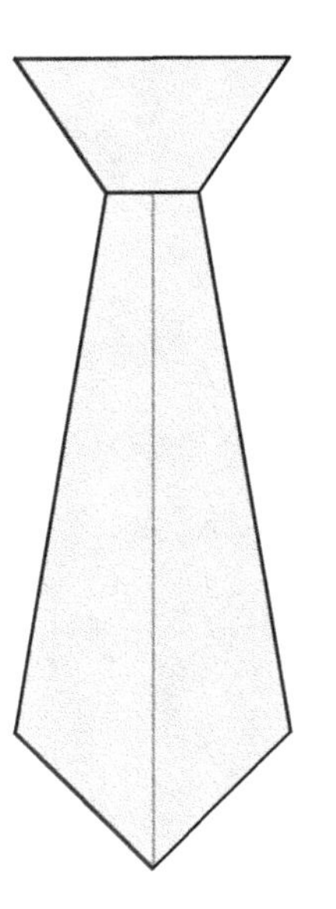

Repeat the previous step on the left side, then flip the figure over.

Tie

Whale

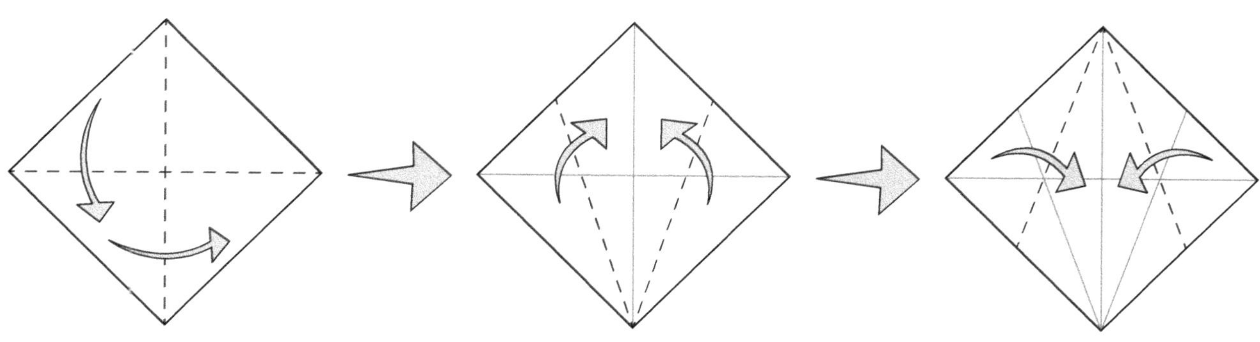

Step 1

Fold the sheet along both diagonals and unfold.

Step 2

Fold the bottom edges of both sides inward to the midline as shown, then unfold it.

Step 3

Now repeat for the top edges of both sides.

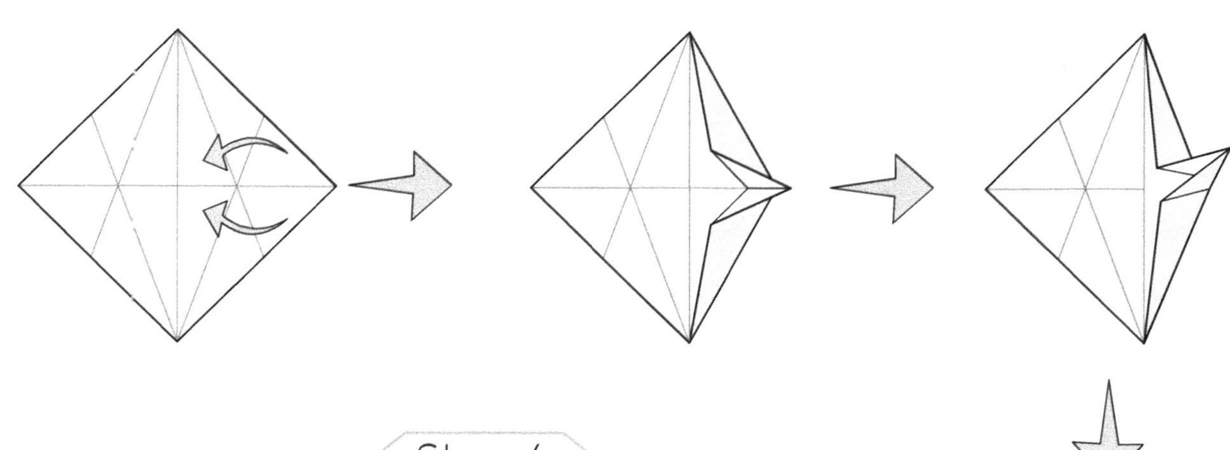

Step 4

You'l see that the creases from Step 2 and 3 form an X. Fold the right corner in along the inner creases of that X. (Longest ones). The shorter creases of the X will form a flap that sticks out, fold it up and flatten. Then flip the figure over.

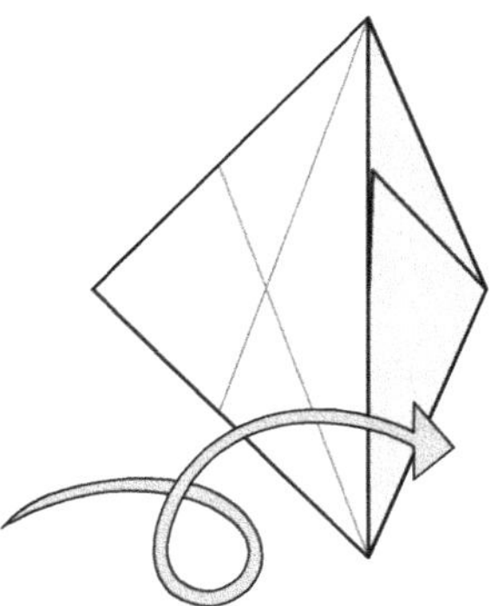

Whale

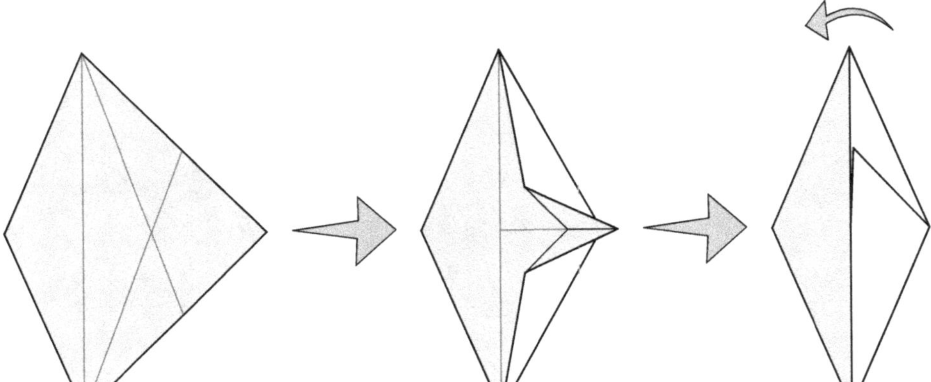

Repeat the previous step on this side, then rotate the figure counterclockwise.

Fold the flap down, then fold the left corner back as shown.

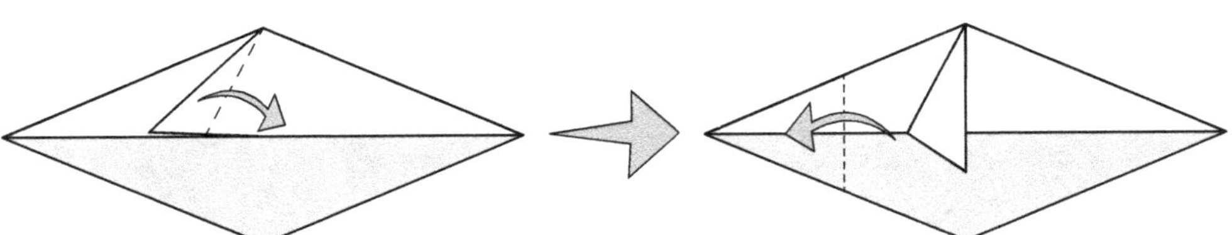

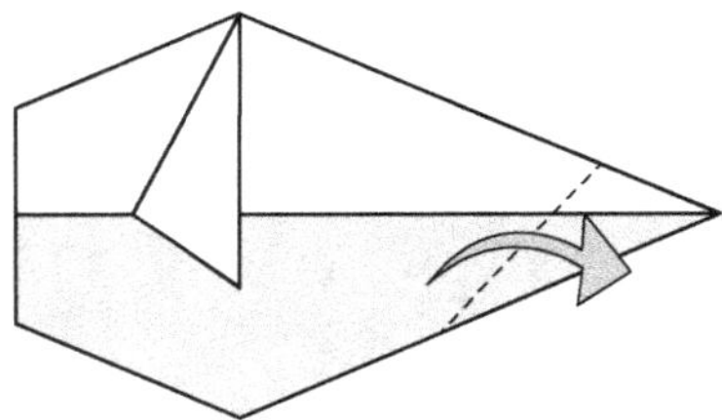

Fold the right corner diagonally back as shown to make the tail.

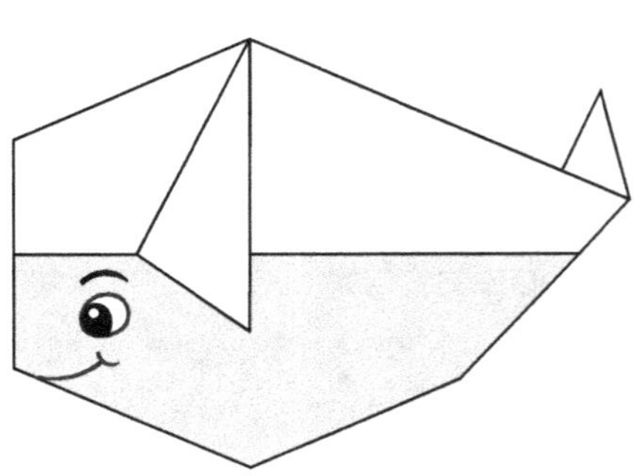

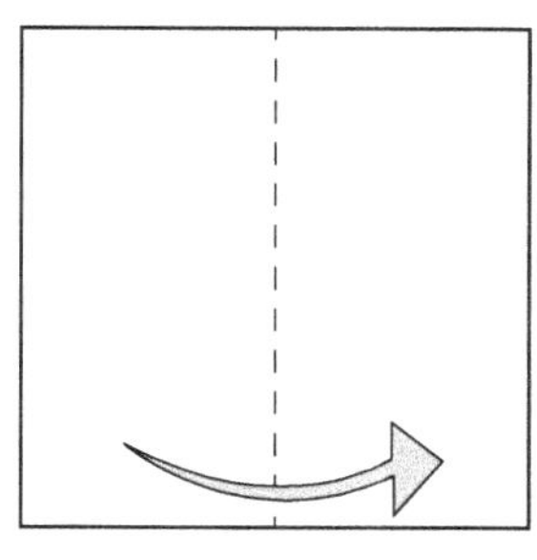

Fold the paper in half leng-hwise and unfold it.

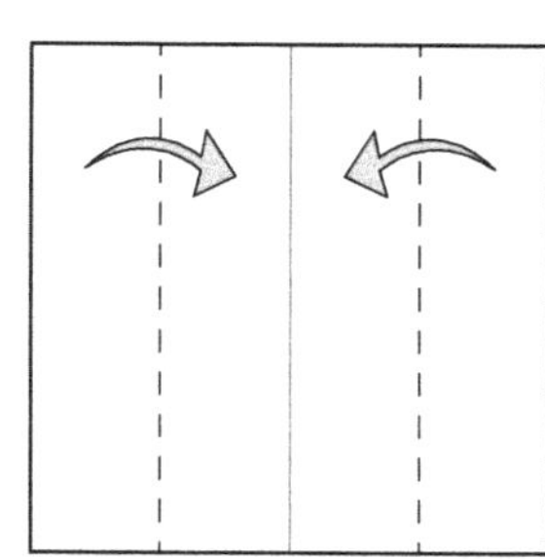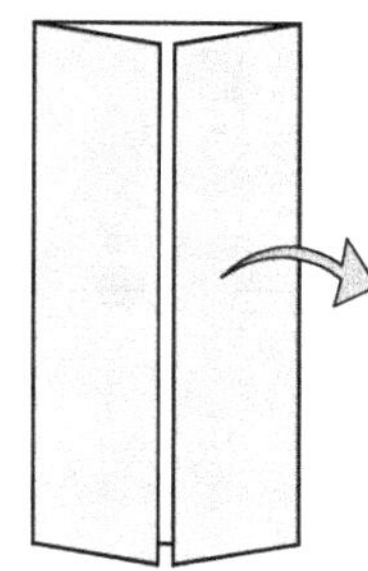

Bring both side edges to the vertical midline.

Unfold the right edge.

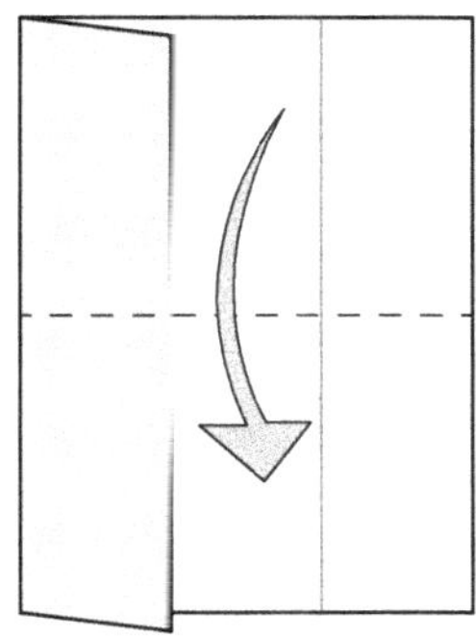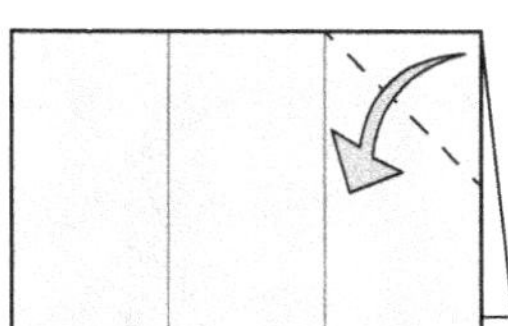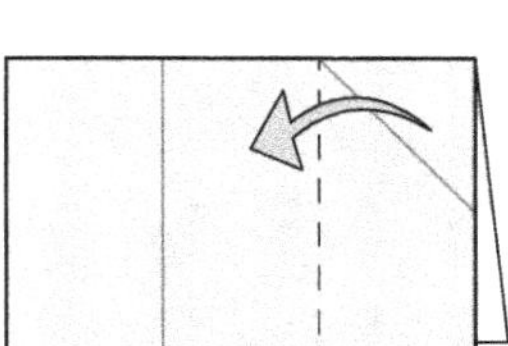

Fold the figure down in half.

Fold th upper right corner diagonally down and unfold to make a crease.

Bring the top layer of the right side in along the crease you just made and flatten.

Chair

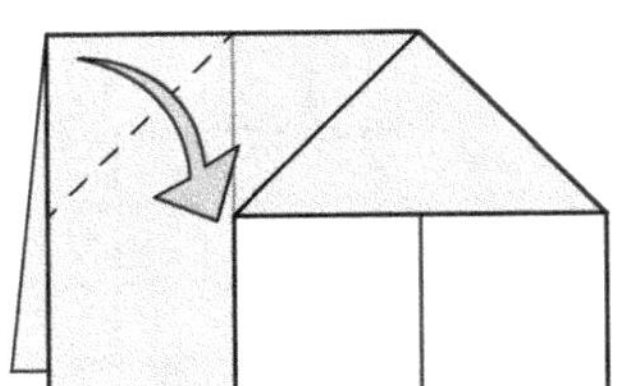  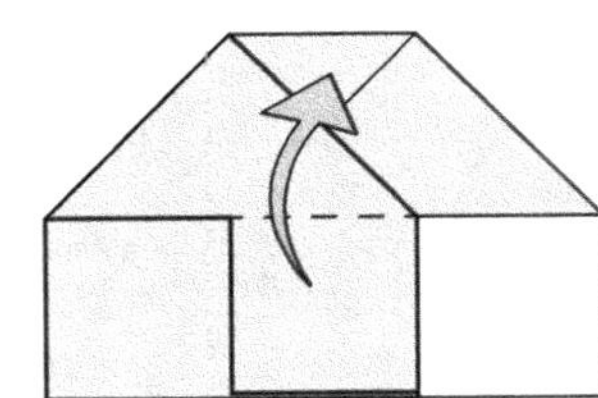  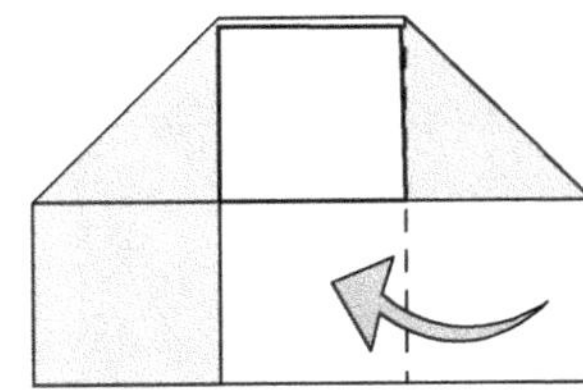

Step 7

Repeat steps 5 and 6 on the left side.

Step 8

After steps 5, 6 and 7 there are two overlapping flaps right in the middle of the figure. Fold them up as shown.

Step 9

Fold the right side in as shown.

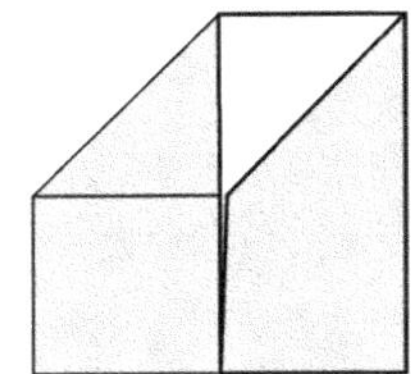  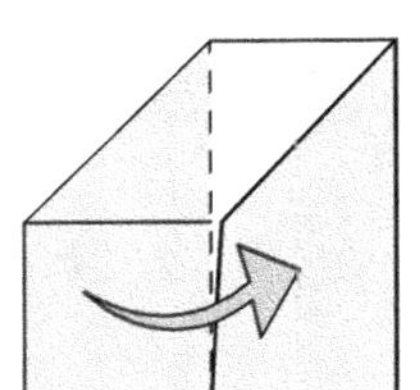

Step 10

Now fold the left side in as shown.

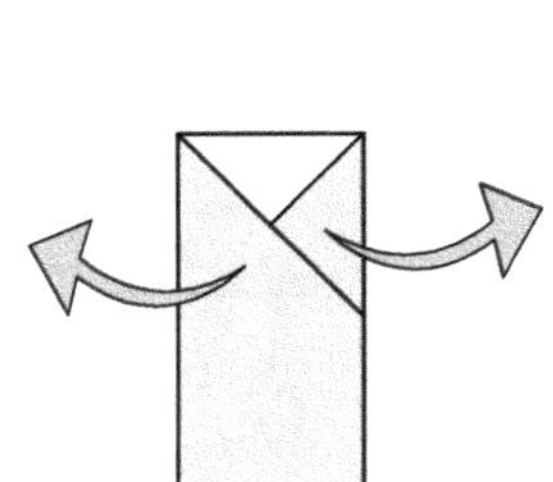  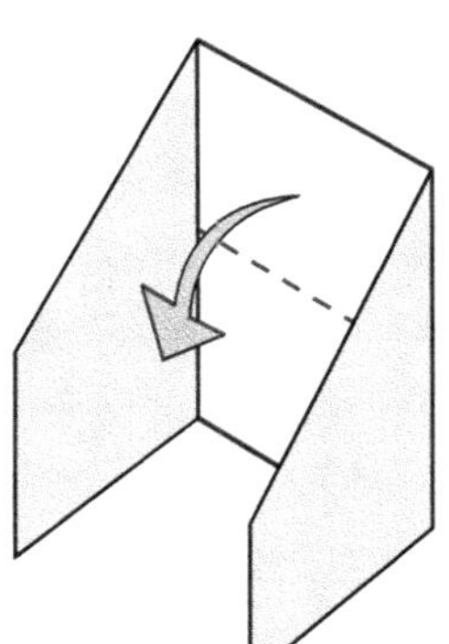

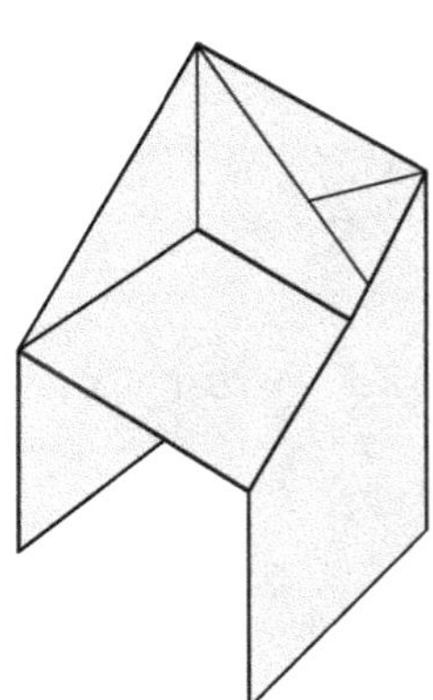

Step 11

Unfold both sides halfway out, then unfold the flaps in the middle on the figure from Step 8 halfway down.

Chair

Table

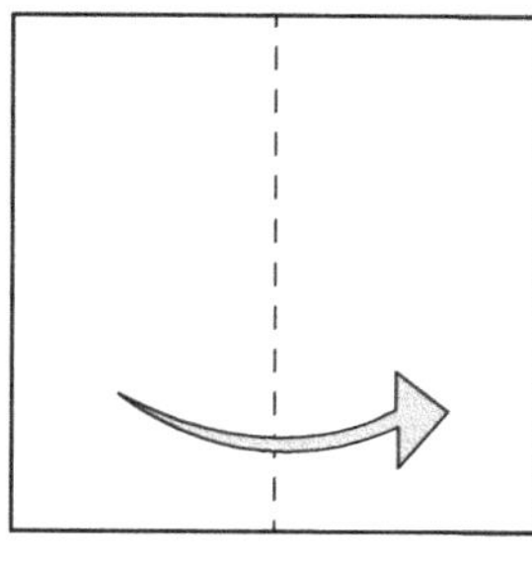  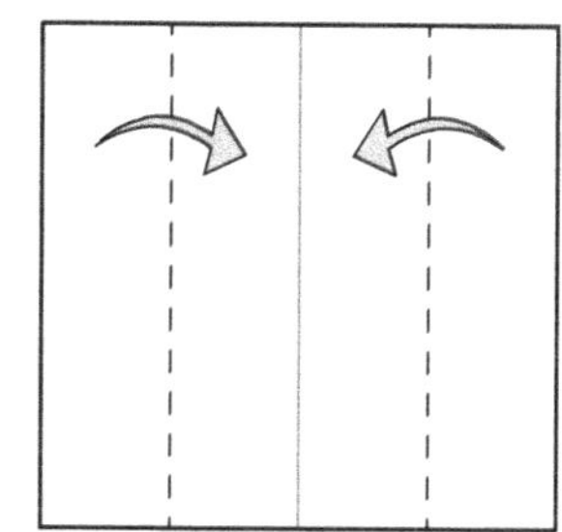  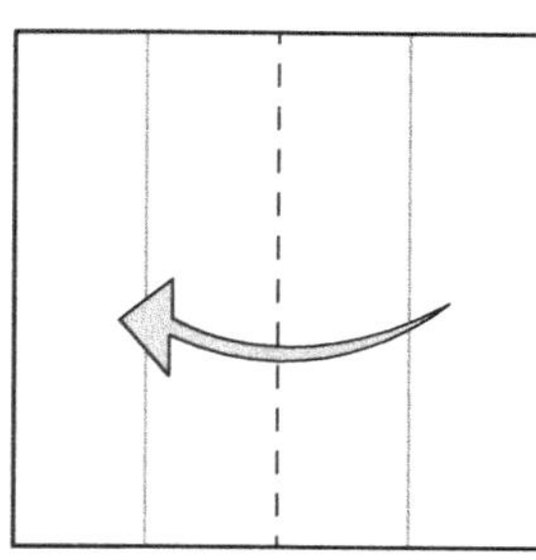

Step 1

Fold the paper in half lengthwise and unfold it.

Step 2

Bring both side edges to the vertical midline and unfold.

Step 3

Fold the sheet in half again.

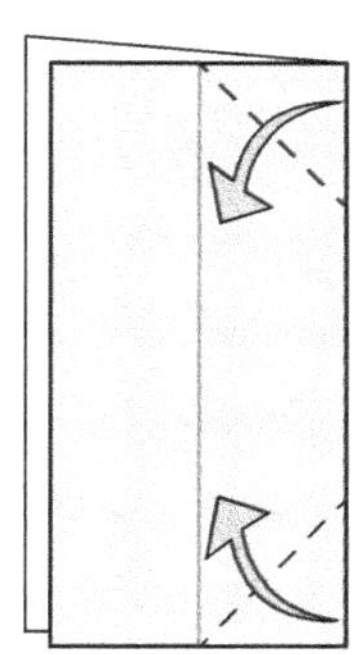  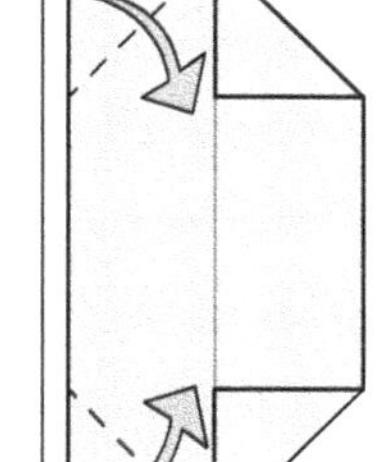 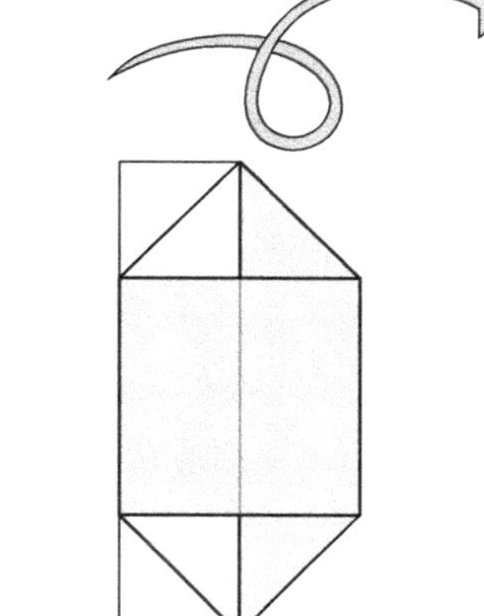

Step 4

Fold the upper right corner diagonally down and the bottom right corner diagonally up as shown.

Step 5

Repeat the previous step on the top layer of the left side.

Step 6

Flip the figure over.

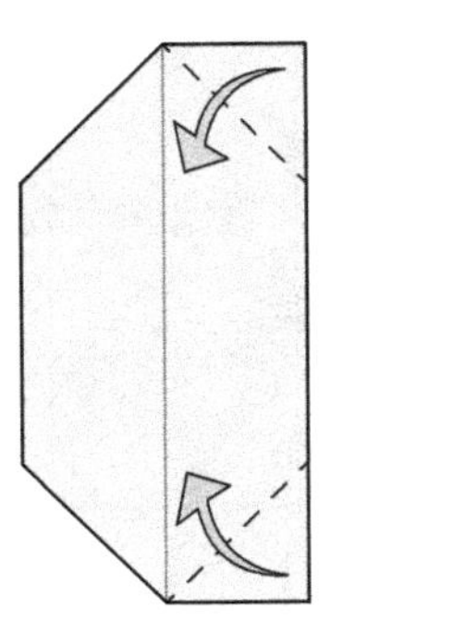  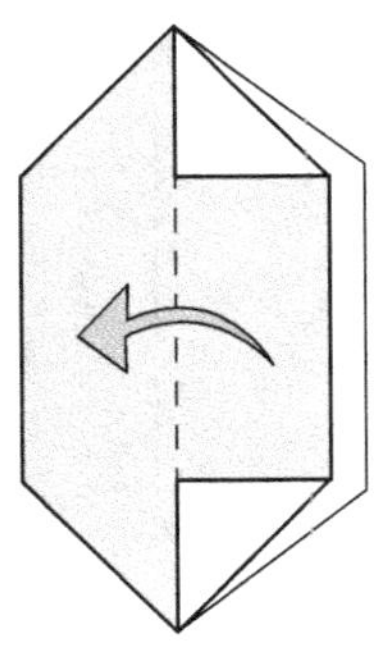  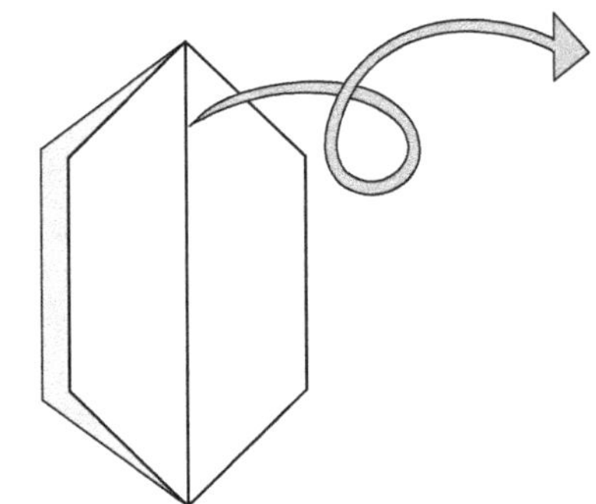

Step 7

Fold the corners of this side in the same way, then fold the top layer of the right side in as shown.

Step 8

Flip the figure over.

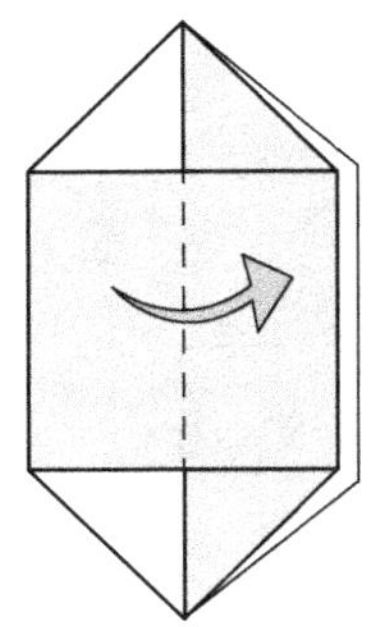  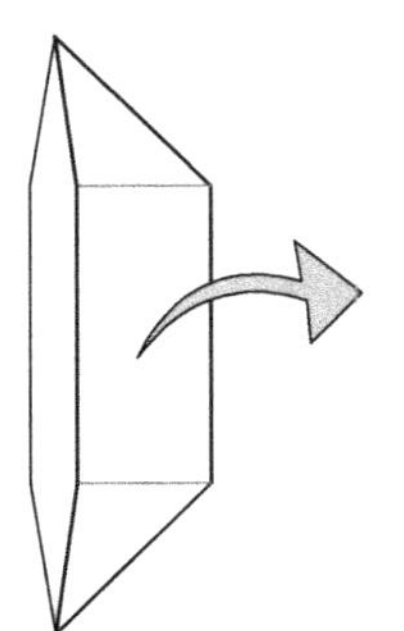

Step 9

Fold the figure in half. Then separate both layers of the figure along the left edge while pushing the top and bottom corners into the space between them. Open the layers and push the corners until all the walls of the figure end up being perpendicular to each other.

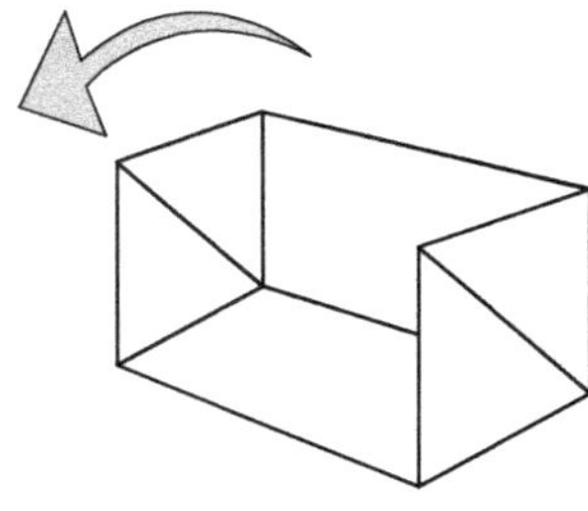

Step 10

Rotate the figure until it matches the illustration.

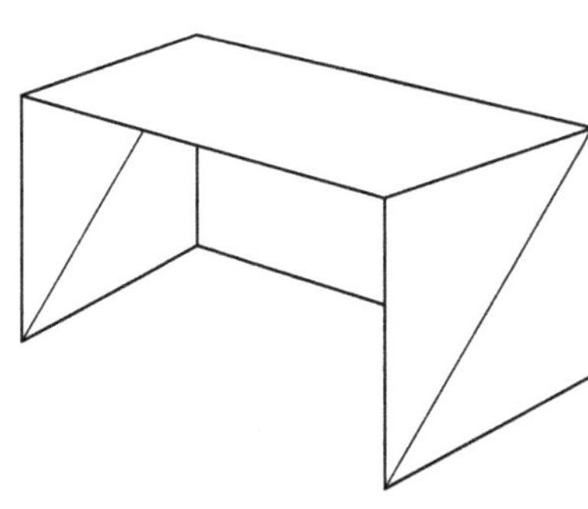

Table

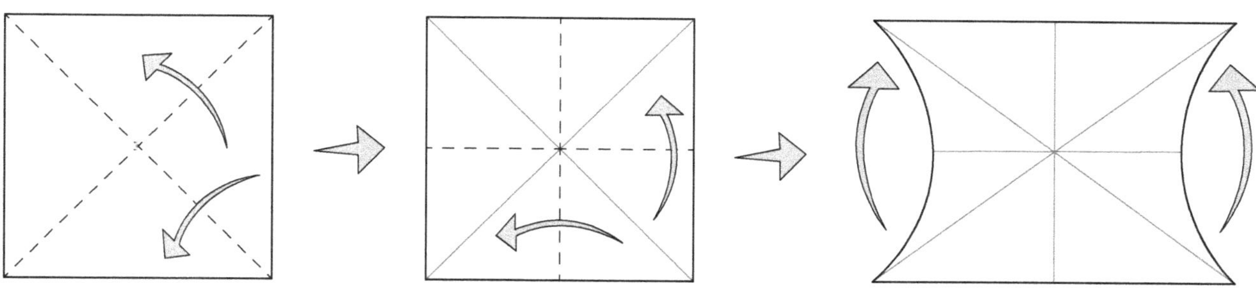

Water Bomb

Step 1

Fold the sheet along both diagonals and unfold it.

Step 2

Now fold it lengthwise and crosswise, then unfold.

Step 3

Bring the bottom edge up to meet the top edge, while you fold both sides in to make a triangle.

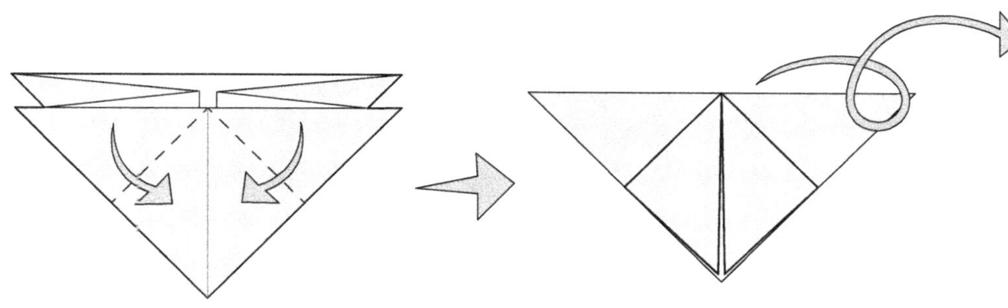

Step 4

Fold the side corners of the top layer diagonally down as shown, then flip the figure over.

Step 5

Fold these side corners diagonally down as well, then fold the sides of the layer in as shown.

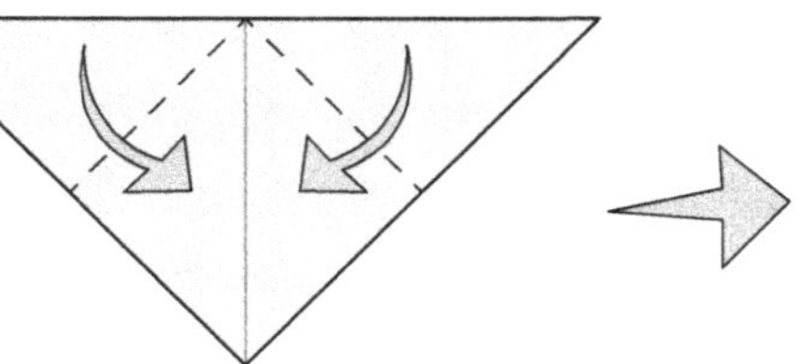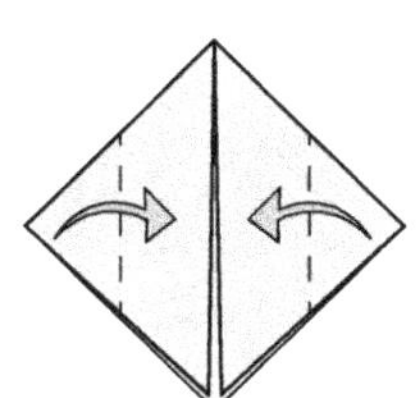

Water Bomb

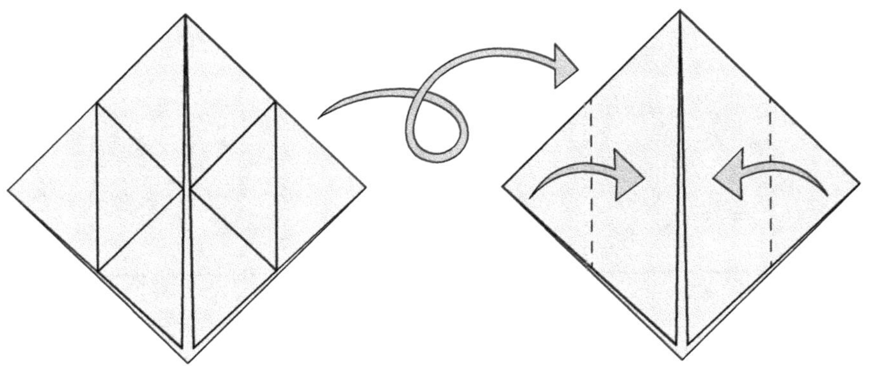

Flip the figure over and fold these side corners in as well.

Step 7

Fold the flaps at the bottom up and tuck them under the flaps you just made. Then repeat on the back side.

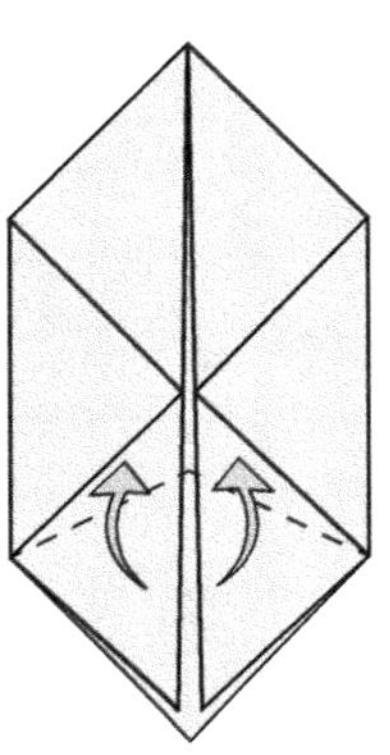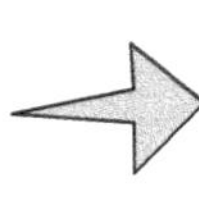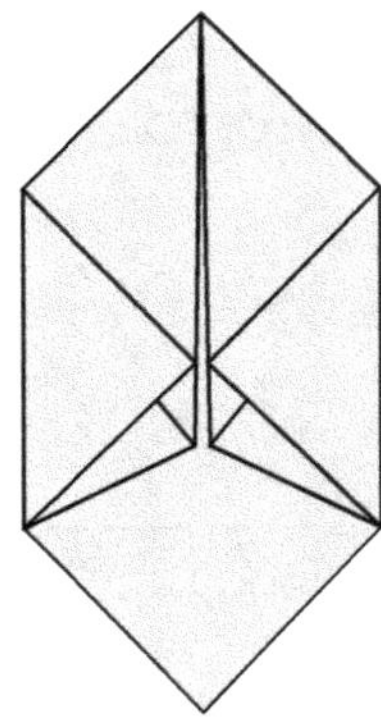

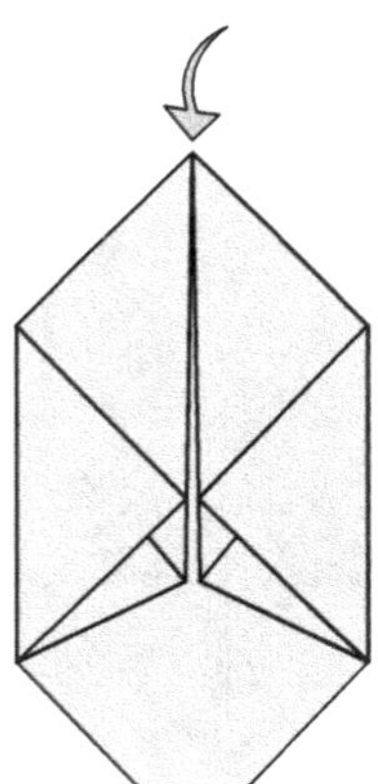

Step 8

Fill the figure with air through the top tip and the water bomb will be ready.

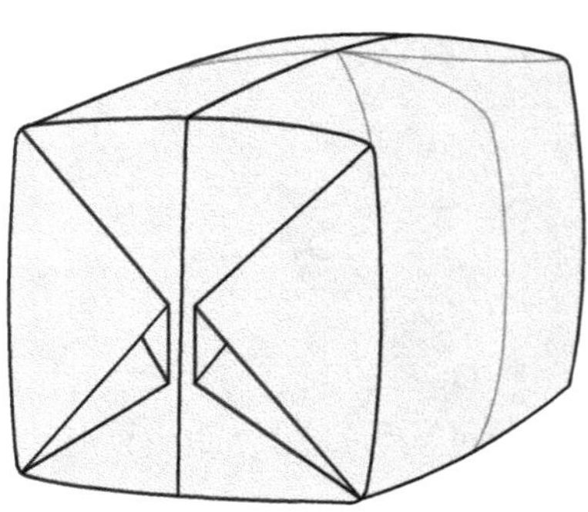

Nodding Dog

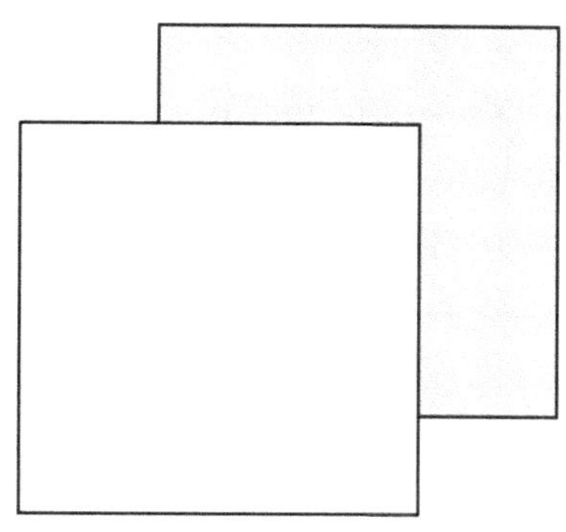

Tip

You will need 2 square sheets to make this Nodding Dog.

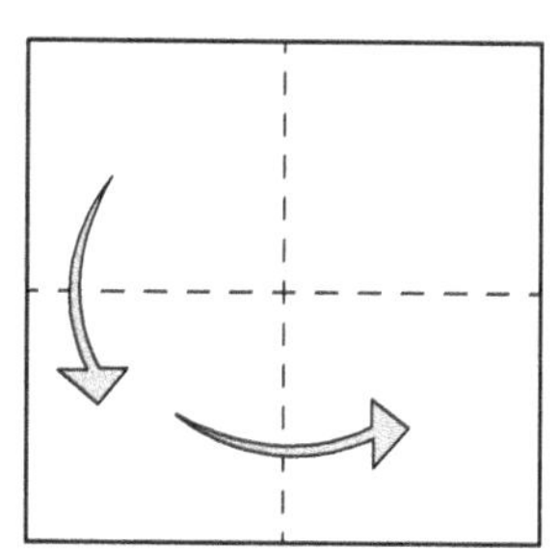

Step 1

Fold one of the paper sheets in half lengthwise and crosswise, then unfold.

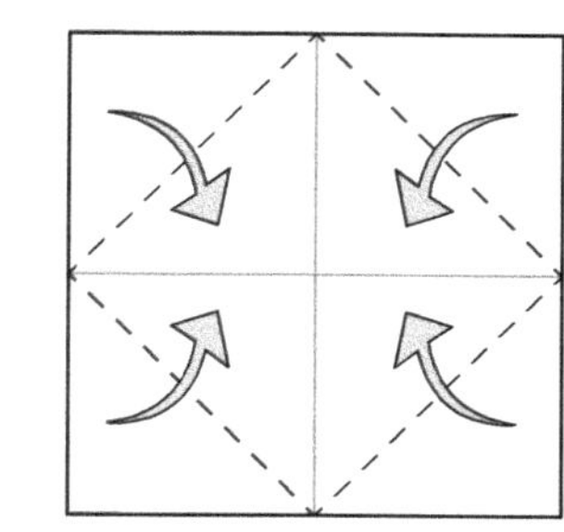

Step 2

Bring all the corners to the center of the sheet.

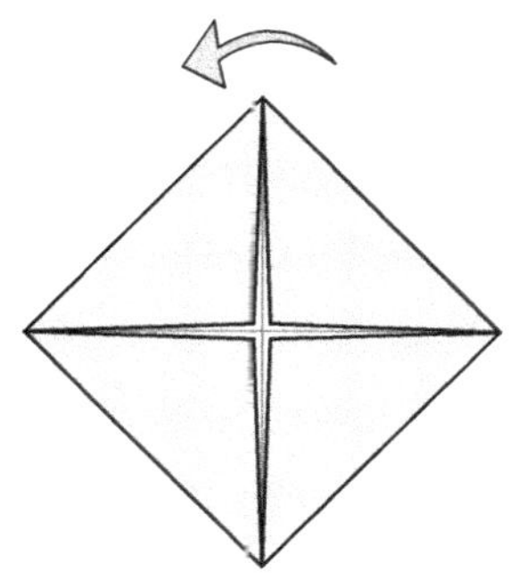

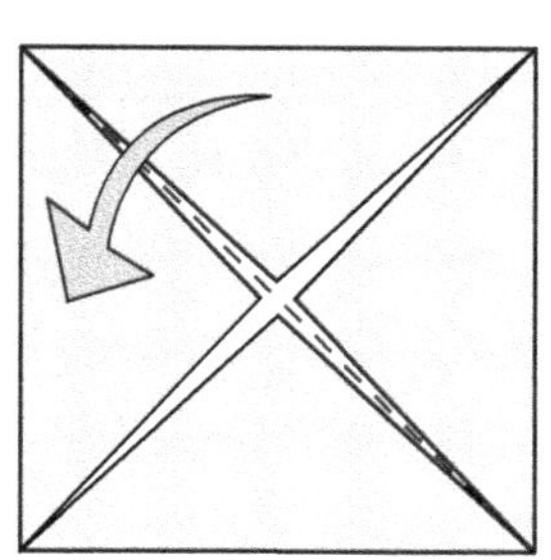

Step 3

Rotate the figure, then fold it diagonally down to make the triangle that will be Dog's body.

Step 4

Fold the tip of right corner in to make the dog's tail. The body is ready, let's move on to the head.

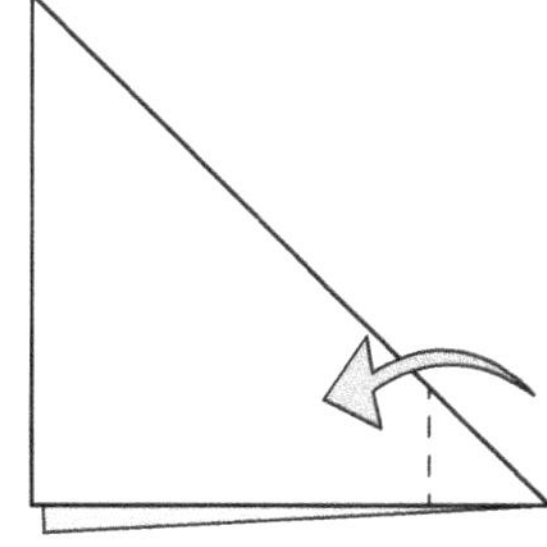

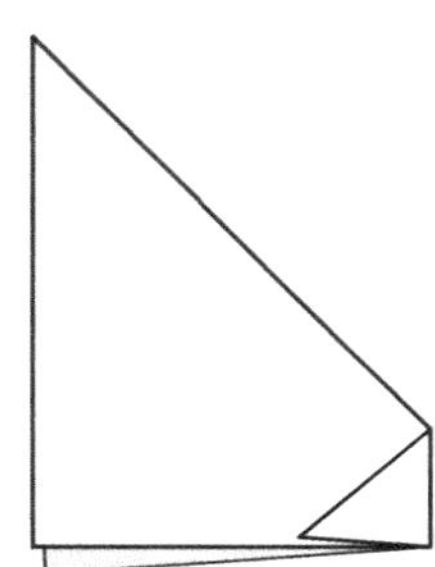

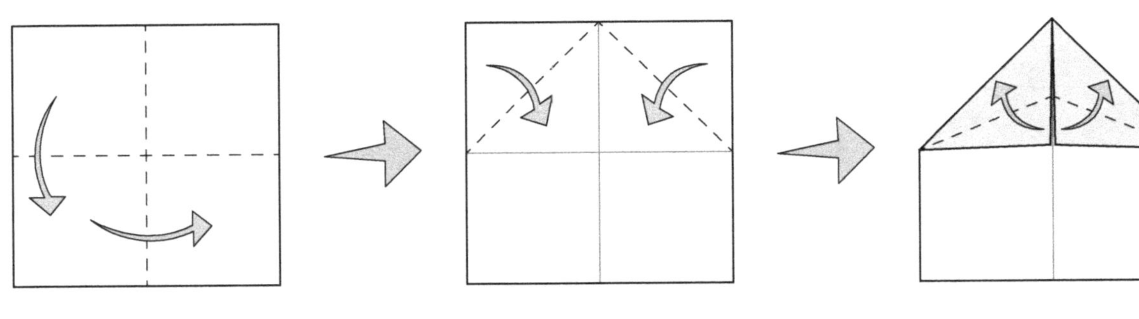

Step 5

Fold the second paper sheet in half lengthwise and crosswise, then unfold.

Step 6

Fold both corners diagonally down.

Step 7

Fold those flaps halfway up, so that their bottom edge meet the sides of the figure as shown.

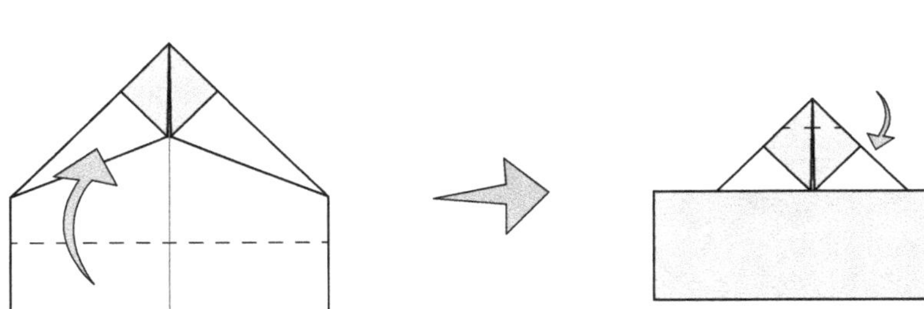

Step 8

Fold the bottom edge up to meet the folds from the previous step as shown, then fold the top tip down.

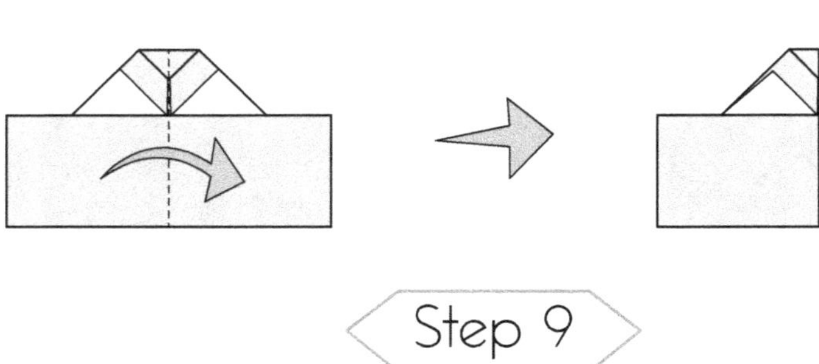

Step 9

Fold the figure backward in half and insert the body between both layers as shown. Gently press the nose and you will see how the head moves up and down.

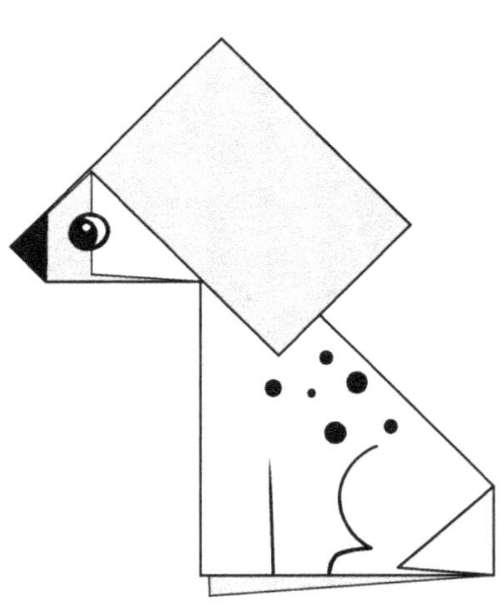

Nodding Dog

Crown

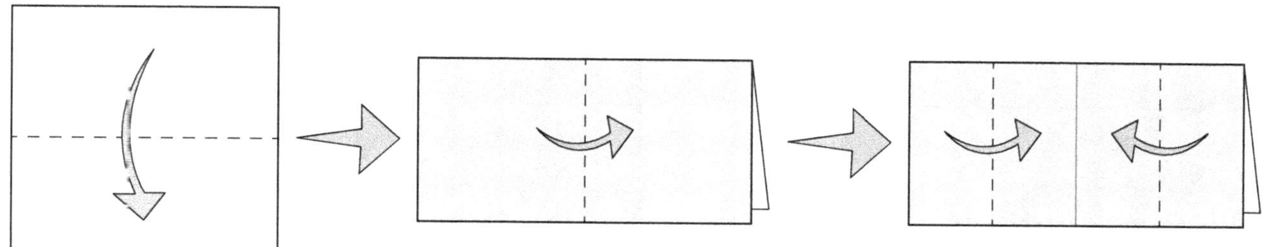

Step 1

Fold the paper in half crosswise.

Step 2

Fold the figure in half and unfold it to make a crease.

Step 3

Fold both side edges in to the vertical midline you just made.

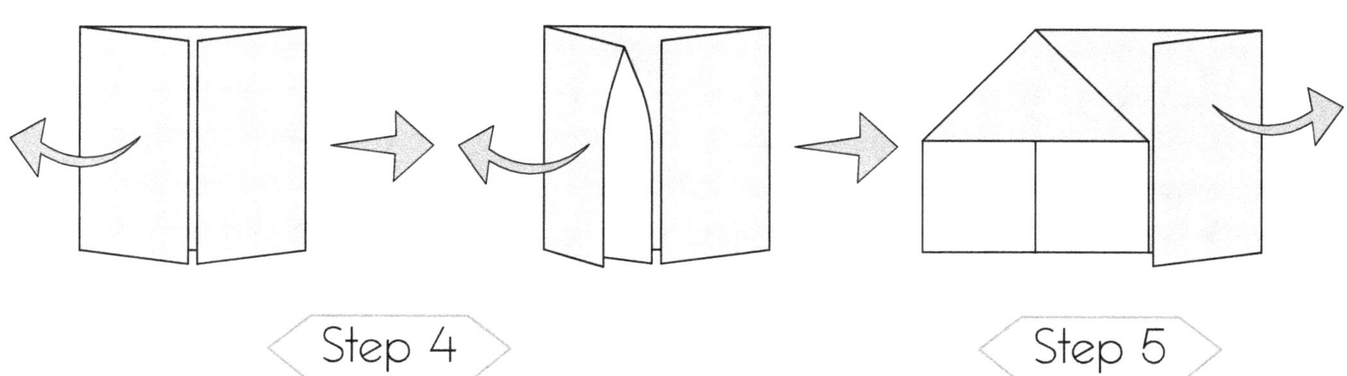

Step 4

Bring the top layer of the left flap back out cnd flatten the top to make a triangle.

Step 5

Repeat on the right side.

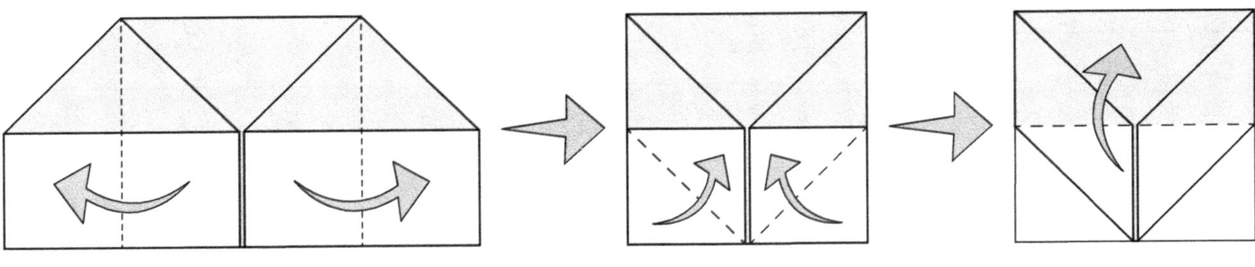

Step 6

Fold both sides backwards
as shown.

Step 7

Fold both bottom corners
of the top layer diagonally
up to make a triangle.

Step 8

Fold the triangle
up as shown.

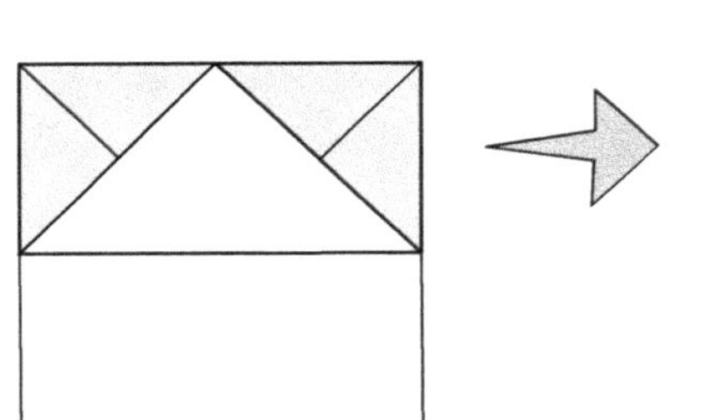

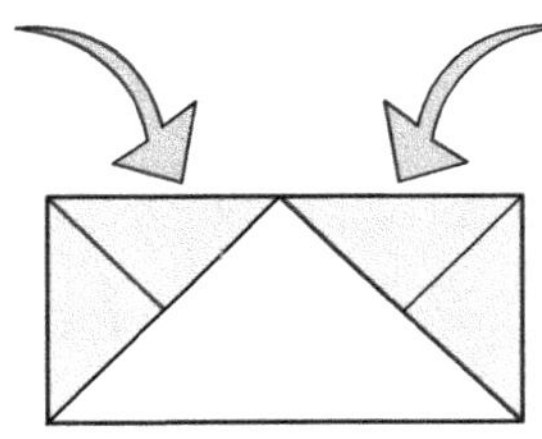

Step 9

Repeat Step 7 and 8
on the back side
of the figure.

Step 10

Now separate the front
and back bottom edges
while gently pushing the
middle layer on top of
the figure.

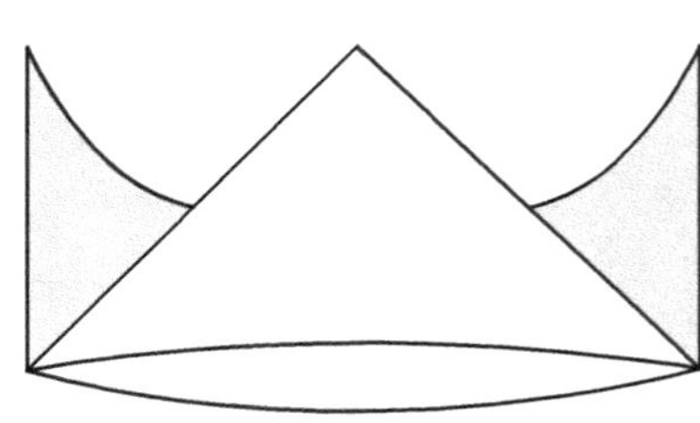

Crown

Hen

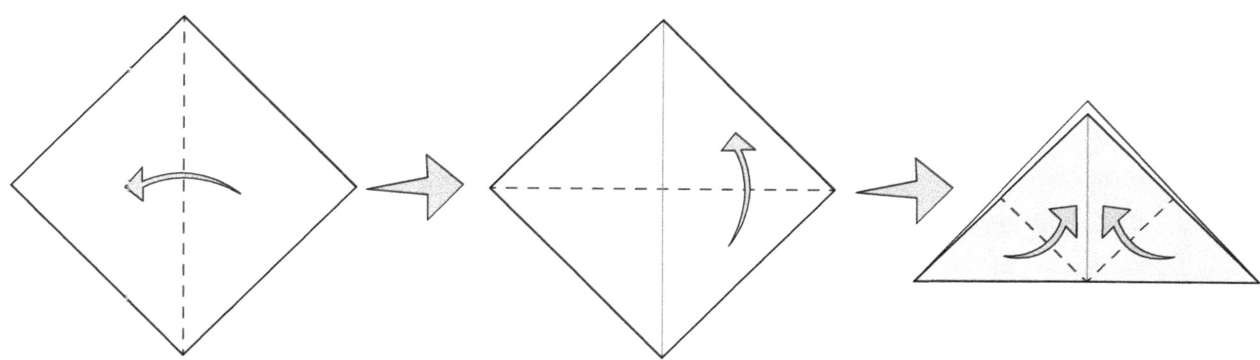

Step 1

Fold the sheet diagonally to the left and unfold it.

Step 2

Then fold it diagonally up in half to make a triangle.

Step 3

Bring both side corners up to the vertical midline.

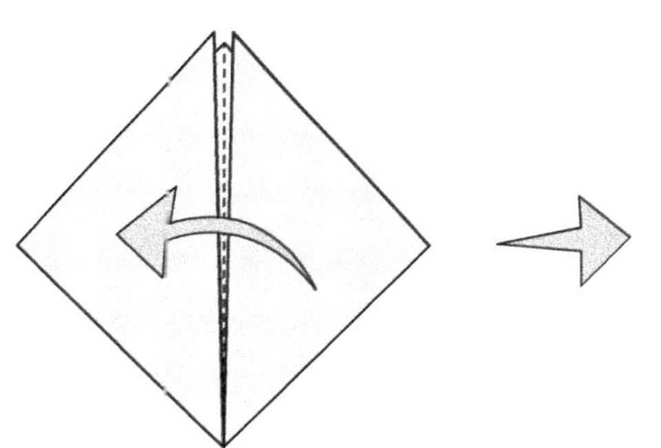
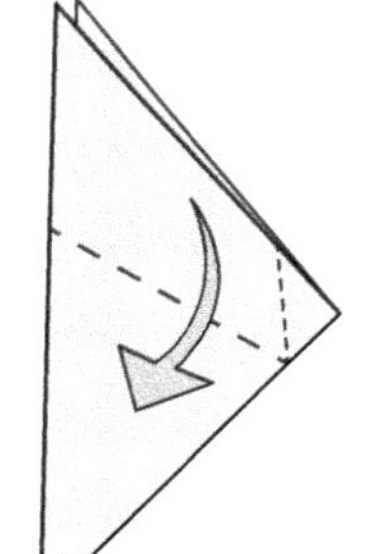

Step 4

Fold the left half of the figure back, then fold the tip of the right corner and unfold it to make a crease. Now use that crease to bring the top layer of the top corner down until you get something like the illustration below.

Step 5

Flip the figure over and repeat for the other side.

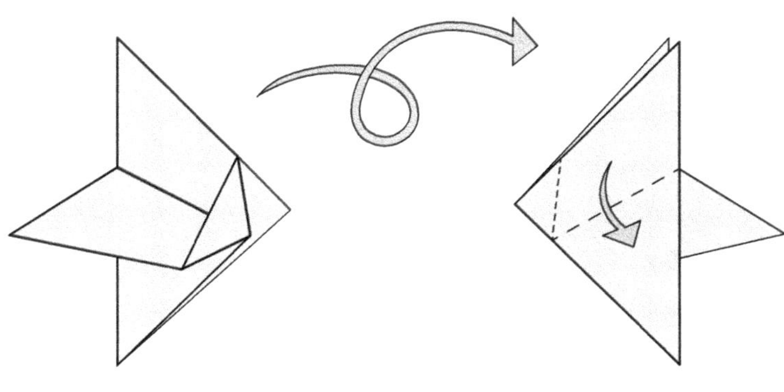

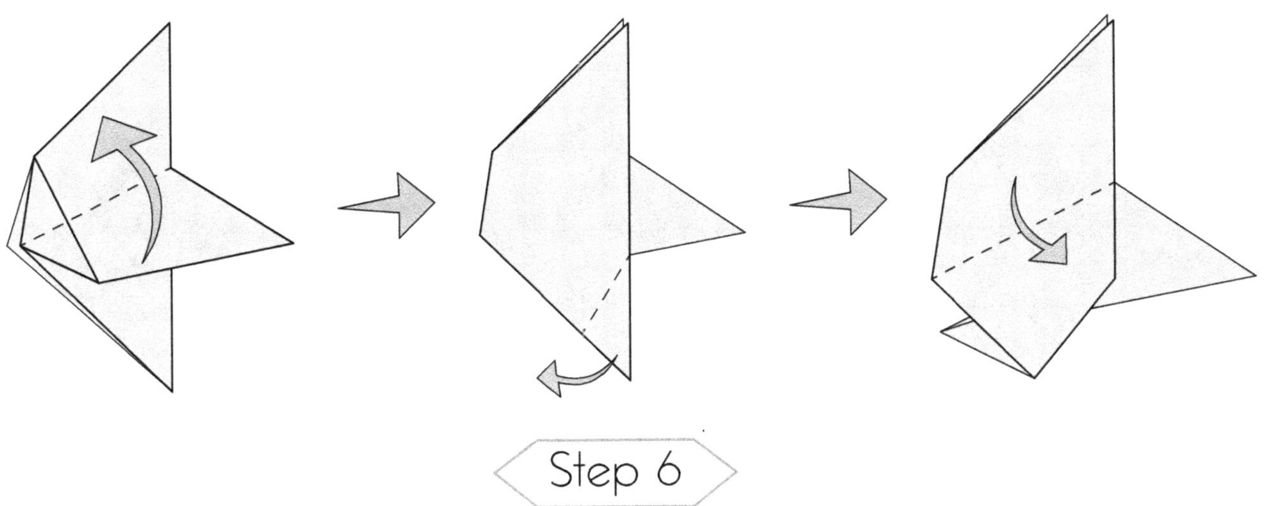

Fold this side back up as shown to make an inside reverse fold at the bottom corner, then fold the top layer down again.

Fold the tip of the top layer down at an angle as shown.

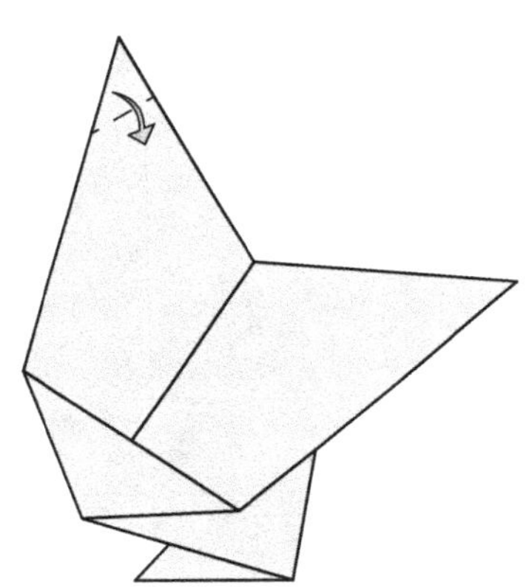

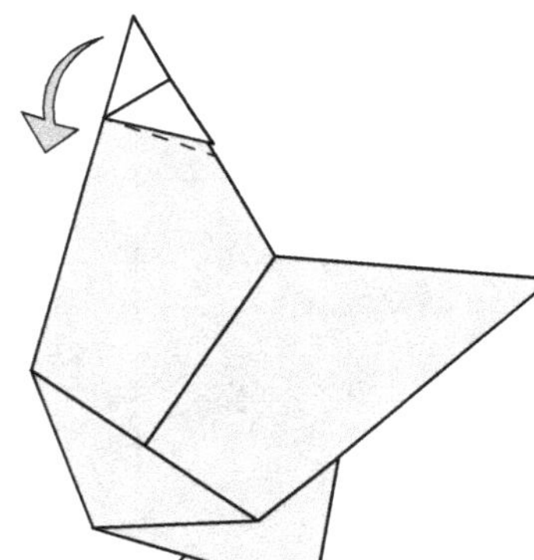

Make an inside reverse fold at the tip of the bottom layer to make the hen's beak.

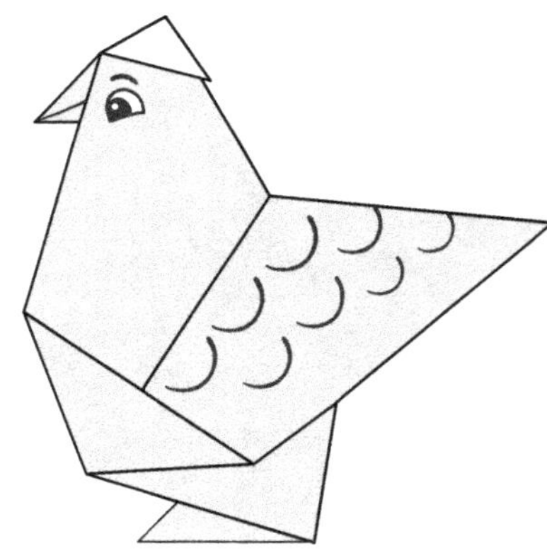

Dove

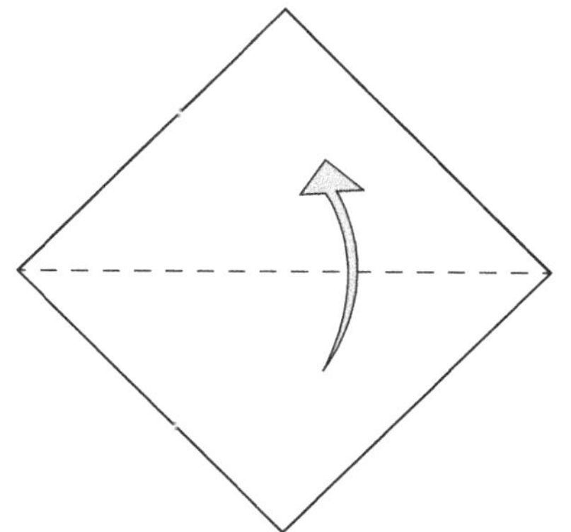 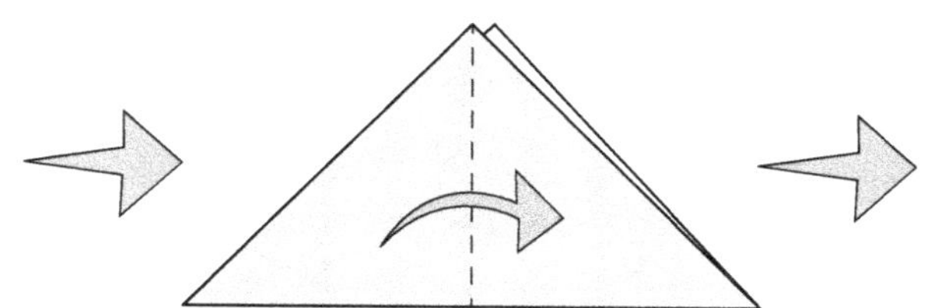 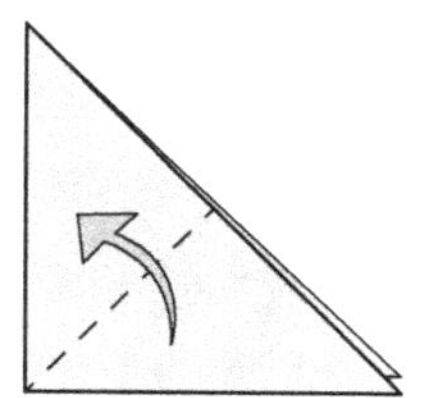

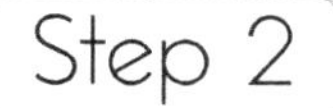

Step 1

Fold the sheet diagonally up in half.

Step 2

Fold the triangle you just made in half.

Step 3

Fold the top layer diagonally up.

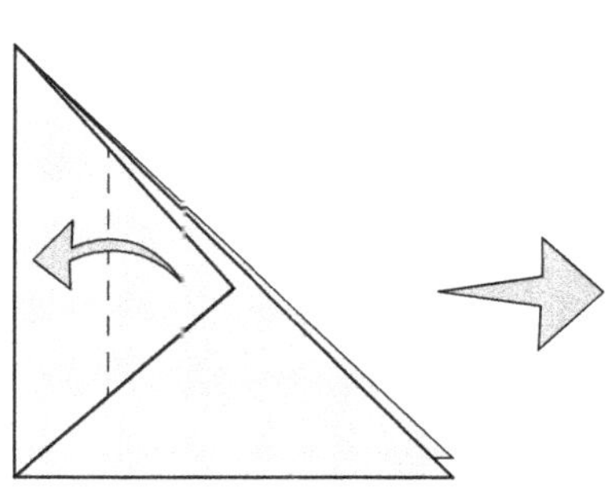 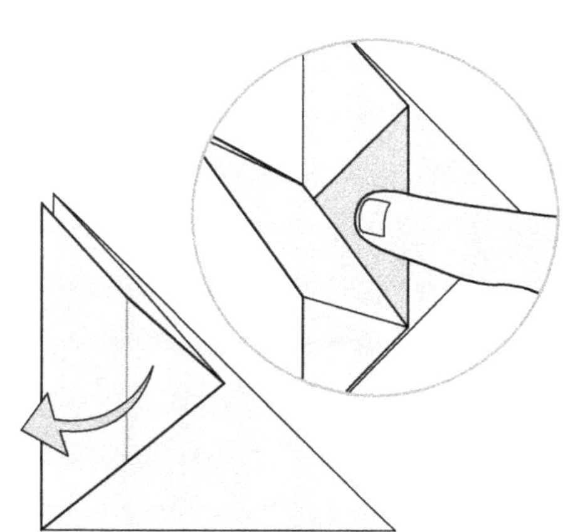

Step 4

Fold out the corner you just made right in the middle of the figure, then use it to make an inside reverse fold.

Step 5

Fold the top layer down as shown, then flip the figure over.

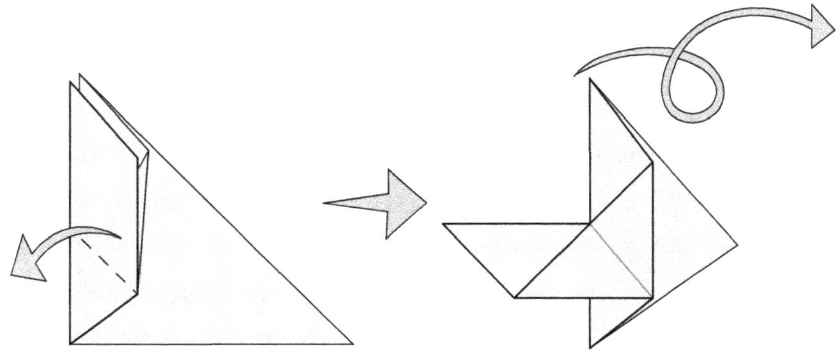

Dove

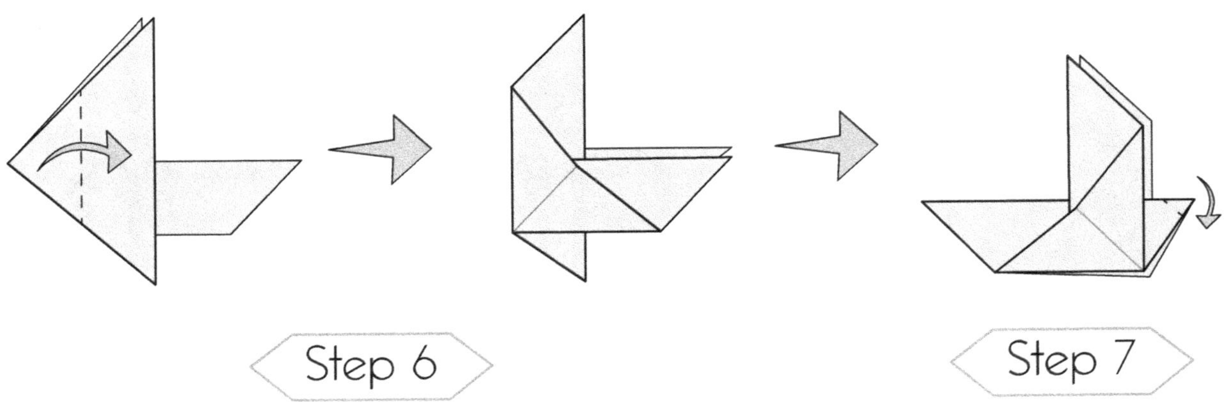

Step 6

Repeat step 3 through 5 on the other side, then rotate the figure counterclockwise.

Step 7

Make an inside reverse fold on the right corner.

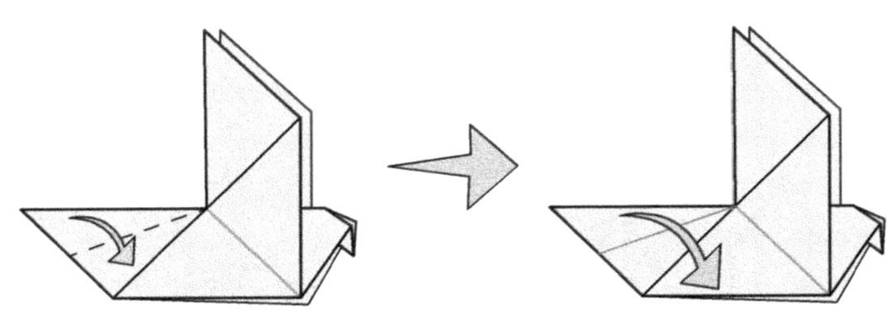

Step 8

Fold the left corner in half as shown, then unfold it to make a crease. Pull that crease forward down to make the tail and flatten.

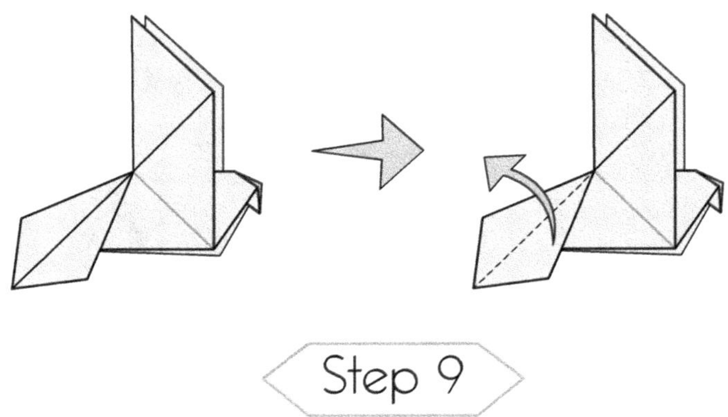

Step 9

Fold half of that tail backward as shown.

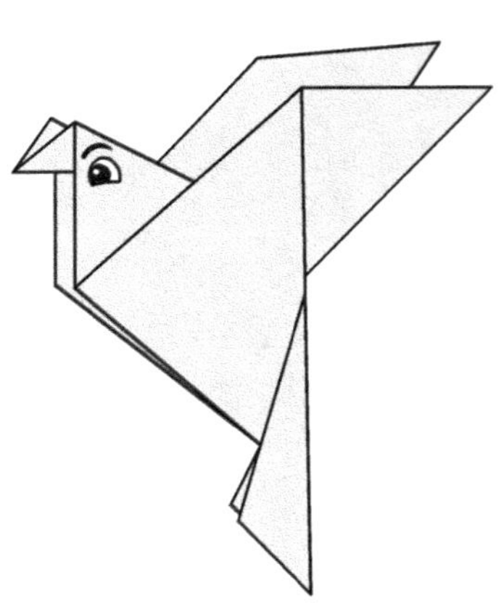

Dove

Rocket

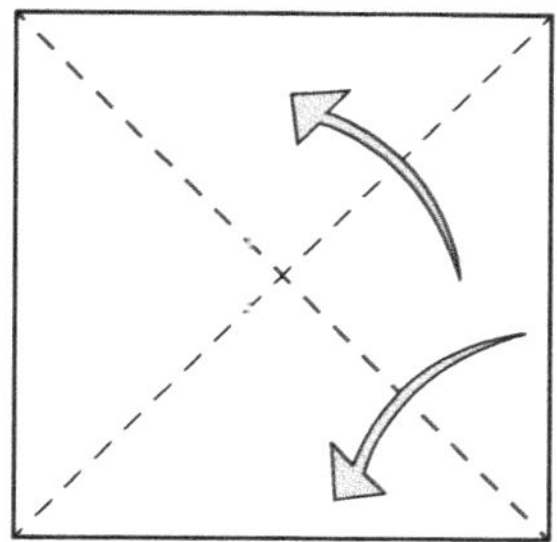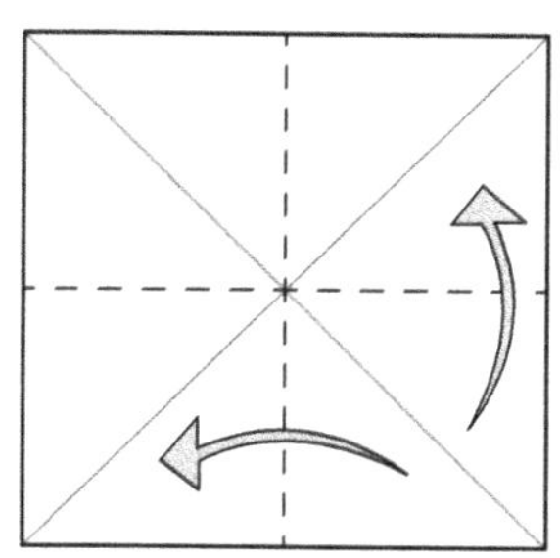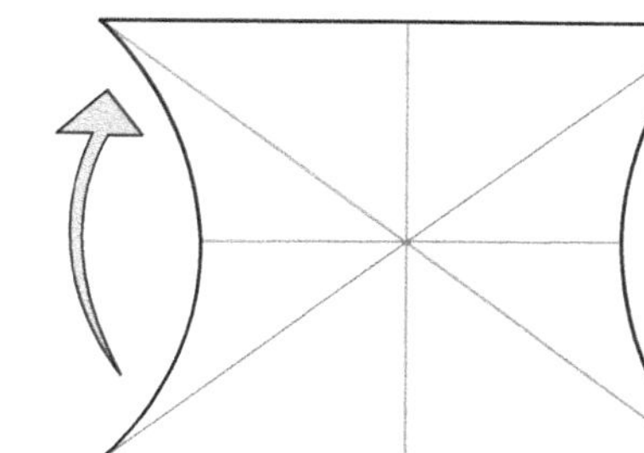

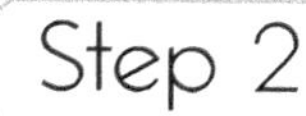

Step 1

Fold the paper sheet ciagonally and unfold it.

Step 2

Fold the paper sheet crosswise and lengthwise and unfold it.

Step 3

Bring the top edge down to meet the bottom edge, while you fold both sides in to make a triangle.

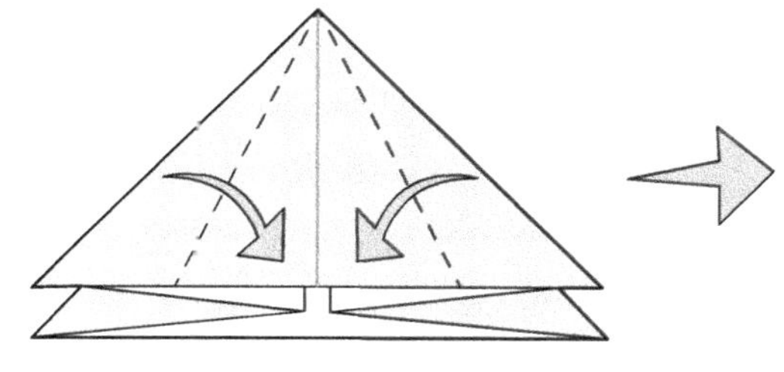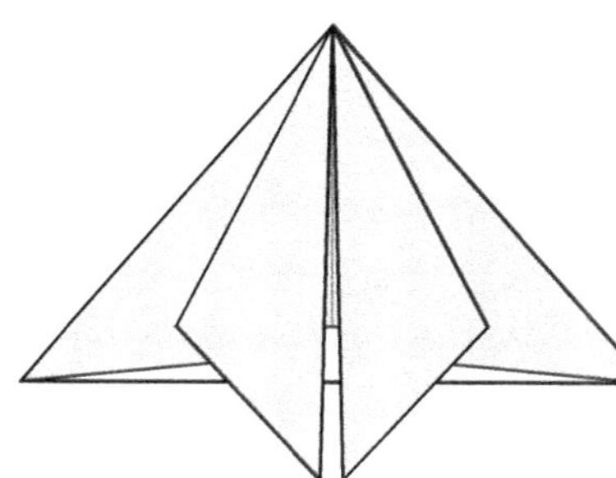

Step 4

Fold both side corners down as shown.

Step 5

Fold the side corners of the flaps you just made in to the vertical midline.

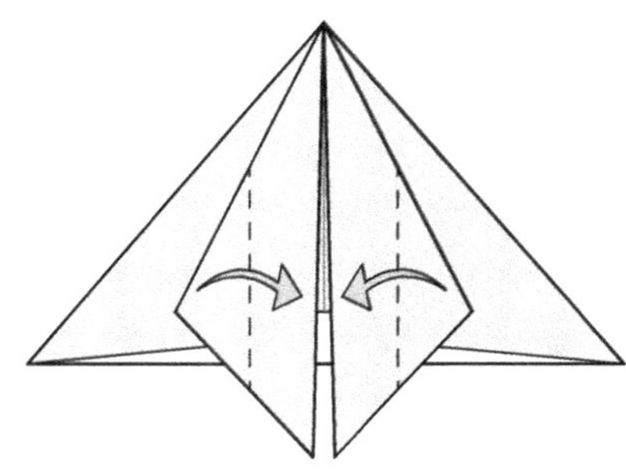

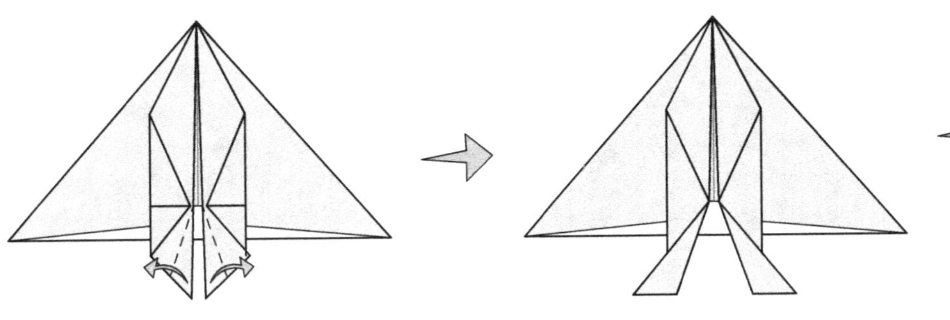

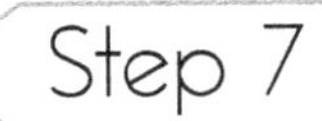

Step 6

Fold the bottom tips of those same flaps outward so their edges meet the folds from the previous step.

Step 7

Repeat steps 4 to 6 on the other side of the figure.

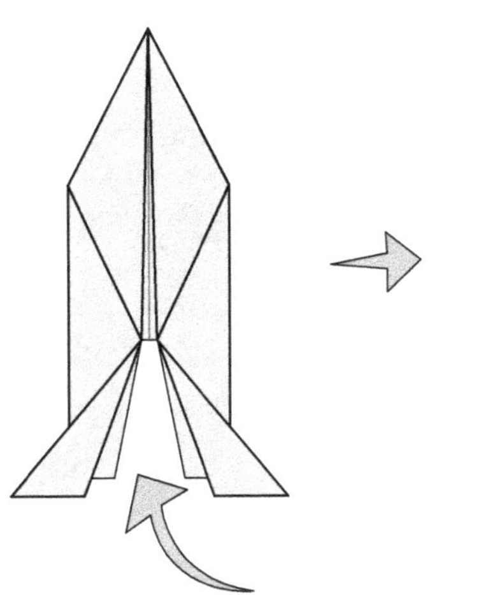

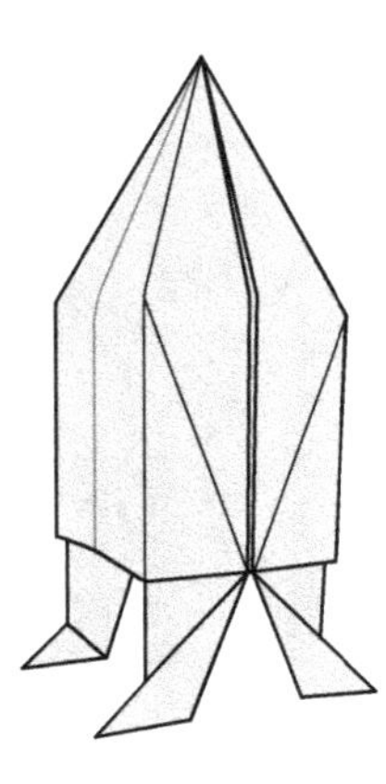

Step 7

Then open it carefully to shape your rocket.

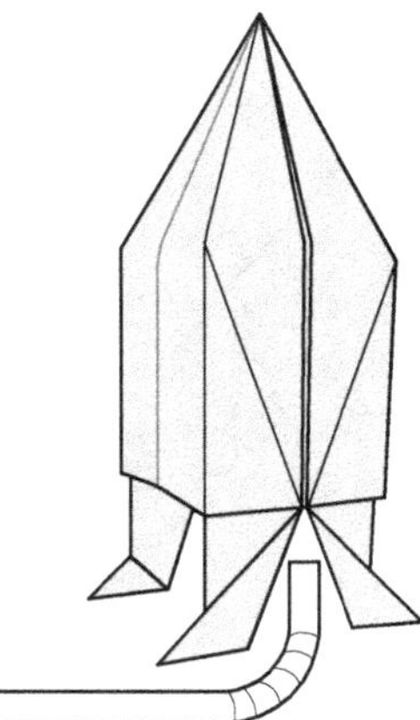

Step 8

Insert a straw into the bottom of the rocket and blow to see it fly!

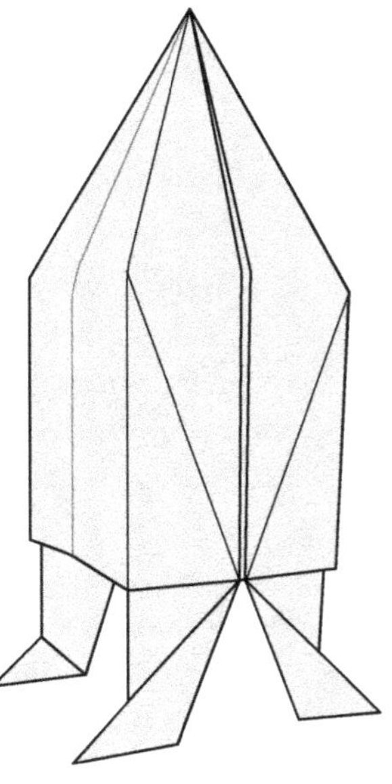

Rocket

Rabbit

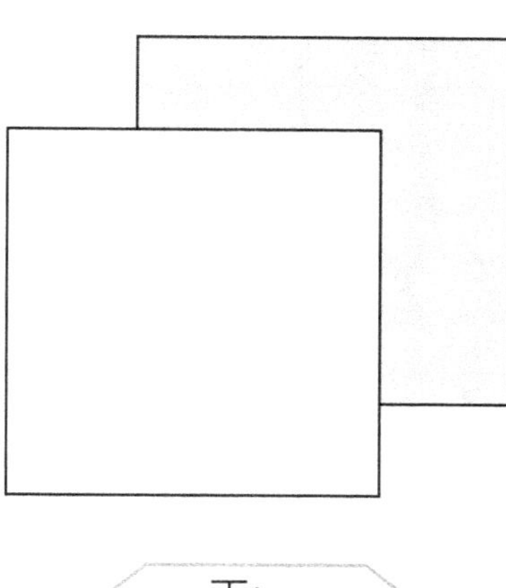

You will need 2 square sheets to make this rabbit.

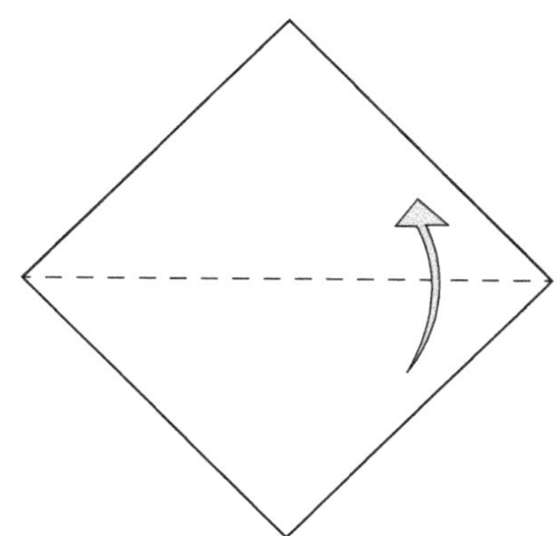

Fold one of the sheets diagonally up in half.

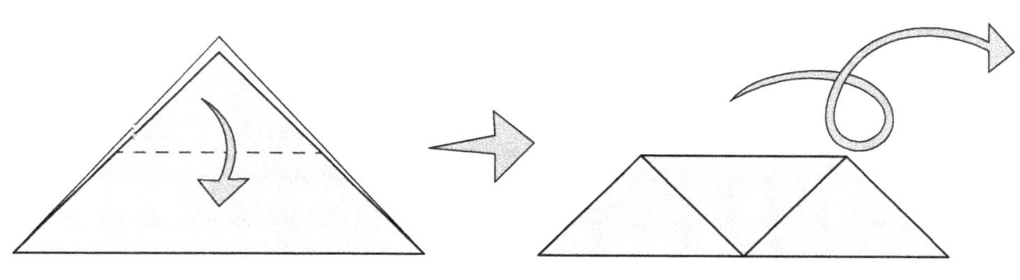

Fold the triangle down in half again, then flip the figure over.

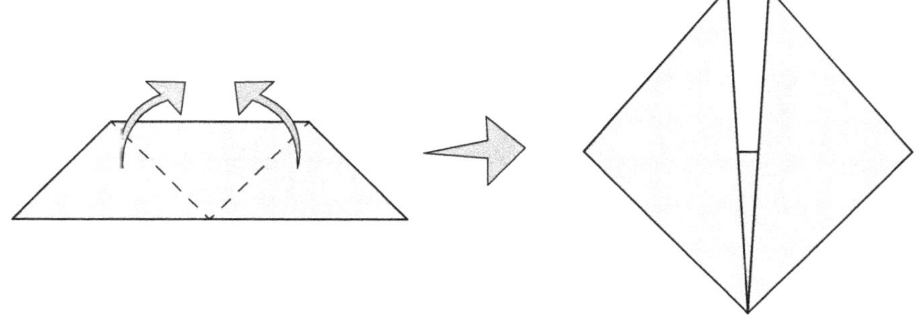

Fold both side corners up at an angle as shown.

Rabbit

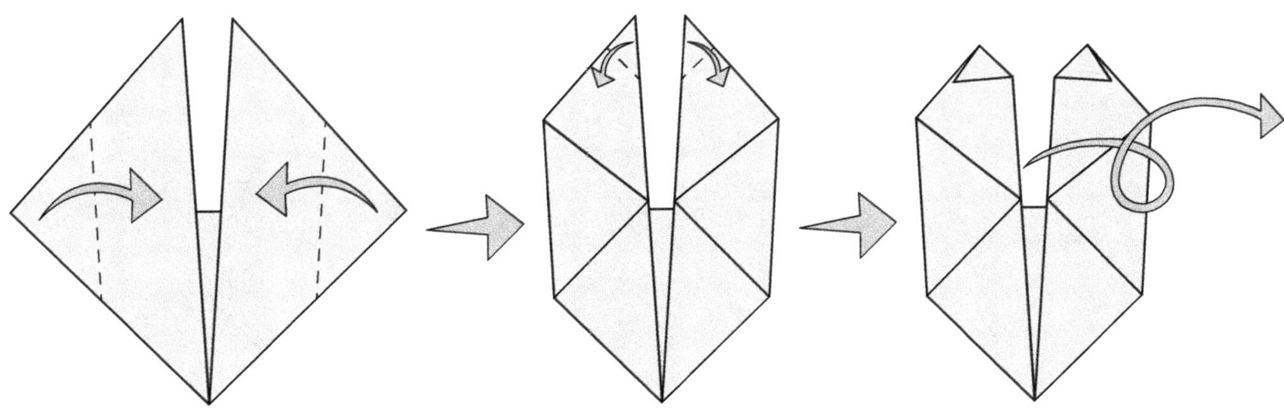

Step 4

Fold the side corners inward until they meet the inner edges of the flaps you just made.

Step 5

Fold the top tips down as shown, then flip the figure over.

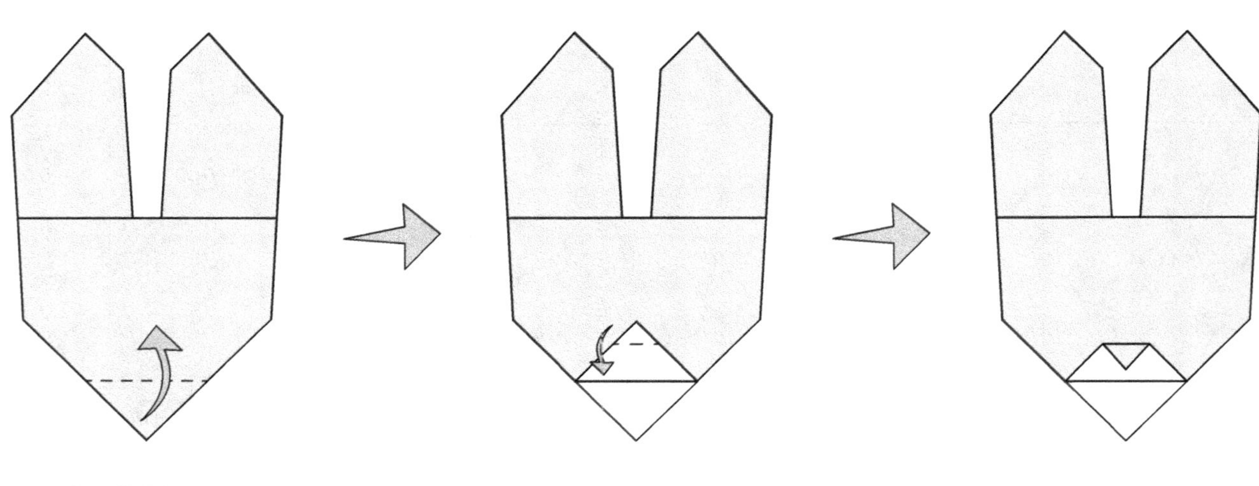

Step 6

Fold the top layer of the bottom corner up as shown.

Step 7

Fold the tip back down to make the rabbit's nose. The rabbit's head is ready, let's move on to its body.

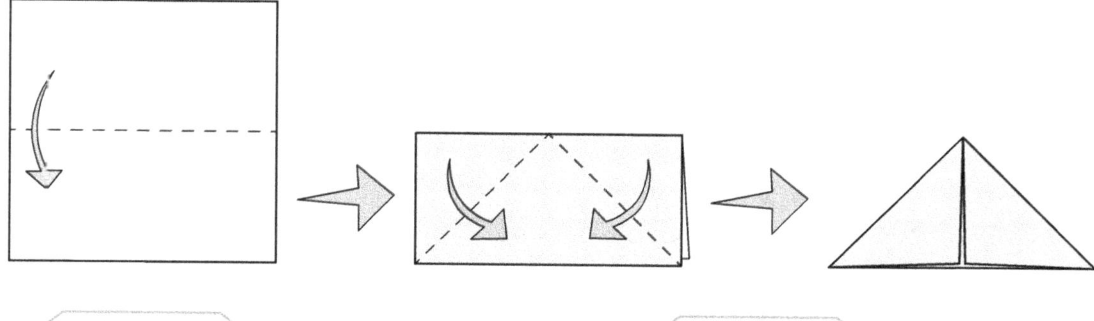

Step 8

Fold the second paper sheet in half crosswise.

Step 9

Fold the top corners diagonally down to make triangle.

Step 10

Fold both side corners down as shown, then fold them up so their tips stick out from the sides.

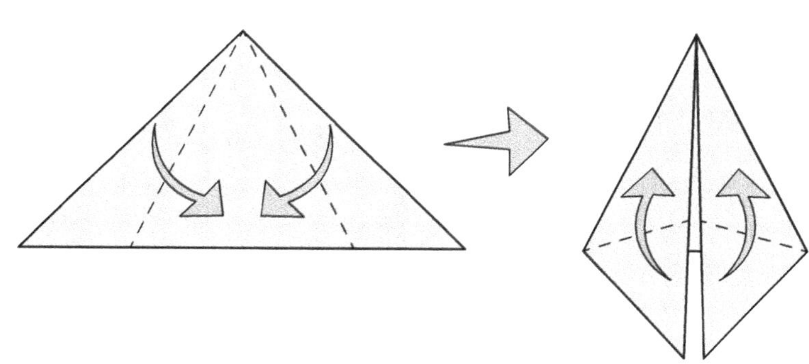

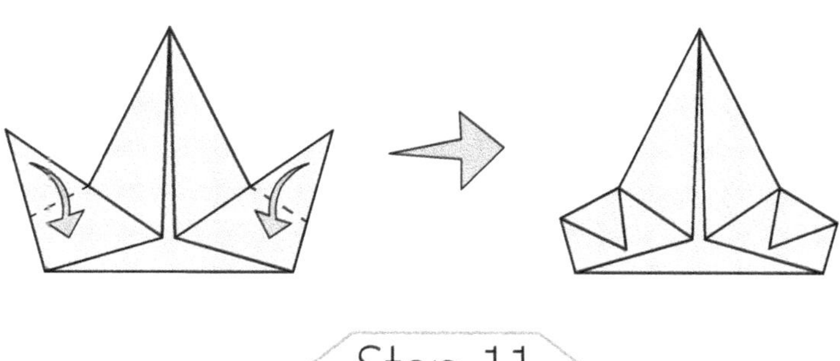

Step 11

Fold the side corners back down as shown. Then tuck the top corner into bottom edge of the head and the rabbit is ready.

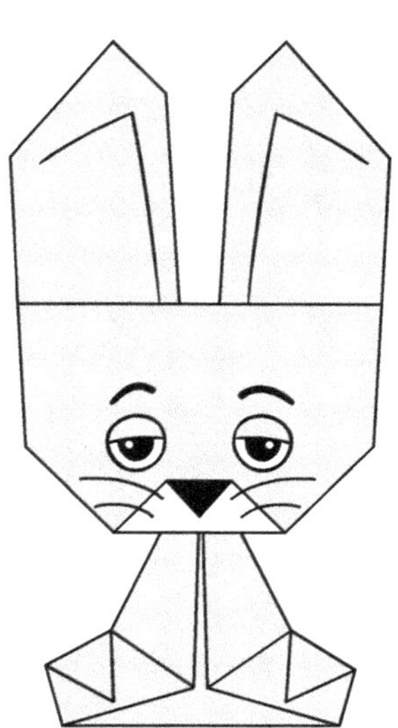

Rabbit

Ghost

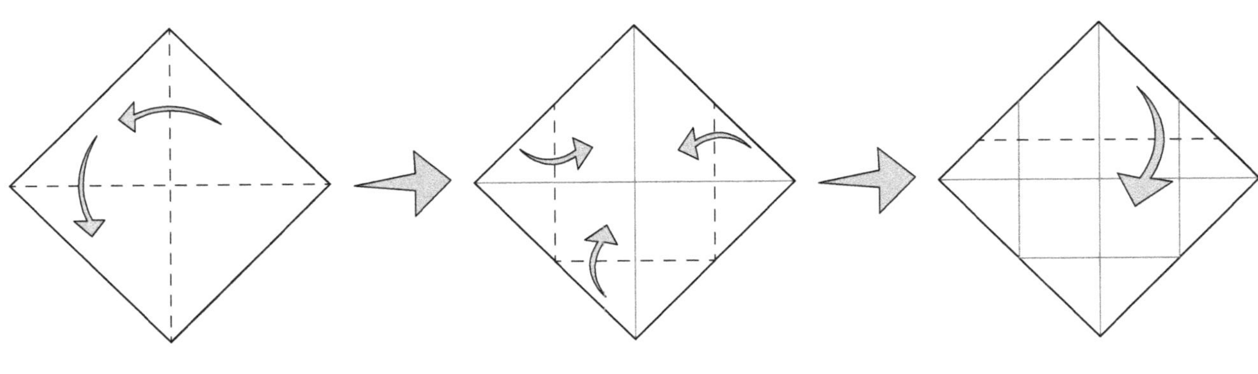

Step 1

Fold the sheet along both diagonals and unfold it.

Step 2

Bring the bottom and side corners to the center of the sheet and unfold again.

Step 3

Fold the top corner down to meet the crease made by the bottom corner as shown.

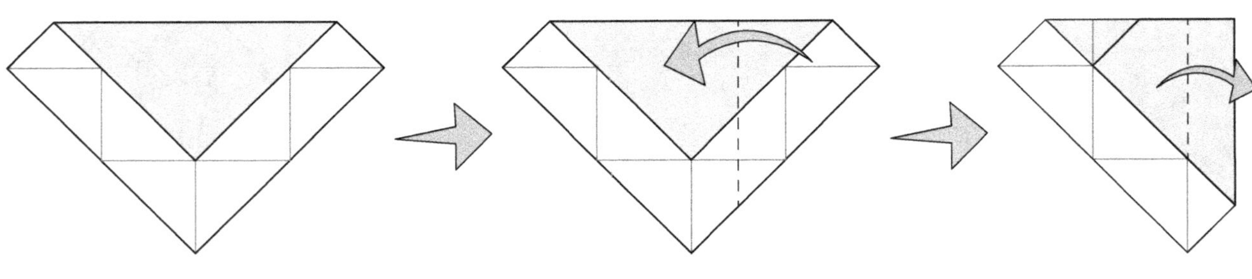

Step 4

Fold the right corner in to meet the crease made by the left corner on step 2.

Step 5

Fold the right corner back out at the midline as shown.

Ghost

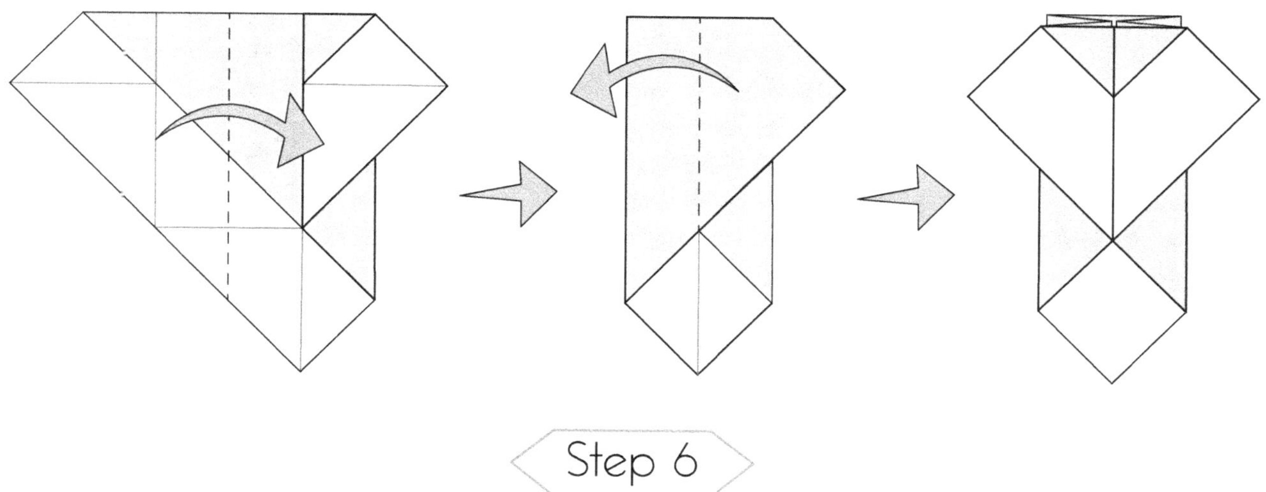

Repeat steps 4 and 5 for the left side of the figure.

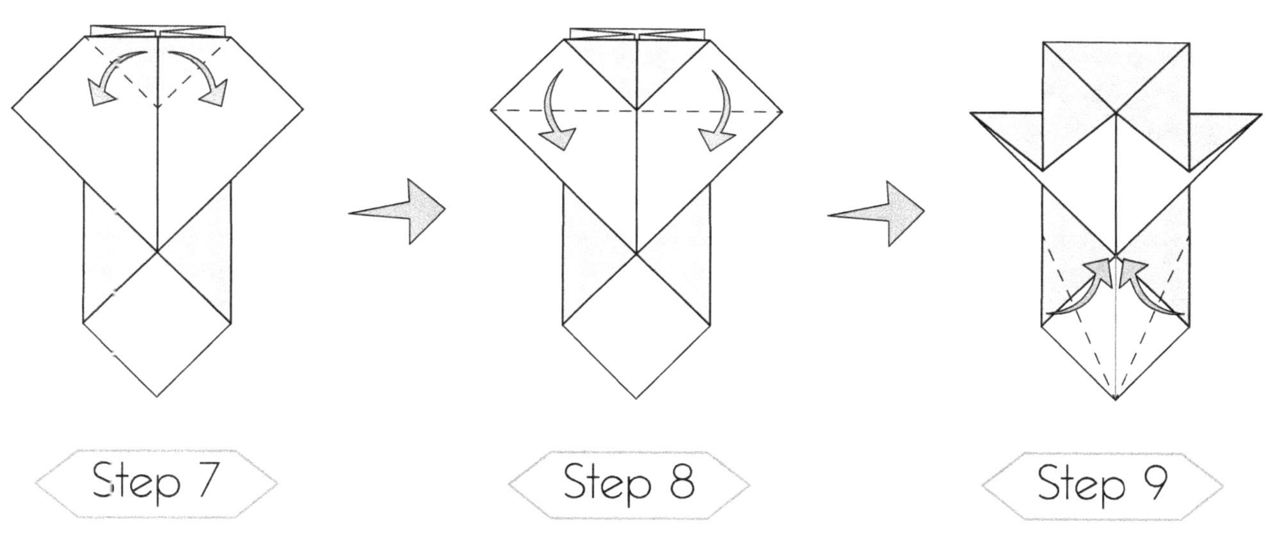

Fold the top corners
of the top layer
diagonally down as
shown and unfold.

Fold the top layer of the
figure down as shown,
using the creases you just made
to flatten the layer just below.

Fold the bottom sides
up to the vertical midline.

Ghost

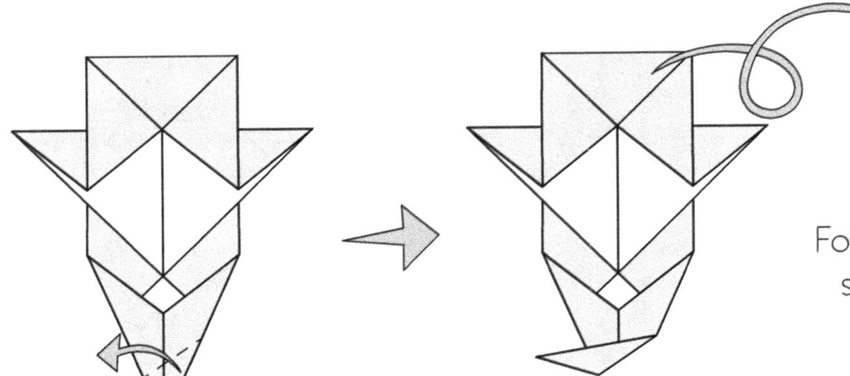

Step 10

Fold the bottom corner to the side at an angle as shown, then flip the figure over.

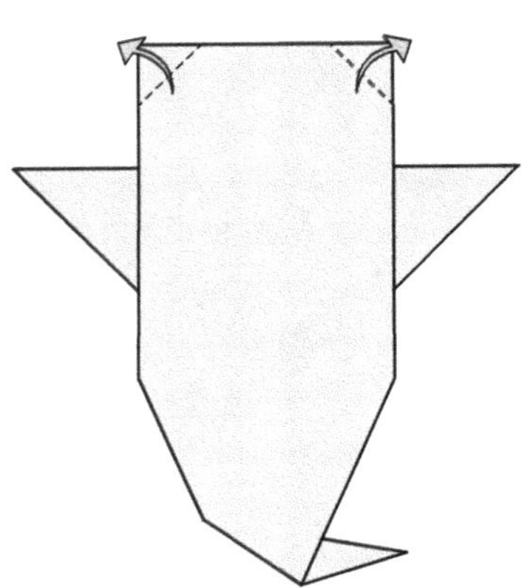

Step 11

Fold the top corner diagonally back as shown.

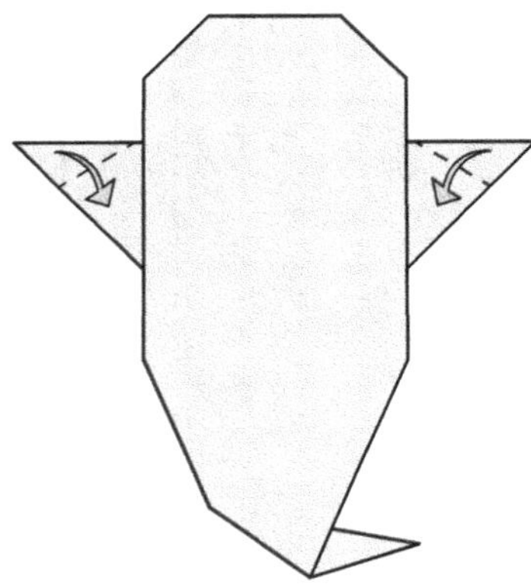

Step 12

Fold the side corners down at an angle as shown. The ghost is ready!

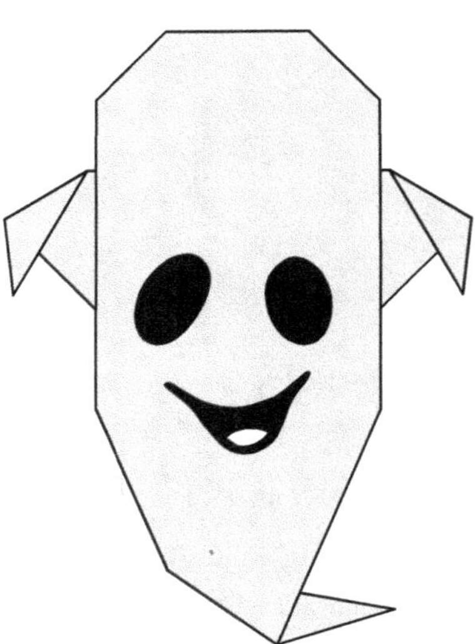

Ghost

Heart Envelope

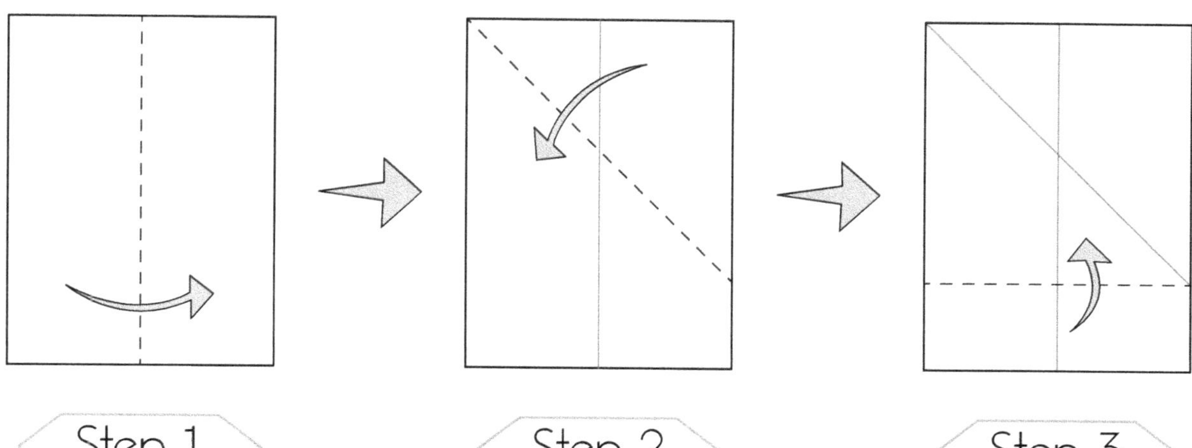

Step 1

Take an A4 sheet and fold it in half lengthwise, then unfold it.

Step 2

Fold the upper right corner diagonally down and unfold it to make a crease.

Step 3

Fold the bottom edge up at the point where the crease you just made meets the right edge.

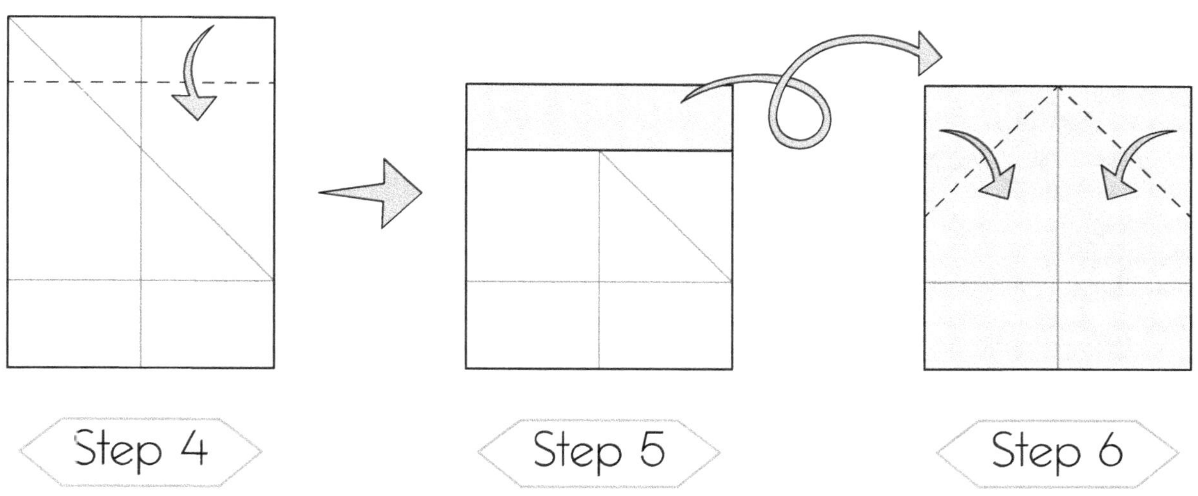

Step 4

Fold the top edge down at the point where the crease from step 2 meets the vertical midline.

Step 5

Flip the figure over.

Step 6

Fold both top corners diagonally down.

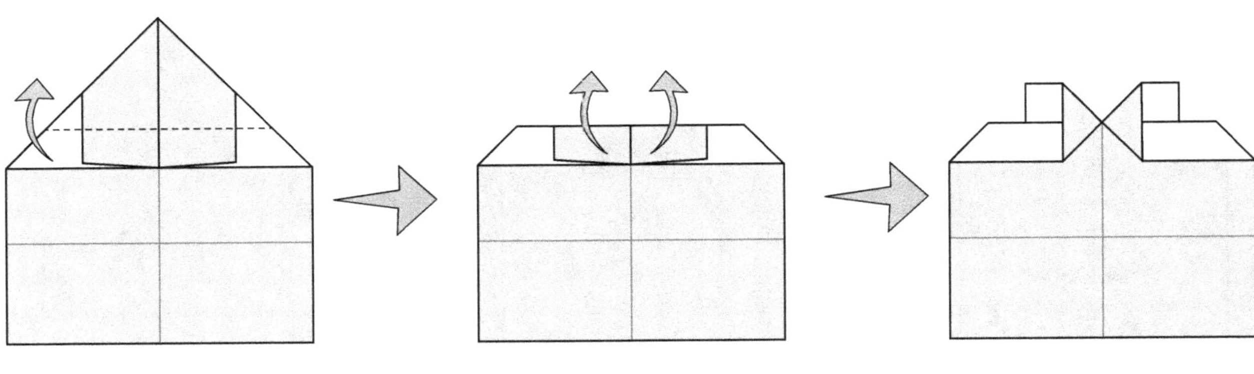

Step 7

Fold the top corner backward as shown.

Step 8

Open the flaps on the top layer and flatten to make two triangles as shown.

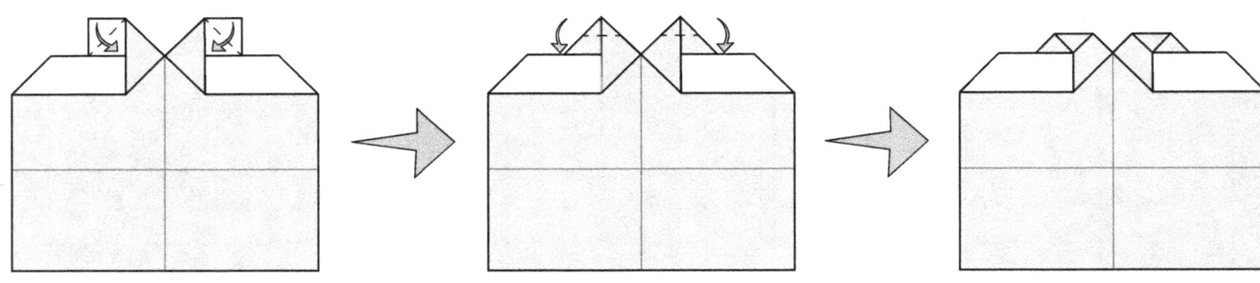

Step 9

Fold the outside corners of those flaps diagonally down.

Step 10

Fold the top tips down in half.

Heart Envelope

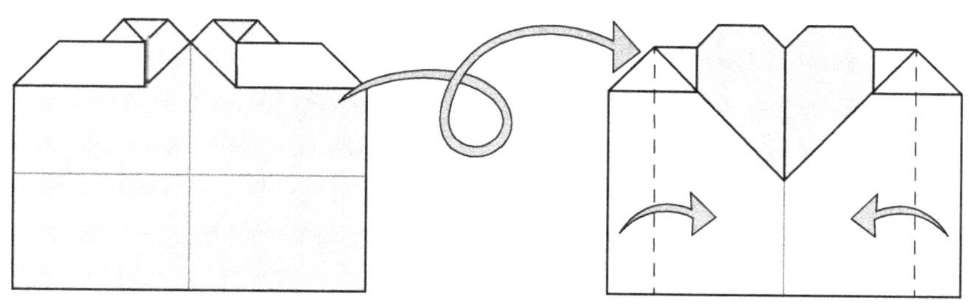

Step 11

Flip the figure over, then fold both side edges in as shown.

Step 12

Fold the heart-shaped flap up, then fold the bottom of the figure up in half.

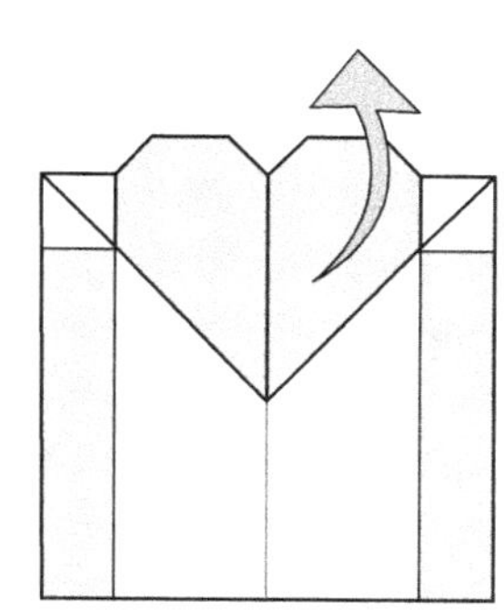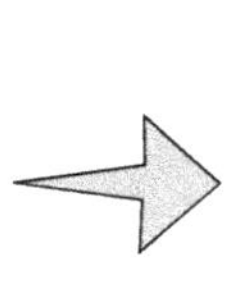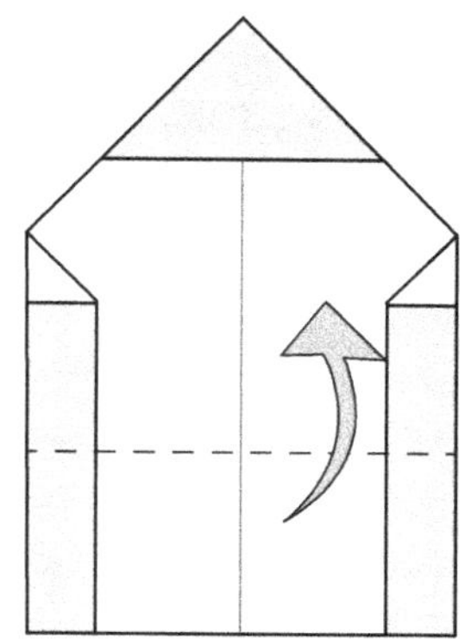

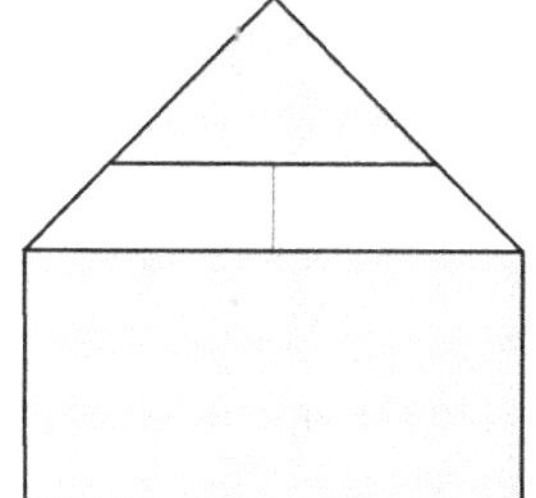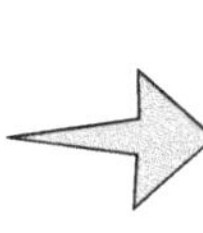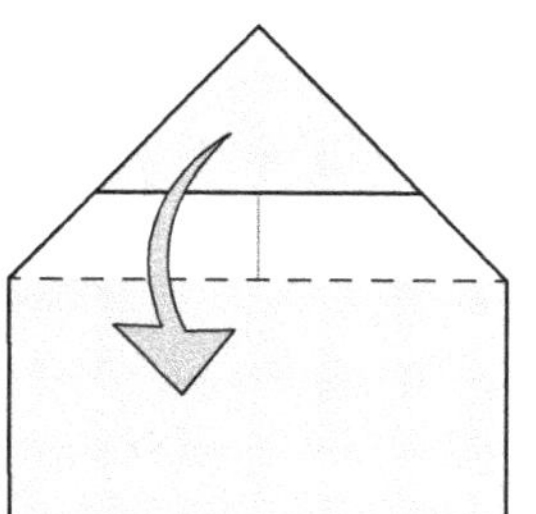

Step 13

Fold the heart-shaped flap back down.

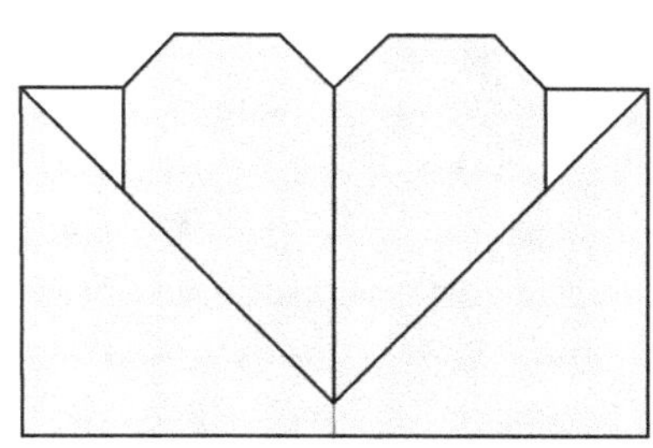

Heart Envelope

Pecking Crow

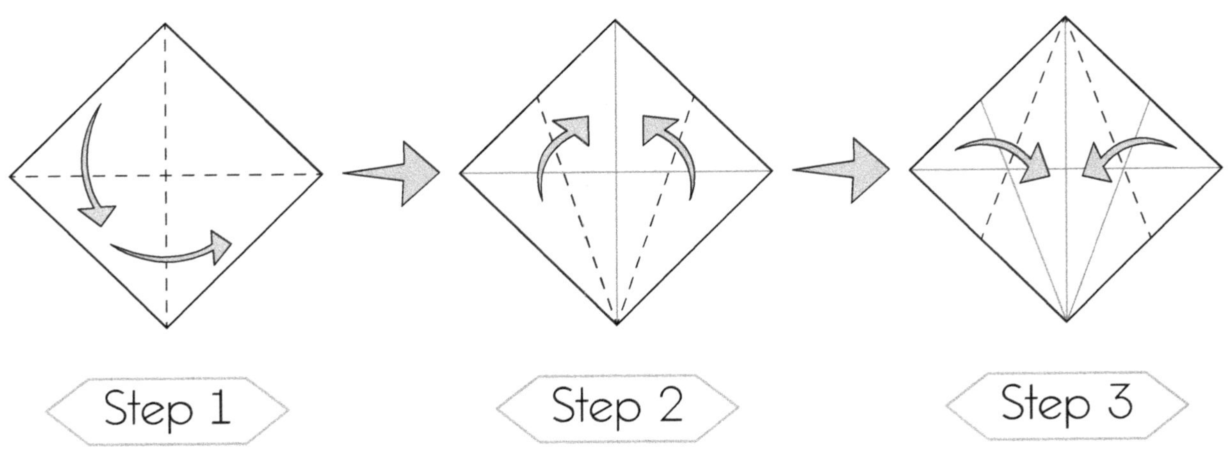

Step 1

Fold the sheet along both diagonals and unfold.

Step 2

Bring the bottom sides up to the vertical midline you just made and unfold.

Step 3

Repeat with the top sides.

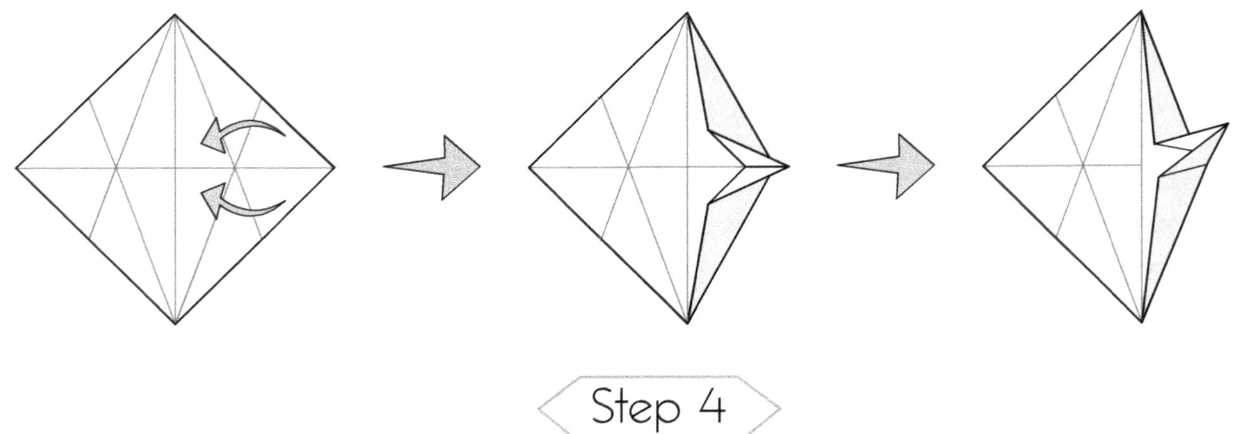

Step 4

You'll see that the creases from steps 2 and 3 form an X on each side of the figure. Fold the right corner i along the inner creases of that X (the longest ones). The shorter creases of the X will form a flap that sticks out, fold it up and flatten.

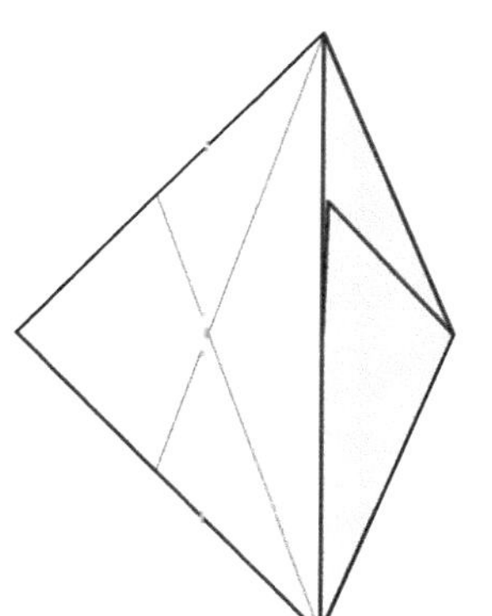  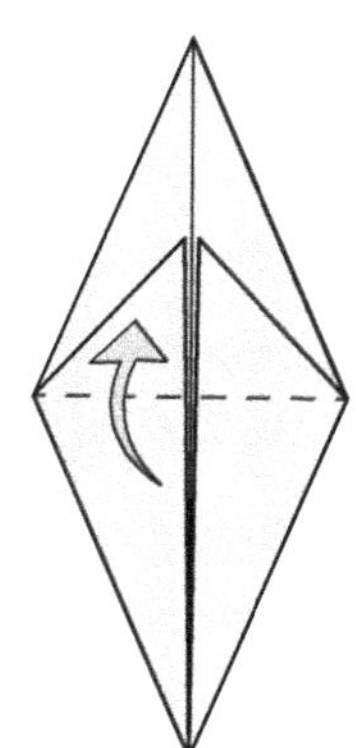 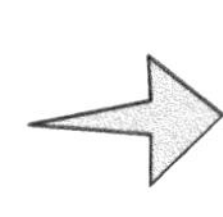 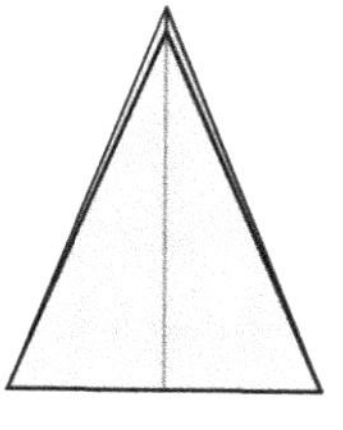

Step 5

Repeat the previous step for the left side, then fold the figure up in half as shown.

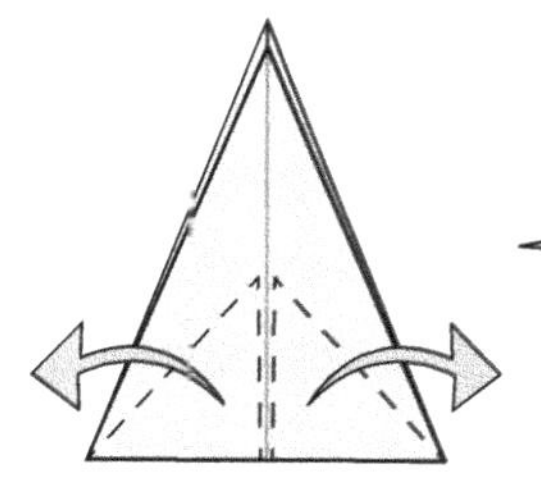 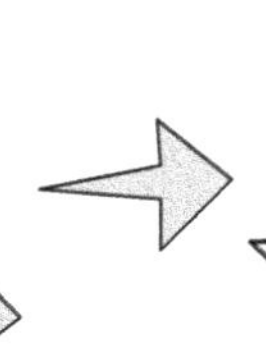 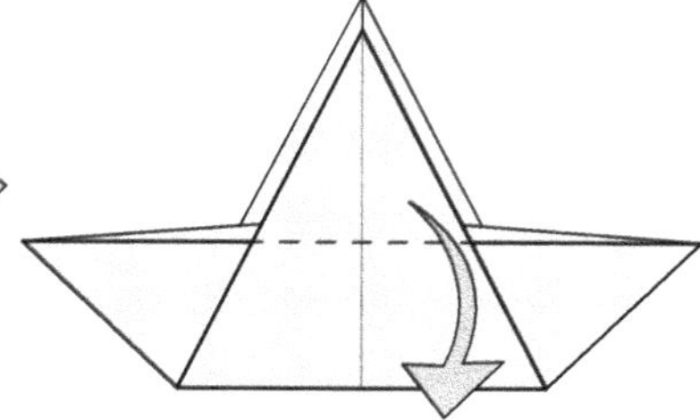 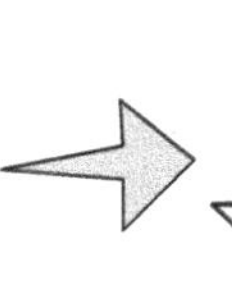 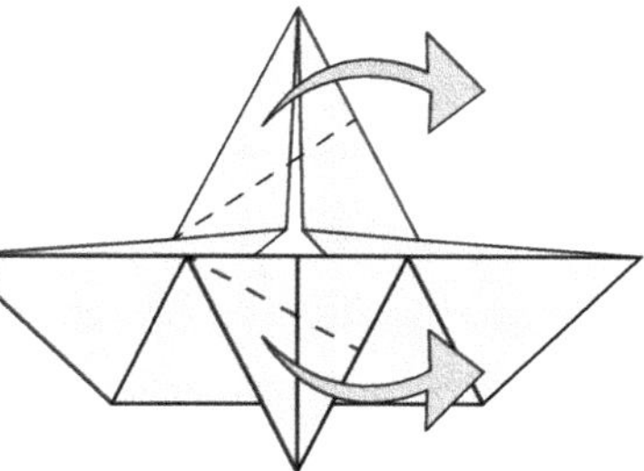

Step 6

Pull the flaps under the top layer you just folded outward (see dotted lines) and flatten.

Step 7

Fold the top corner of the top layer down as shown.

Step 8

Fold both corners to the right as shown.

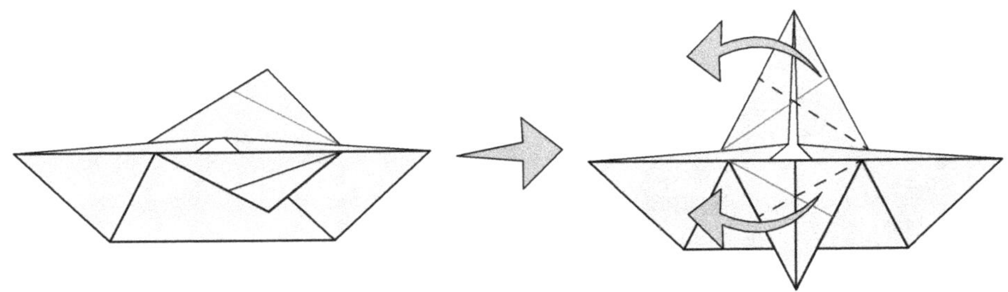

Unfold both corners
and fold them to
the left now, then
unfold again.

Use those creases to valley
fold both corners as shown
(just like you did on step 4)

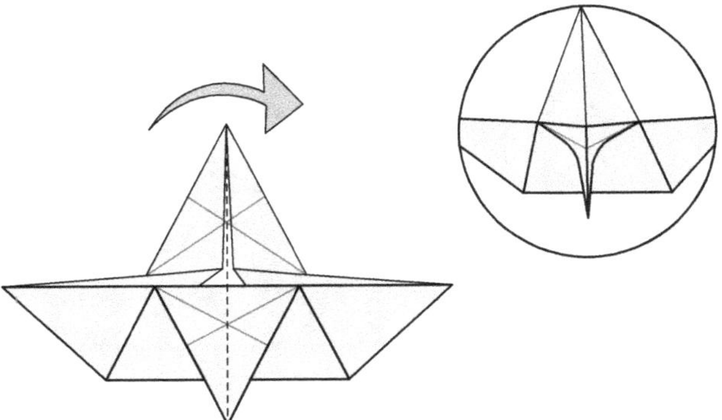

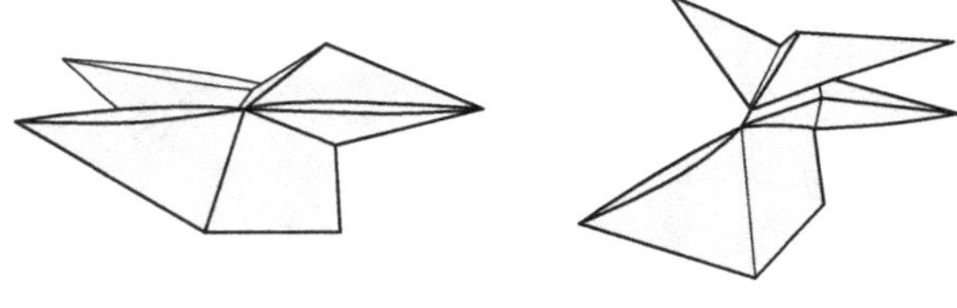

Fold the sides of the figure backward
to see how the crow's beak closes and unfold
them to see it open again.

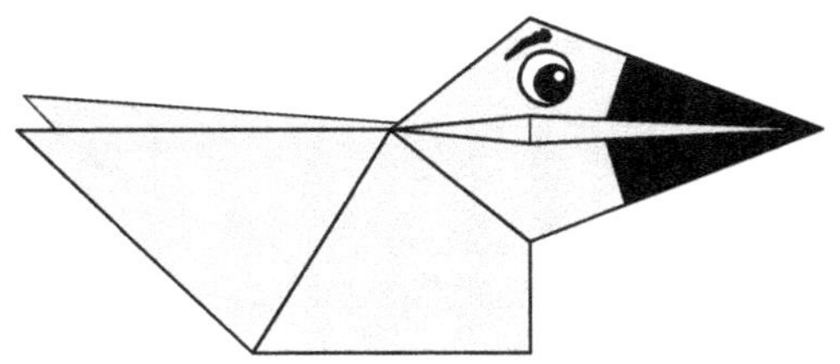

Pecking Crow

Moving Lips

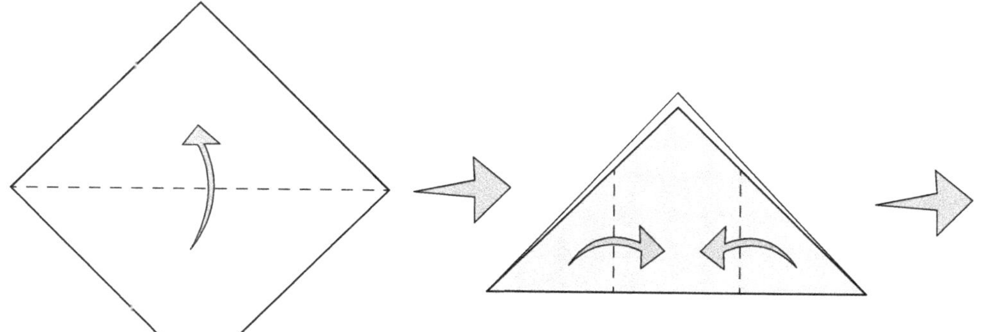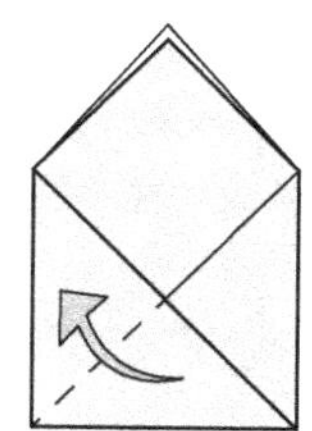

Step 1

Fold the sheet diagonally up to make a triangle.

Step 2

Fold the triangle into three equal parts, so that when you fold the side corners in, they overlap perfectly as shown. Make sure the left corner sits on top of the right corner.

Step 3

Fold the top layer (left corner from the previous step) up in half.

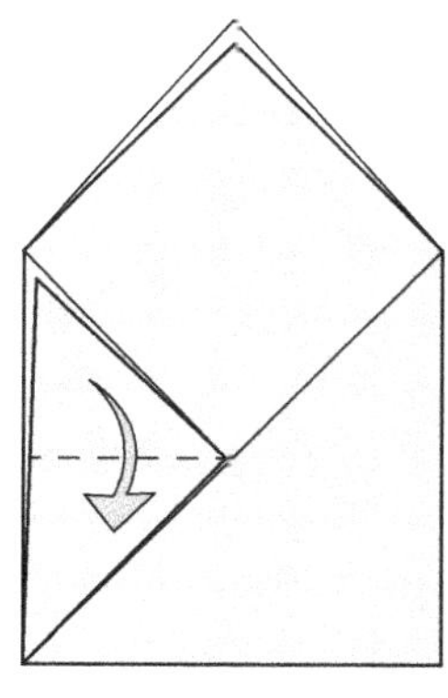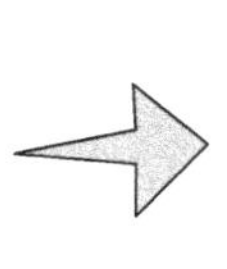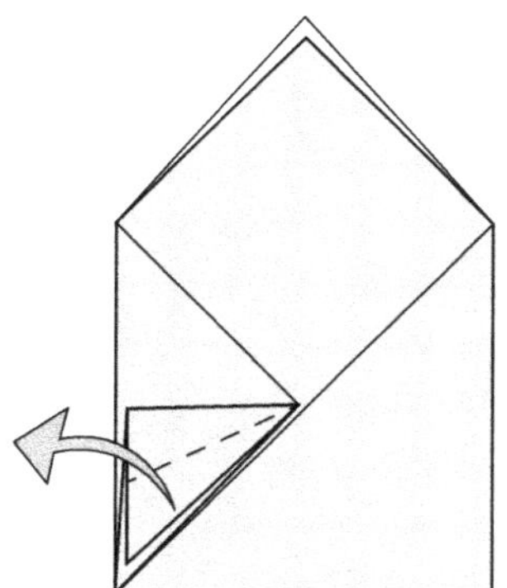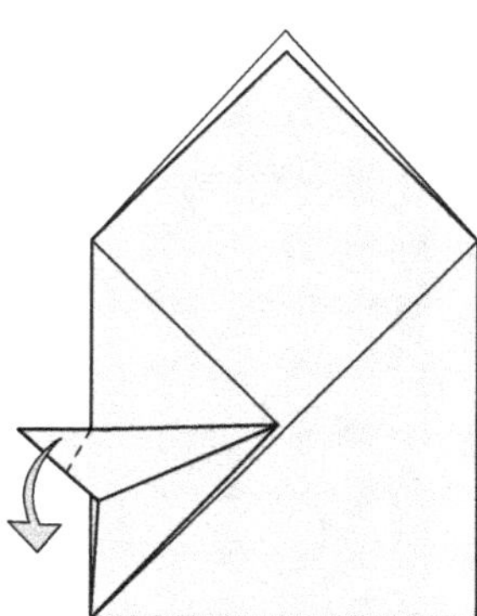

Step 4

Fold the same flap cown in half as shown.

Step 5

Fold it up again in half.

Step 6

Fold its tip down to meet the edge of the figure as shown.

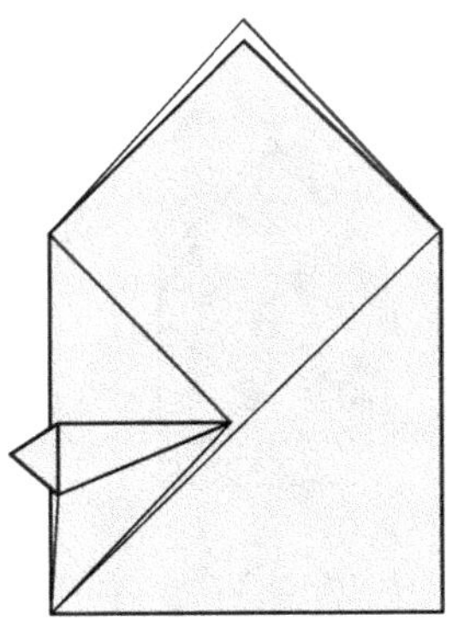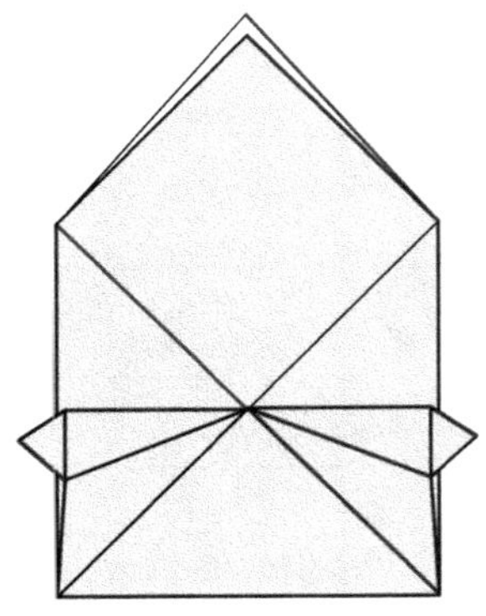

Repeat steps 3 through 6 on the right side of the figure, then unfold everything you've done so far.

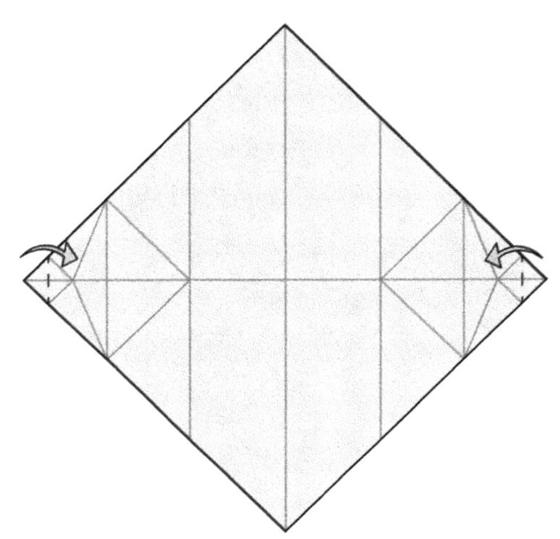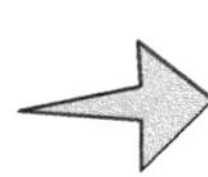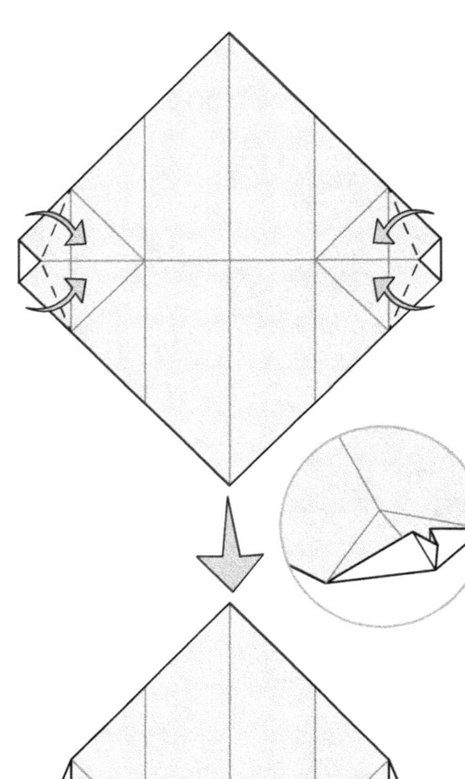

From now you're going to use all the creases you've made so far. Fold the side tips inward as shown, then use the X-shaped creases to fold those corners inward again. Pinch the flap that will stick out on both sides to flatten it. Flip the figure over.

Moving Lips

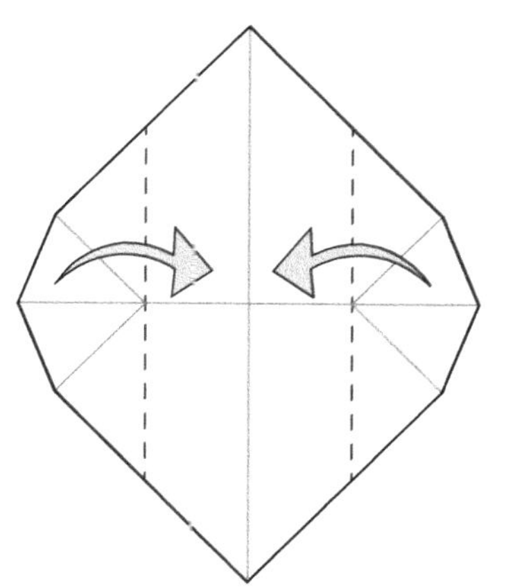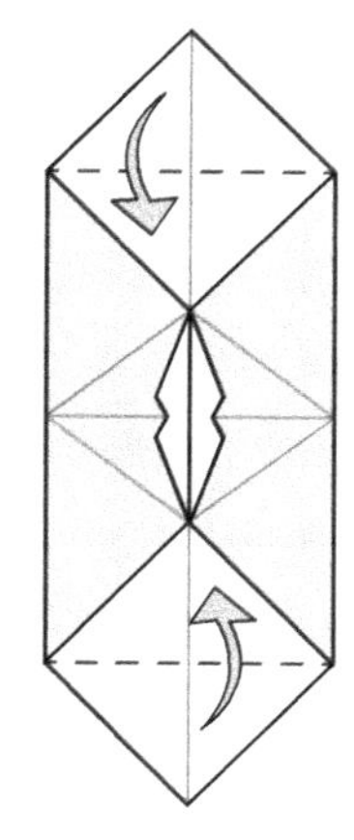

Fold both sides in along the vertical creases on either side of the midline, these are the lips. Then fold the top and bottom corners to match these folds you just made.

Step 10

Fold the top and bottom edges until they meet the edges of the lips.

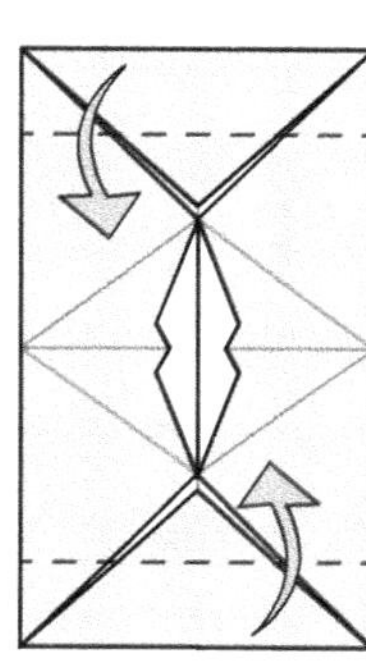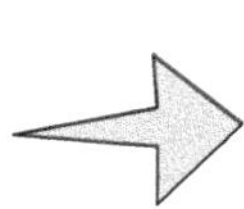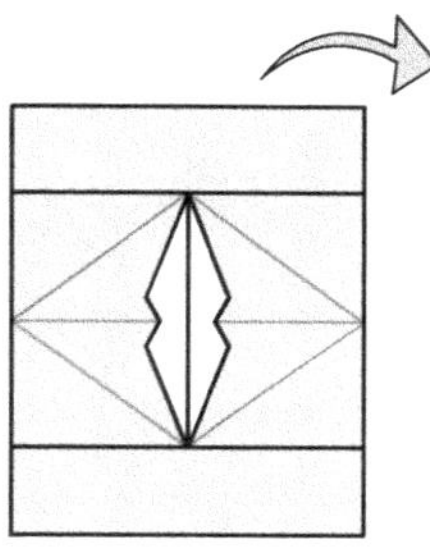

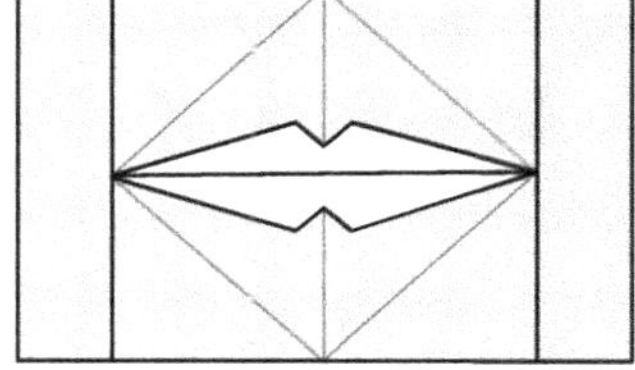

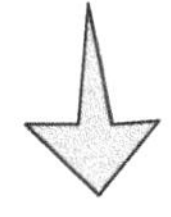

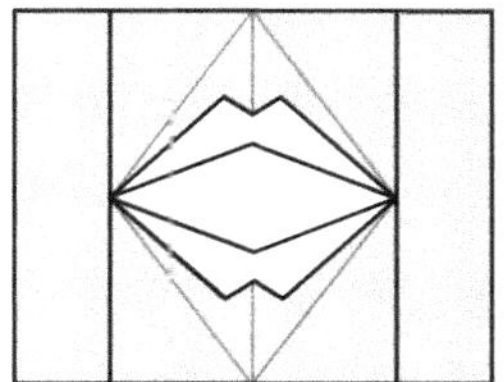

Step 11

Now that the lips are ready, grab the figure by its sides and fold it back and forth to see how they open and close!

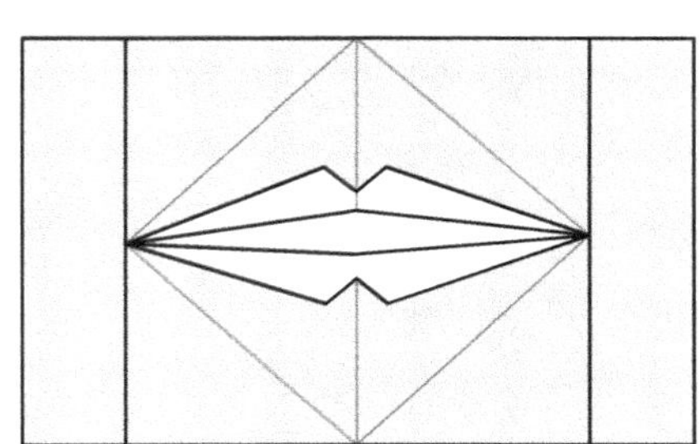

Chinese Boat

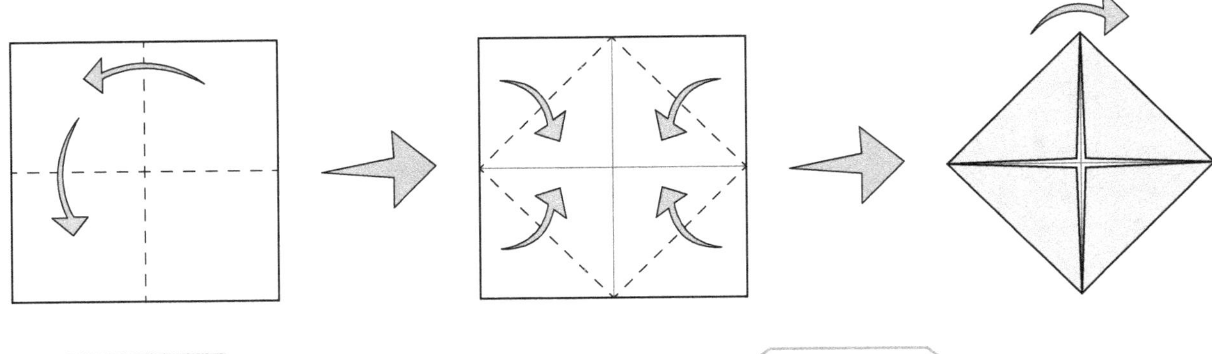

Step 1

Fold the sheet in half lengthwise and clockwise then unfold.

Step 2

Bring all the corners in to the center of the sheet (where the two crease from the previous step meet)

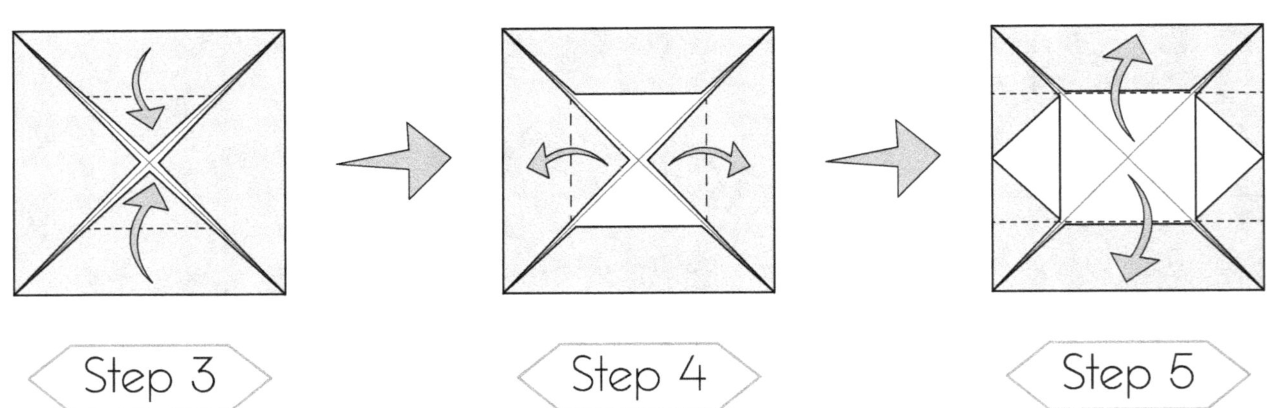

Step 3

Fold the top and bottom corners in half backward as shown.

Step 4

Fold the side corners back out in half as shown.

Step 5

Fold the sheet along both diagonals and unfold. Then bring the top and bottom edges to meet the center of the sheet at the back of the figure.

Chinese Boat

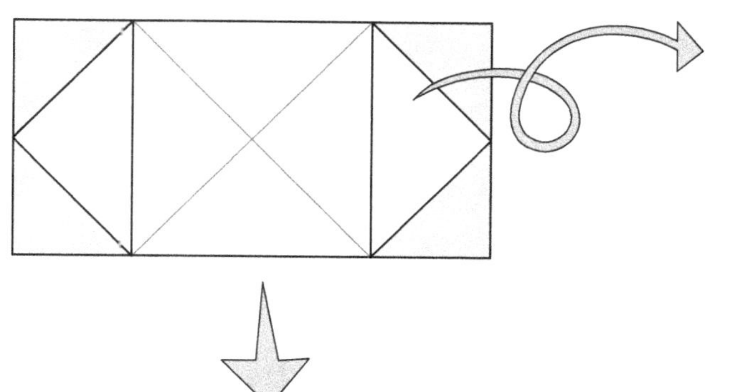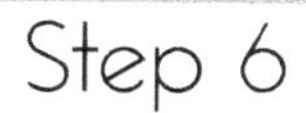

Flip the figure over.

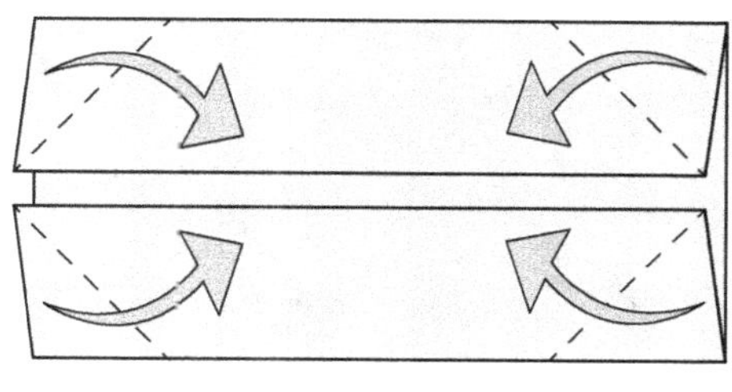

Step 7

Fold all the corners diagonally inward
as shown.

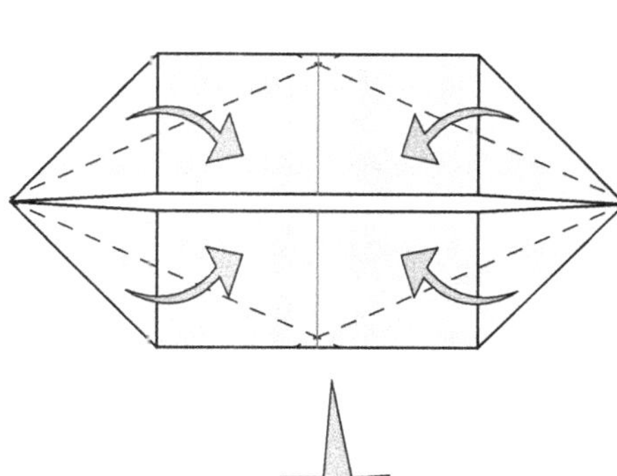

Step 8

Fold the corners on the left side to the
horizontal midline, then repeat for the right
side. You will see that the flaps on the right
side slightly overlap those on the left side.

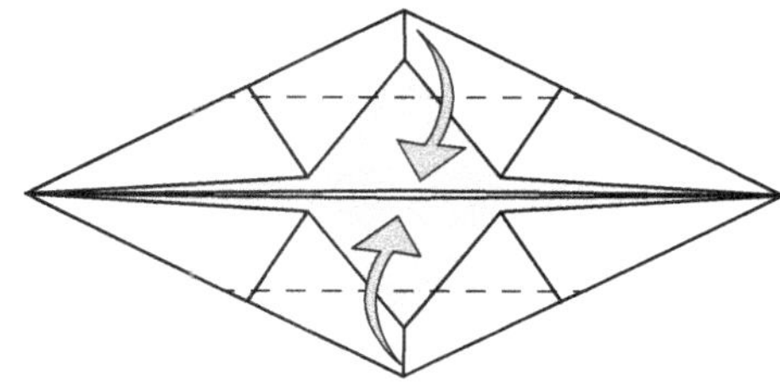

Step 9

Bring the top layer of the top and bottom
corners to the horizontal midline as shown.

Chinese Boat

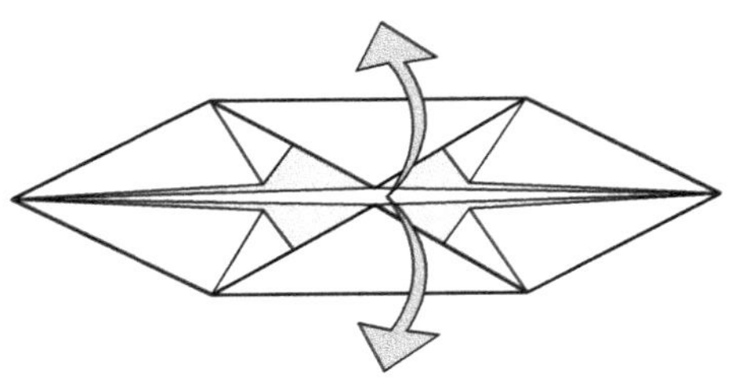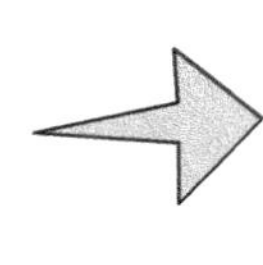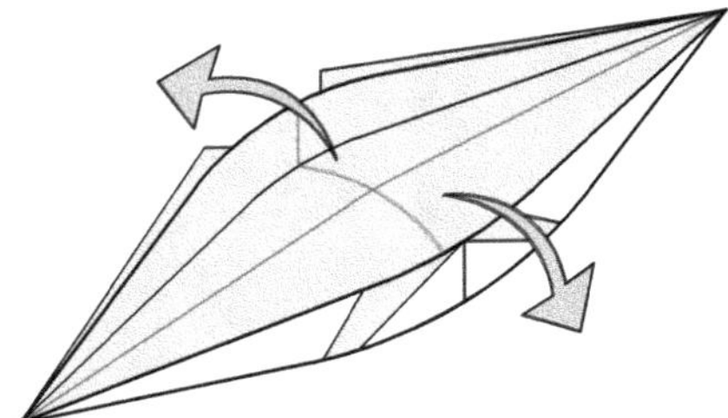

This is the tricky part of this design, but don't worry, it's easy and you can do it! Stick a finger under each side of the horizontal midline and separate them to completely turn the entire figure inside out. Then flip the figure over.

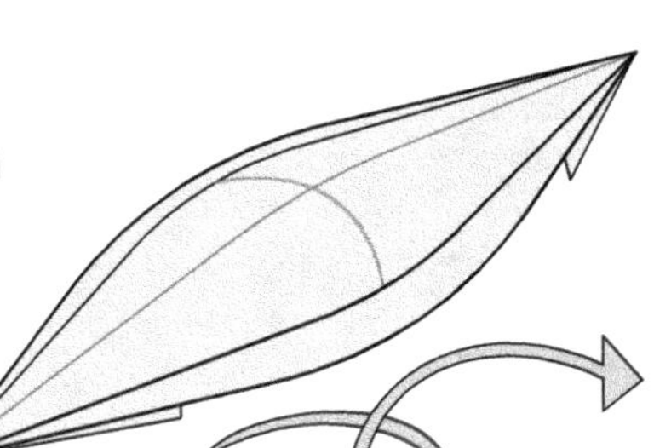

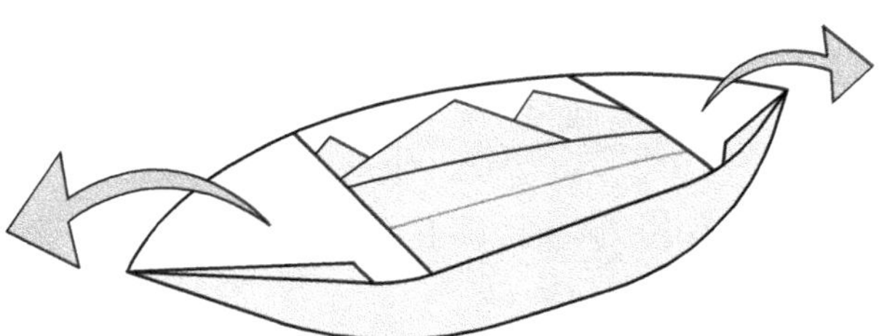

Carefully pull the flaps that you will see in each corner of the figure to finish shaping your boat.

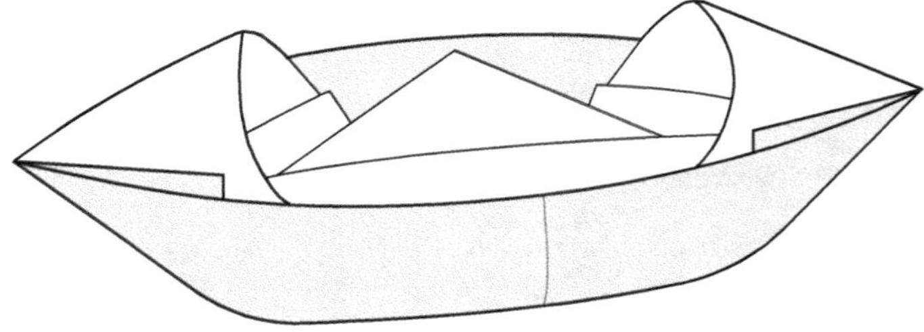

Dinosaur

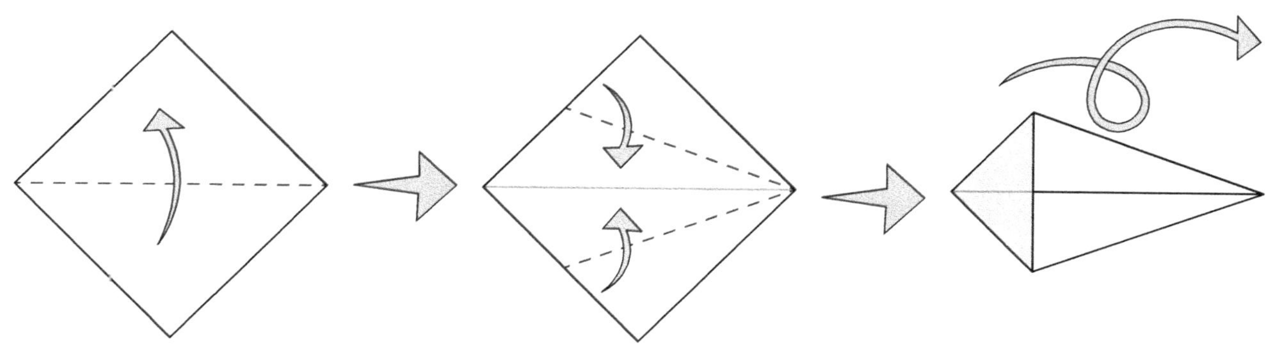

Step 1

Fold the sheet diagonally up in half and unfold.

Step 2

Bring the top and bottom corners to the horizontal midline as shown.

Step 3

Flip the figure over.

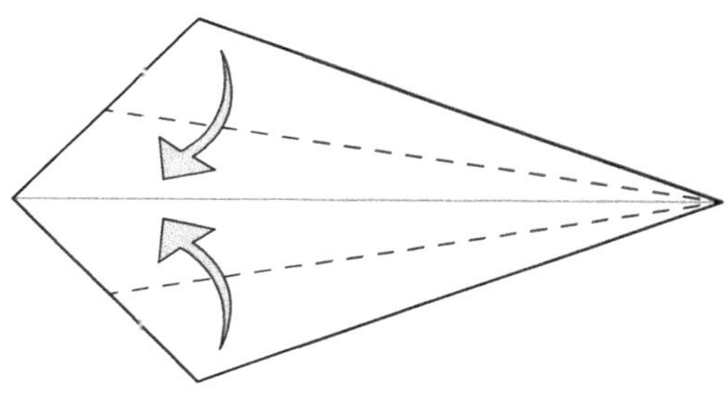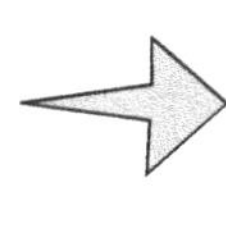

Step 4

Bring the top and bottom corners to the horizontal midline again as shown.

Step 5

Unfold the flaps you made on step 2 and flatten.

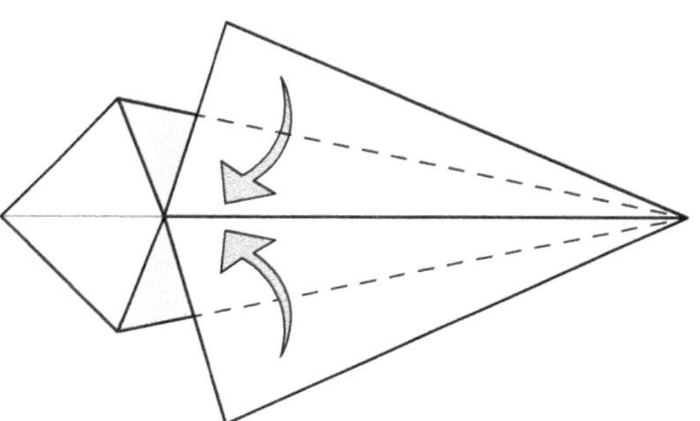

Step 6

Now bring those same flaps to the horizontal midline.

Dinosaur

Step 7

Bring the top and bottom corners of the top layer to the horizontal midline.

Step 8

Unfold both corners.

Step 9

Fold the entire figure to the right at the point marked by the creases from the previous step as shown.

Step 10

Unfold it.

Step 11

Let's focus on the top half of the figure: Open the bottom corner of the top layer to the right using the crease from step 7 to make a triangle then flatten.

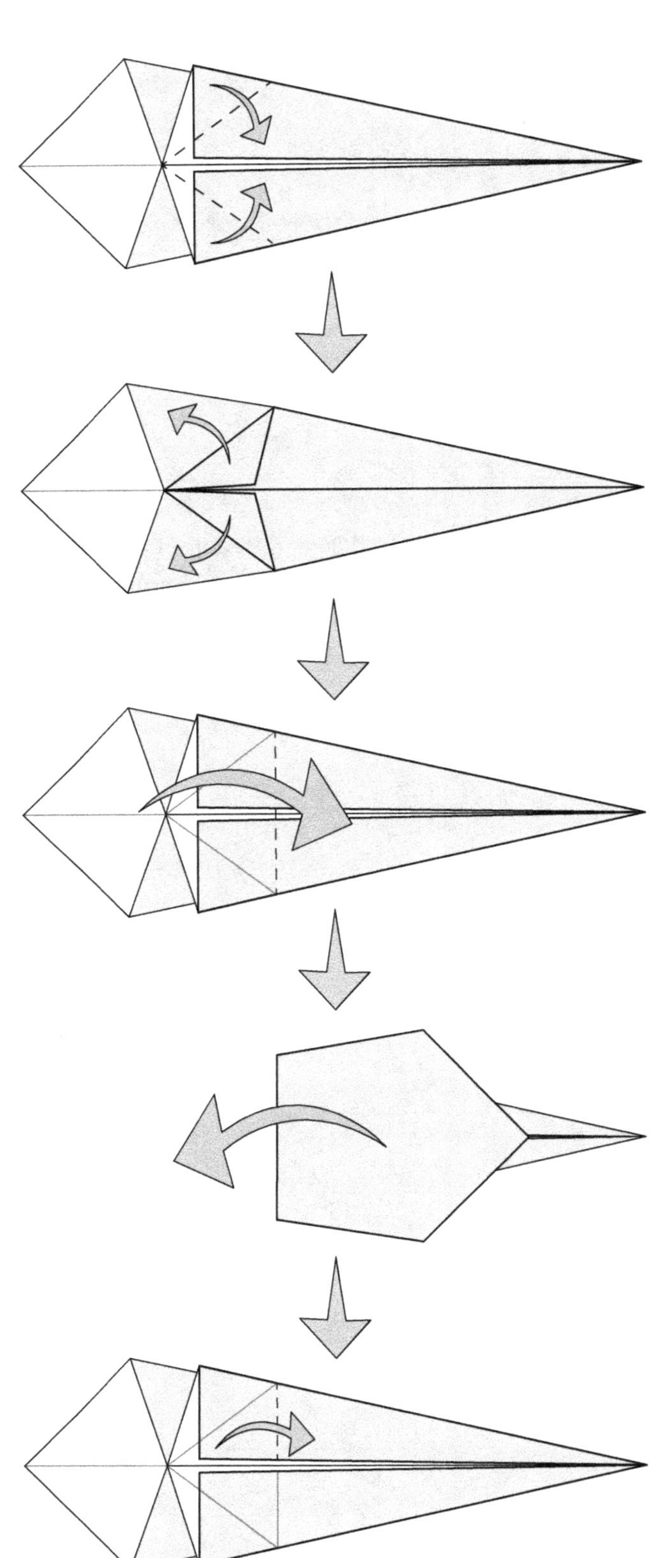

Step 12

Repeat the previous step
on the bottom half of the figure.

Step 13

Fold the top and bottom corners of
the back layer forward to the
horizontal midline, then unfold.

Step 14

Now repeat steps 11 and 12
for these corners.

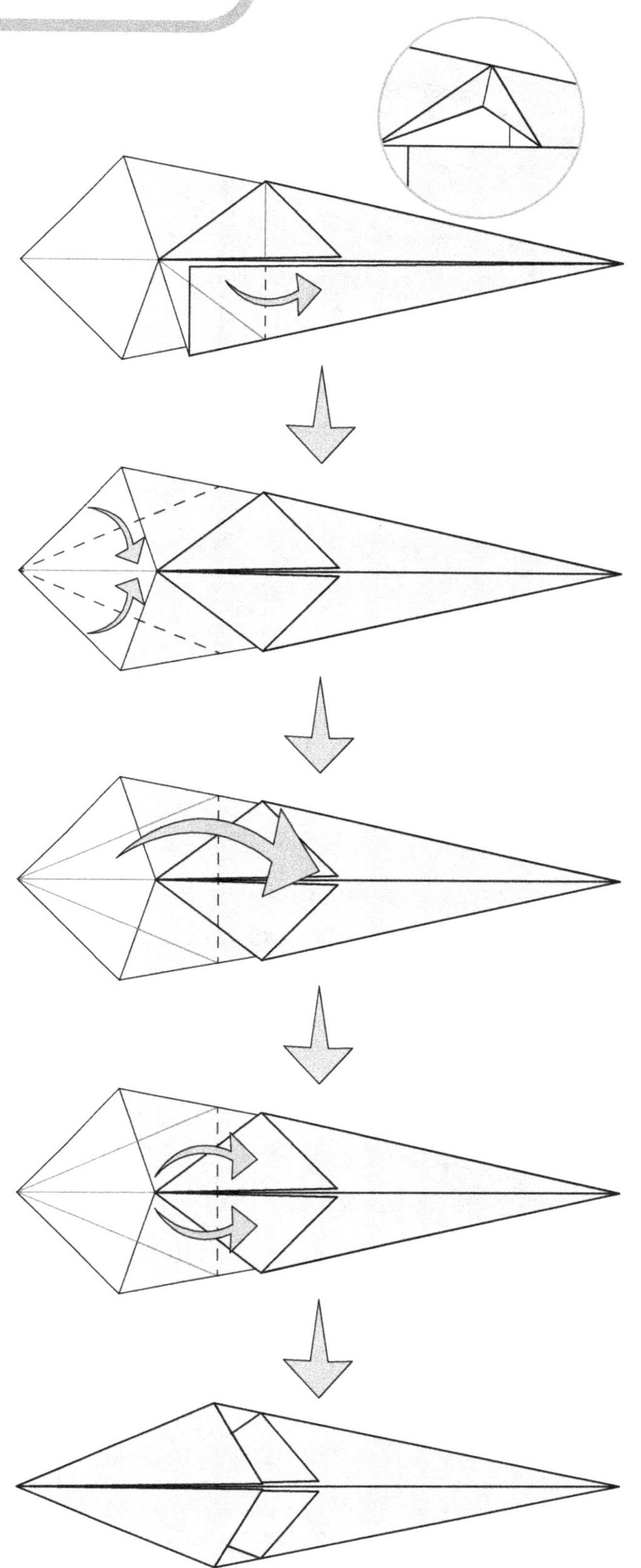

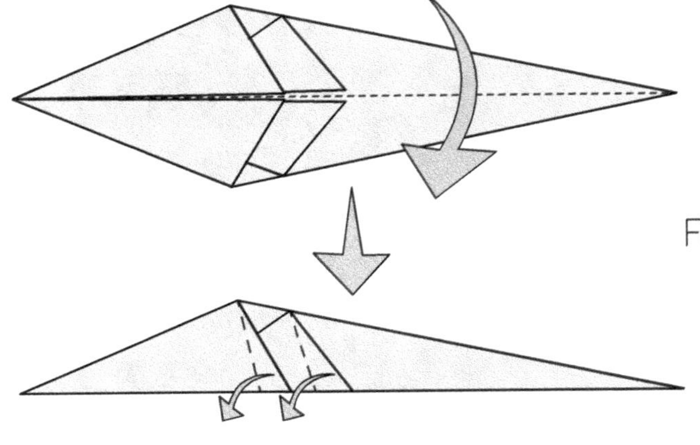

Fold the figure back up in half, then fold the flaps in the middle of the figure so that their edges end up vertical and their tips stick out from the bottom of the figure.

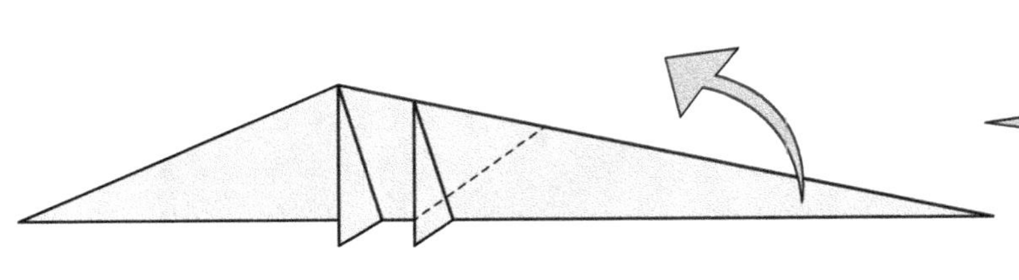

Fold the right side up as shown and unfold it to make a crease, then use it to make an inside reverse fold.

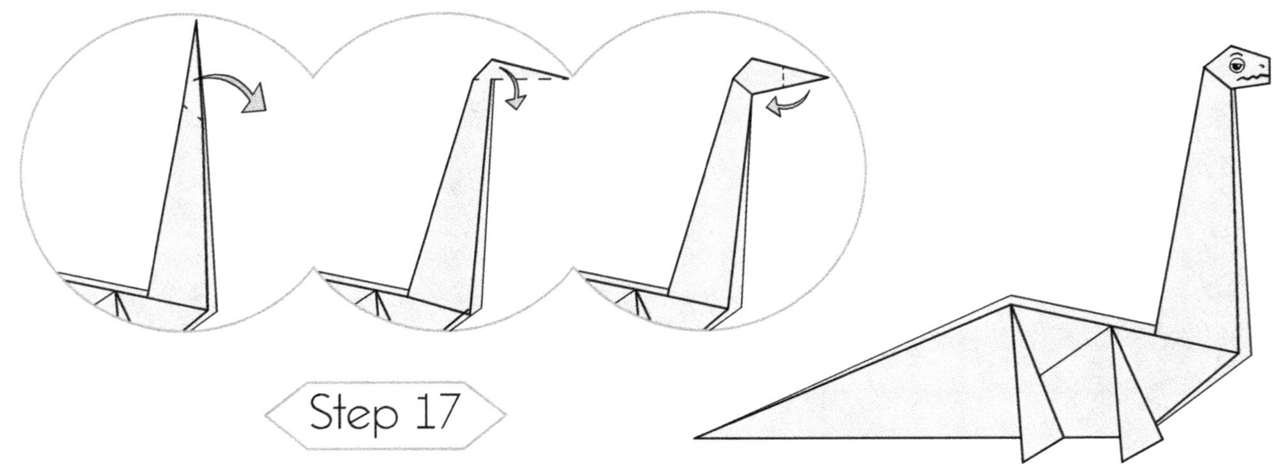

Now make an outside reverse fold on top of that same section to make dinosaur's head. Then fold the tip inward as shown.

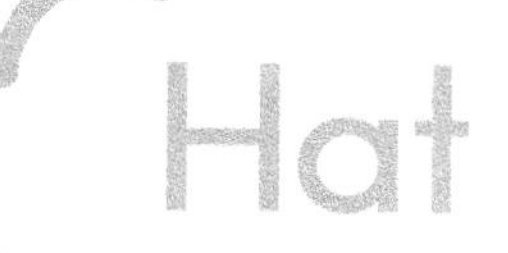 Hat

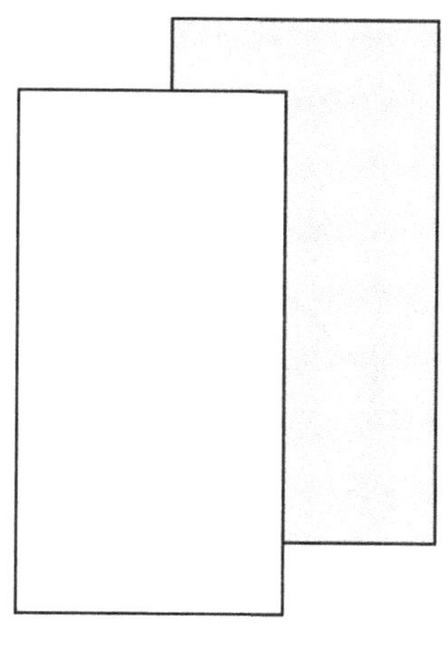

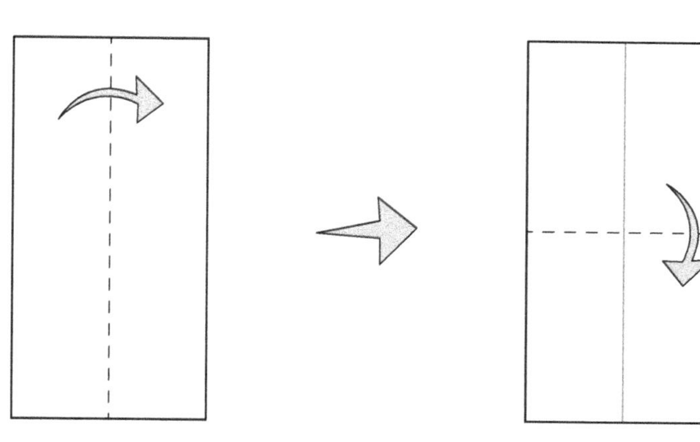

Tip

You will need two sheets to make this cap. Sheets should be twice as tall as they are wide, for example, 10 x 20 cm.

Step 1

Fold the paper in half lengthwise and unfold it to make a crease. Then fold the sheet in half crosswise.

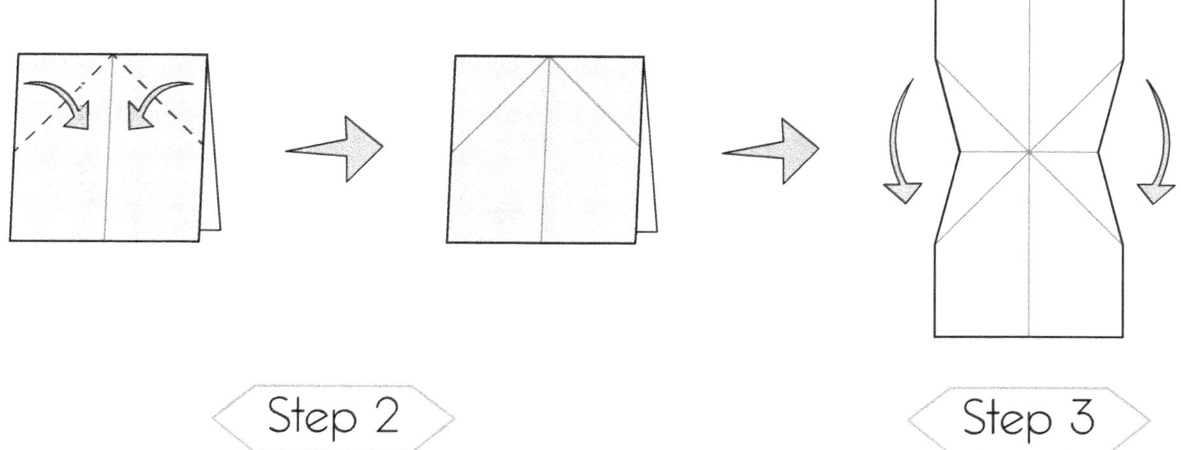

Step 2

Fold both top corners diagonally down and unfold them to make creases, then unfold the entire figure.

Step 3

Fold the figure down in half and use the creases from the previous step to fold those corners in to make a triangle at the top of the figure.

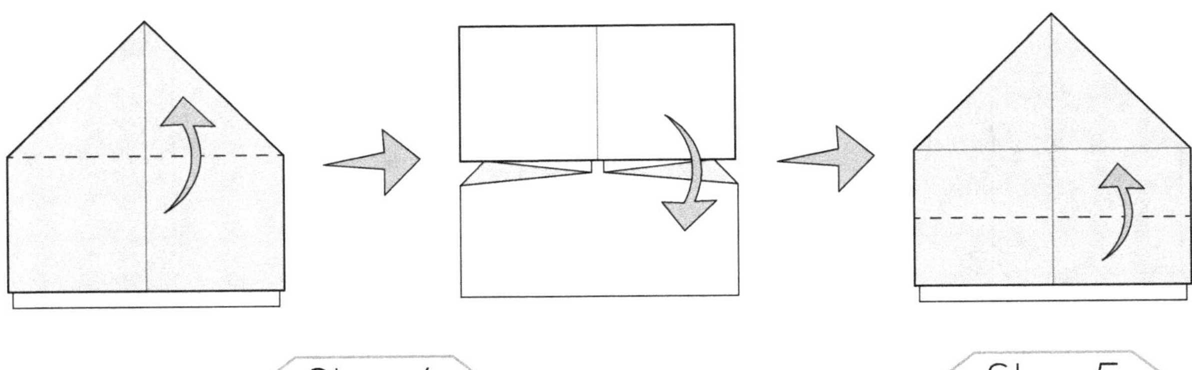

Step 4

Fold the top layer of the bottom edge up as shown, then unfold it to make a crease.

Step 5

Fold the same edge back up to meet the crease you just made.

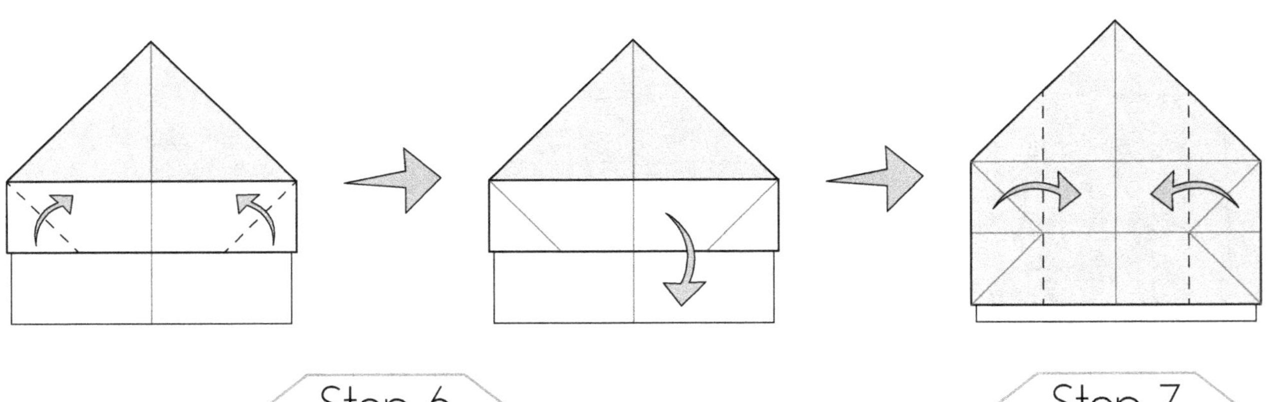

Step 6

Fold the corners of the flap you just made diagonally, then unfold them. Bring that edge back down as shown.

Step 7

Bring both side edges of the top layer in to the vertical midline.

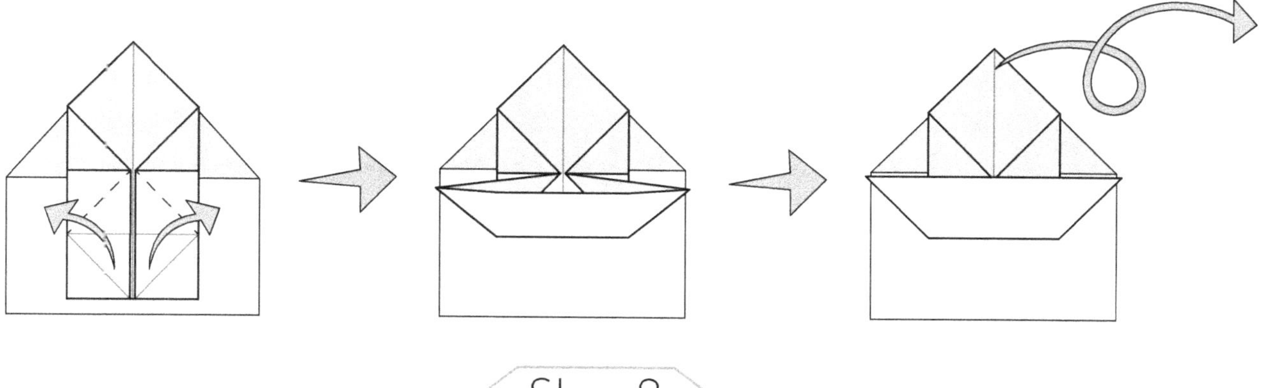

Step 8

Use the creases you made in step 6 to bring the corners out as shown and flatten. Flip the figure over and repeat everything on the other side.

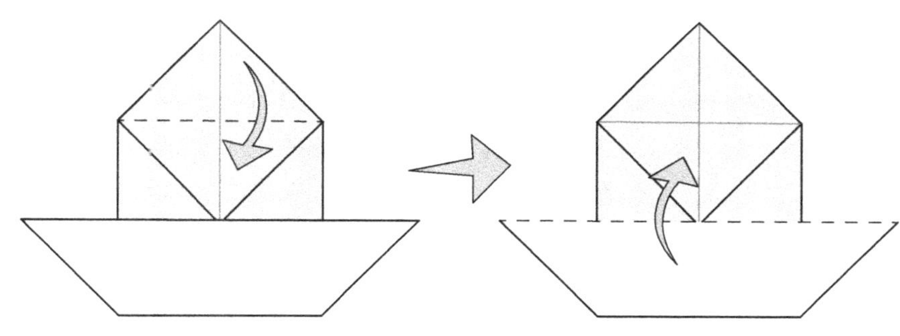

Step 9

Fold the top corner down and unfold it. Then bring the bottom edge of both sides of the figure up as shown.

Step 10

Pull both layers of the figure apart while pushing the top corner down to flatten it and shape the cap.

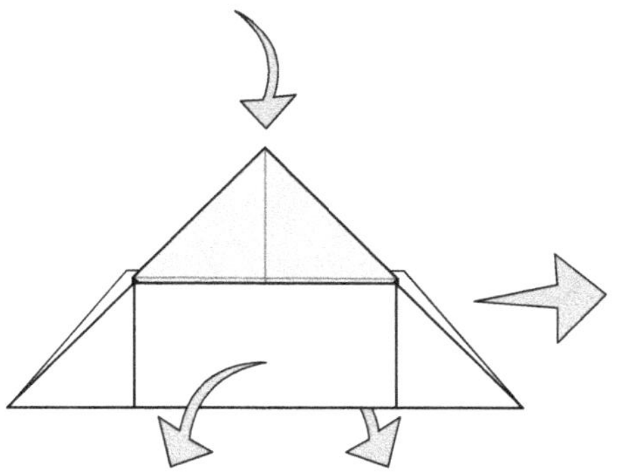

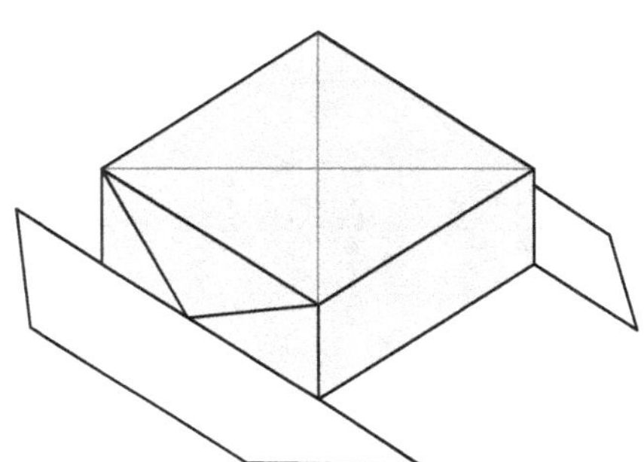

Hat

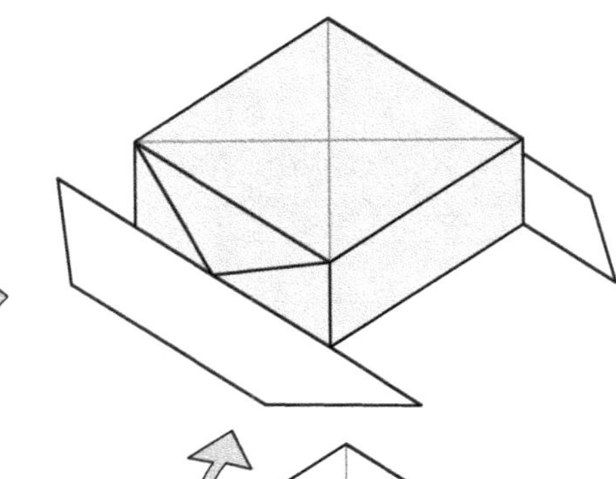

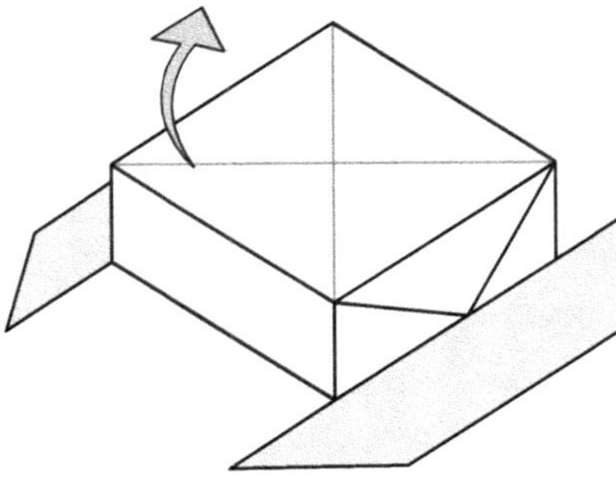

Rotate this figure and insert it under the first figure you made, making sure the flaps of both figures are on different sides as shown.

Take the other sheet and repeat all the steps so far.

Fold one of the corners of the upper figure as shown.

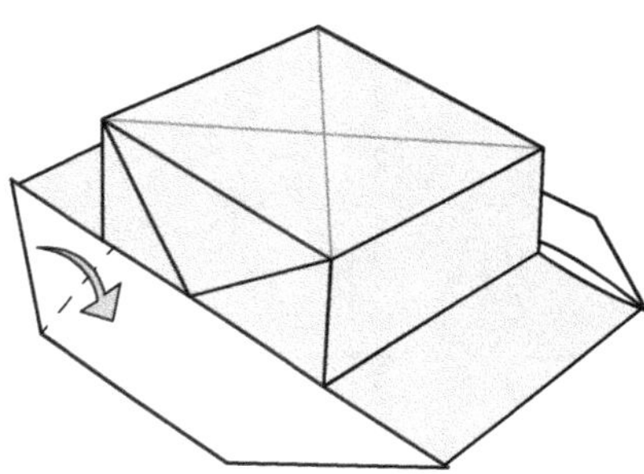

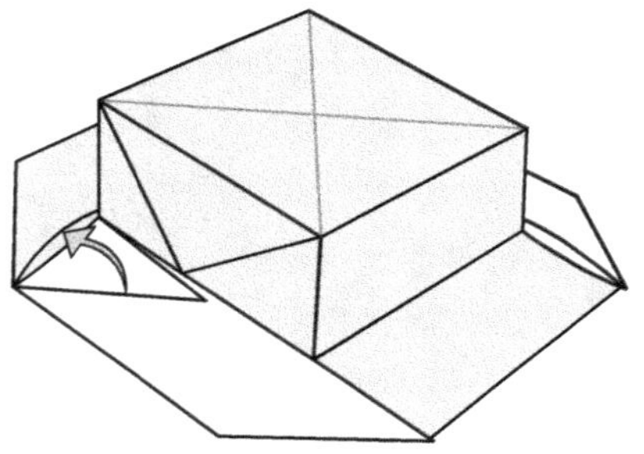

Now tuck that corner into the corner of the figure below as shown. Repeat for all corners.

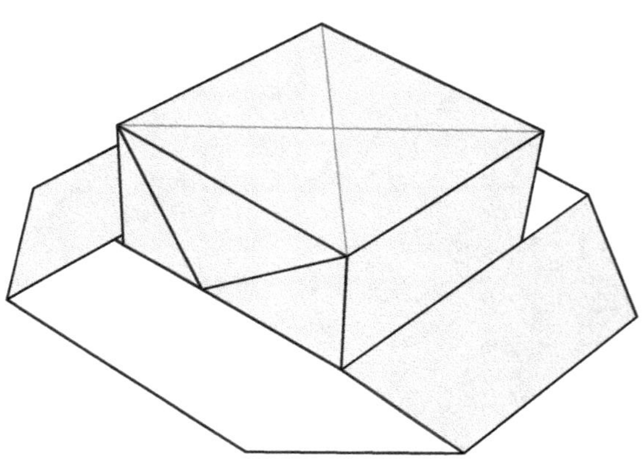

Chatterbox

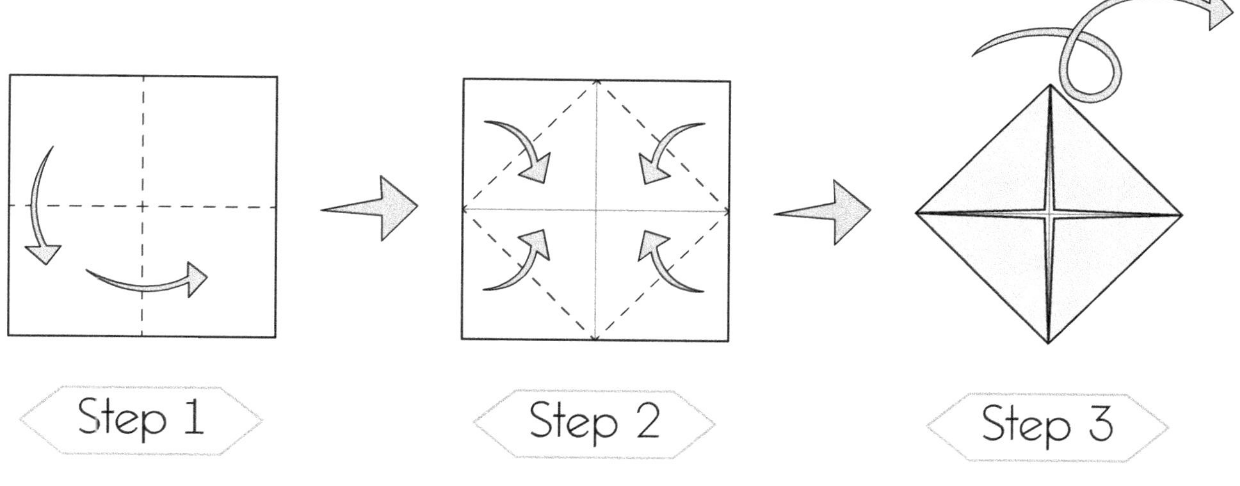

Step 1

Fold the paper sheet in half lengthwise and crosswise. Then unfold it.

Step 2

Bring all corners to the center of the sheet.

Step 3

Flip the figure over.

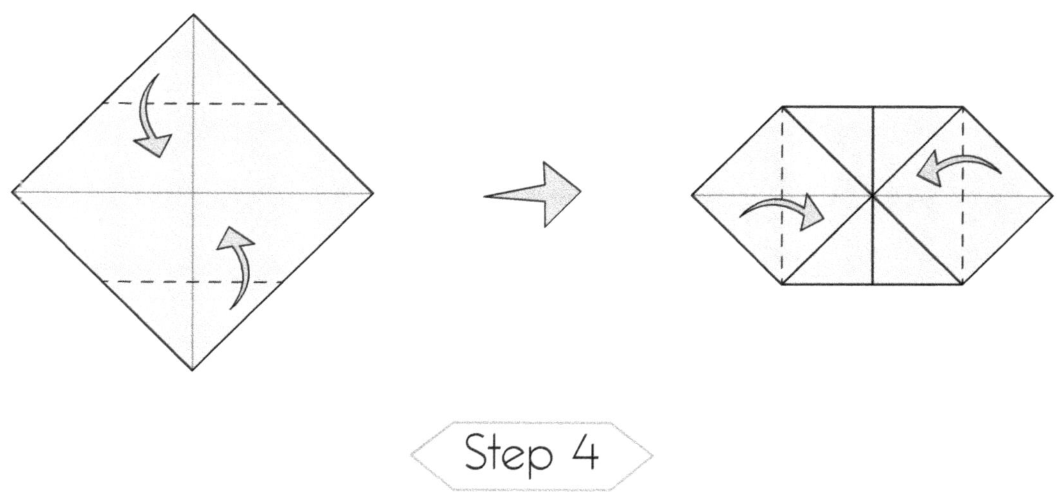

Step 4

Bring all corners to the center of sheet again and flatten it.

Chatterbox

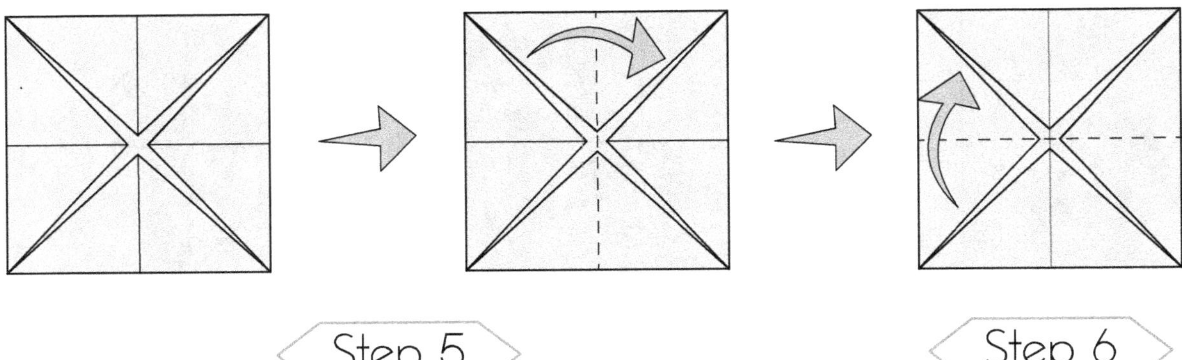

Step 5

Fold the figure in half lengthwise
and unfold it to make a crease.

Step 6

Now fold the figure in half
crosswise.

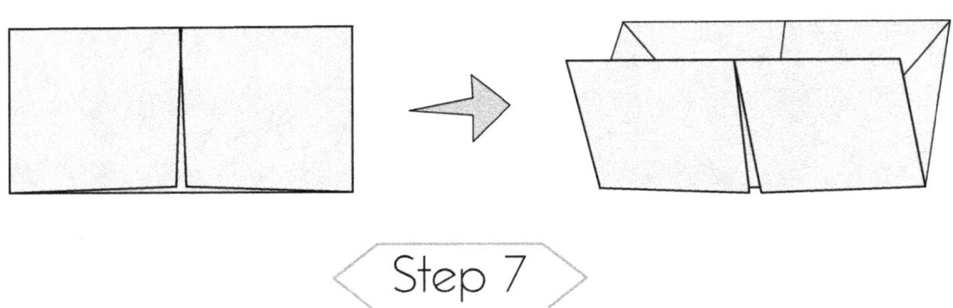

Step 7

Insert your fingers into the flaps in each corner
and your chatterbox is ready to play!

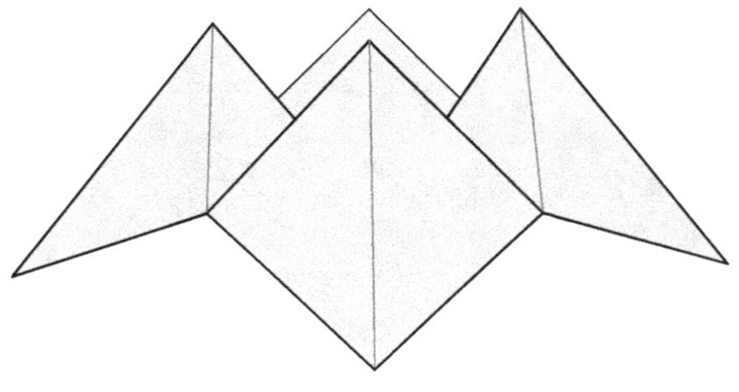

Chatterbox

Now that your chatterbox is ready, it's the funniest moment: let's decorate it and play! The good thing about your chatterbox is that you can decorate it however you like and use as many colors as you want. Once you have a colorful chatterbox you can use it to play fun games at home with friends and family, during car trips, birthday parties, holidays... Even on your own just for fun!

The chatterbox has 3 layers or levels where you can color or write:

- The outer side of the flaps where you insert your fingers to open and close it, which is the visible part when it's completely closed and which will be the 'top layer' from now on.

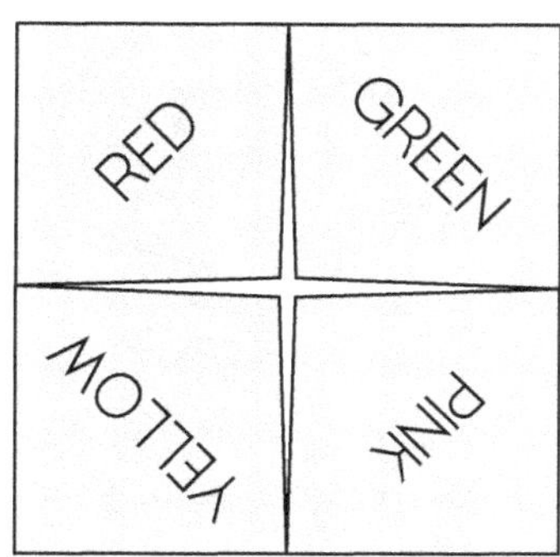

- The inner side of those flaps that is only visible when you open the chatterbox a little and that will be the 'middle layer'.

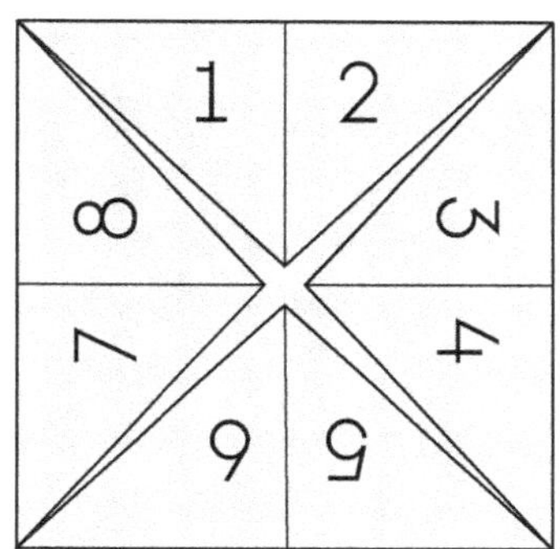

Chatterbox Games

- The layer below all of the above, which is only visible if you lift the inner side of the flaps and which will be the 'bottom layer'.

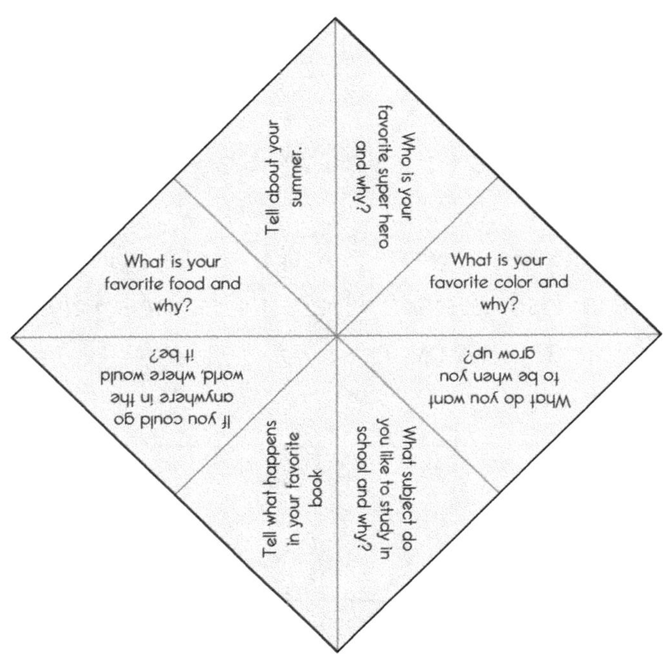

On the top layer you can use different colors, patterns, shapes... Anything you can think of! In the middle layer you can put numbers or drawings related to the theme of the game you choose, for example, animals or flowers. And on the bottom layer write actions or questions to have fun and have a great time with your friends or family.

You can play as many games as you can think of with your chatterbox, so here are just a few examples to get you started and the rest is up to your imagination!

Chatterbox Games

Game #1: Nature

- Top layer: Draw different flowers, leaves or seeds on each flap.
- Middle layer: Write numbers from 1 to 8 or draw insects.
- Bottom layer: Write actions for each number or drawing, here are some ideas.

  - Find 3 birds.
  - Look for 3 different insects.
  - Find leaves of 3 different colors.
  - Look for the perfect pet rock.
  - Feel the grass with your bare feet.
  - Hug a tree.
  - Run between two trees 3 times.
  - Find a tree with rough bark and a smooth one.

Game #2: Animals

- Top layer: Draw different animals or their fur patterns.
- Middle layer: Write numbers or draw animal tracks.
- Bottom layer: Write actions for each number or drawing, here are some ideas.

  - Bark like a dog.
  - Jump like a frog.
  - Walk slowly like a snail.
  - Sing like a rooster.
  - Moo like a cow.
  - Meow like a cat.
  - Pretend you can fly like a bird.
  - Jump around like a monkey.

Chatterbox Games

Game #3: Exercise

- Top layer: Draw people exercising or gym stuff.
- Middle layer: Write numbers or sports.
- Bottom layer: Write actions for each number or drawing, here are some ideas.

  - Jump 10 times.
  - Run around the house or the park.
  - Stand on one foot for 10 seconds.
  - Run on the spot for 20 seconds.
  - Dance for 30 seconds.
  - Do 10 jumping jacks.
  - Good luck! No exercise for you.
  - Walk backwards until your next turn.

Game #4: What would you do....?

- Top layer: Draw question marks of different colors or things related to the questions.
- Middle layer: Write numbers, letters, shapes...
- Bottom layer: Write questions that start with 'what would you do...?' for each number or drawing, here are some ideas.

  - What would you do if you could go anywhere?
  - ... If you could only eat one thing for the rest of your life?
  - ... If you had a lot of money right now?
  - ... If you had to choose between having a dog or a cat?
  - ... If you had to choose chocolate or vanilla ice cream forever?
  - ... If you could have whatever you want for dinner?
  - ... If you could fly?
  - ... If you could breathe underwater?

Here's how to play:

1. Ask someone to choose one of the colors or patterns on one of the flaps on the top layer.
2. Open and close the chatterbox by spelling that color or object. For example, if you drew a cow's fur open and close it spelling c-o-w, or if you colored it yellow open and close it spelling y-e-l-l-o-w.
3. Ask that person to choose one of the numbers or drawings on the middle layer.
4. Open it to reveal what they have to do!

Conclusion

Congratulations on making it to the end of this Origami book. After mastering the designs in this book and our others you will be able to create an Origami world of your own!

I hope this trip was fun and you have learned more about the art of folding paper.

If you enjoyed this book, we would really appreciate your feedback on Amazon. This way, we can grow together and create more quality Origami books!